More Praise for *Extra Virginity*

"Engrossing history, vivid contemporary reporting and a cogent call to action, expertly blended in an illuminating text."   —*Kirkus Reviews*, starred review

"*Extra Virginity* offers a smart, well-written crash course. . . . I don't know anyone who has put it all together more thoroughly or entertainingly than Mueller."   —Russ Parsons, *Los Angeles Times*

"This book expands the scope of [Mueller's] earlier work and makes unsettling reading for anyone who imagines that what they purchase in many supermarkets is actually high-quality olive oil, with all of its attendant life-enhancing attributes."   —Bruce Palling, *Wall Street Journal*

"A sparkling, stylish, sharply observed narrative that entertains and educates. . . . [Mueller] gives us scandals, romance, history, personalities and pop references galore. . . . Readers will find themselves becoming ravenous as they read *Extra Virginity*, and by book's end, their appetites will be whetted for a bottle of authentic olive oil."   —Joyce Sáenz Harris, *Dallas Morning News*

"In *Extra Virginity*, Mueller explores the long history of olive oil . . . and the long history of olive oil fraud—which is as old as the production of the oil itself. Along the way he develops a lively cast of characters, from artisanal oil makers and chemical analysts to food activists, and professional oil tasters."
                                                                          —*Daily Beast*

"Skillfully blend[s] international courtroom drama with the rich history of one of the first commodities. . . . Fans of Michael Pollan's The *Omnivore's Dilemma* and Peter Singer and Jim Mason's *The Way We Eat* will find Mueller's indictment of a slippery trade enlightening and entertaining."   —*Library Journal*

"The *New Yorker* writer does for his subject what Susan Orlean did for orchids."
                                                                  —*Columbus Dispatch*

"An eye-opening and brilliantly researched exposé."   —*Times* (London)

"Passionately written yet clear-headed. . . . Mueller builds a convincing case for olive oil as one of the most miraculous and versatile substances in all of nature."   —Jerry Shriver, *USA Today*

"American Italian–domiciled writer Tom Mueller tells this fascinating story in an unusual book packed with facts and figures. It is clear where his feelings lie about an oil made by nature alone, as distinct from wine, harvested by man from a strange and noble tree, sometimes hundreds of years old, a living symbol of peace and fortitude."   —*Sunday Independent* (UK)

"[In a] book filled with twists and turns that would shame the best mystery writer, Mueller tells a riveting tale about an age-old staple."
                                          —Caroline J. Beck, *Olive Oil Source*

"Though he offers a wealth of information, Mueller is never dry. . . . *Extra Virginity* will give you a new appreciation of olive oil."   —*VIVMag*

"Admirable and enjoyable."   —*Irish Times*

"To read Tom Mueller's *Extra Virginity: The Sublime and Scandalous World of Olive Oil* is to fall in love with the history, romance, and intrigue surrounding the olive and its fresh juice. . . . The world of olive oil is filled with passionate advocates, and Mueller draws deft word portraits of many key players. . . . Riveting."   —Catherine Watkins, *inform*

"Sexy title aside, this is the most delicious crime world exposé you can hope to read this month—or probably ever. In this vividly rendered book about everyone's favorite fine food item, Tom Mueller picks apart the wicked and illegal adulterated olive oil industry while doling out history and expert musings on the side. In a climate where it's totally uncool not to know where your edibles are coming from, this book is a must for those of us who keep a tub of the green stuff on hand at all times."   —Emily Temple, *Flavorpill*

"A fascinating book and a timely one too. . . . Tom Mueller masterfully separates strands of information—and misinformation—about a . . . truly sacred substance."   —Deborah Madison, chef and food writer

"Italy resident Mueller . . . is well-situated to interpose olive oil against the Byzantine ways of its present-day production in this intriguing and sumptuously researched book."   —*Publishers Weekly*

"Tom Mueller humanizes the hotbed of olive oil today in a way that is clear, credible and compelling. *Extra Virginity* . . . could well prove to be the olive oil tipping point the world has been waiting for."

—Curtis Cord, *Olive Oil Times*

"[*Extra Virginity*] does for olive oil what Eric Schlosser's *Fast Food Nation* did for hamburgers. Mueller traces the history of this valuable product from antiquity to the present, but the really disturbing part is his exposé of the inferior quality control and outright fraud among today's oil producers."

—Andy Lewis, *Hollywood Reporter*

"You may never eye olive oil the same way again. [*Extra Virginity* is] a fascinating read that spans thousands of years of olive oil production, as well as the oil's cultural, religious and medical significance."

—Jackie Burrell, *Mercury News*

"[*Extra Virginity*] is blowing the lid off an industry that might be built in part on the backs of crooks."   —Mandi Woodruff, *Business Insider*

"Mueller is back with an entertaining . . . account of the olive's glorious history and the oily business practices that now dilute and misrepresent the cherished cooking substance. *Extra Virginity* explains why olive squeezings are worth our love, crediting the olive's green unctuousness with everything from the curing of teenage blemishes to the very establishment of religion and art."   —Bill Kohlhaase, *Pasatiempo*

"Mueller's writing is exceptional, particularly when explaining the properties of olive oil that most of us seek. He gently unfurls the chemistry of great olive oil. . . . Woven throughout are Mueller's stories about life in Italy, his warm interviews with older olive oil producers who still use grinding stones pulled by beasts of burden. . . . For anyone who loves olive oil and vows never to be ripped off by the sinister side of the olive oil business, this book is a must-read."

—Elaine Corn, *HerbalGram*

EXTRA VIRGINITY

The
SUBLIME
and
SCANDALOUS WORLD
of
OLIVE OIL

TOM MUELLER

W. W. NORTON & COMPANY
New York • London

For information about permission to reproduce selections from this book,
write to Permissions, W. W. Norton & Company, Inc.,
500 Fifth Avenue, New York, NY 10110

For information about special discounts for bulk purchases, please contact
W. W. Norton Special Sales at specialsales@wwnorton.com or 800-233-4830

Manufacturing by Courier Westford
Book design by Chris Welch Design
Production manager: Julia Druskin

Library of Congress Cataloging-in-Publication Data

Mueller, Tom.
Extra virginity : the sublime and scandalous world of olive oil / Tom Mueller. — 1st ed.
p. cm.
ISBN 978-0-393-07021-7 (hardcover)
1. Olive oil—History. 2. Olive oil industry—Moral and ethical aspects.
3. Olive—History. 4. Olive—Folklore. 5. Food adulteration and inspection. I. Title.
TP683.M845 2011
664'.362—dc23

2011041459

ISBN 978-0-393-34361-8 pbk.

W. W. Norton & Company, Inc.
500 Fifth Avenue, New York, N.Y. 10110
www.wwnorton.com

W. W. Norton & Company Ltd.
Castle House, 75/76 Wells Street, London W1T 3QT

1 2 3 4 5 6 7 8 9 0

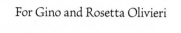
For Gino and Rosetta Olivieri

When a native of the Mediterranean had to leave the shores of the sea, he was uneasy and homesick; like the soldiers of Alexander the Great when he left Syria and advanced towards the Euphrates; or the sixteenth-century Spaniards in the Low Countries, miserable among the 'fogs of the North'. For Alonzo Vázquez and the Spaniards of his time (and probably of all time) Flanders was 'the land where there grows neither thyme, nor lavender, figs, olives, melons, or almonds; where dishes are prepared, strange to relate, with butter from cows instead of oil.'

—Fernand Braudel, *The Mediterranean and the Mediterranean World in the Age of Philip II*

CONTENTS

EXTRA
VIRGINITY

ESSENCES

hen the olive oil reached 28 degrees Celsius, the temperature at which its aromatic substances become volatile, the eight tasters removed the lids from the glasses that contained the first sample of oil, inserted their noses, and began snuffling loudly, some closing their eyes. These were members of the tasting panel of the Corporazione Mastri Oleari, in Milan, one of the most respected private olive oil associations; they sat in individual cubicles of white formica, each equipped with a sink, a pen and a stack of tasting forms, and a yogurt maker with a thermostat, on which sat six tulip-shaped tasting glasses containing samples of oil. They were a diverse group, which included a thirty-three-year-old farmer from Lake Garda, a forty-seven-year-old Tuscan *marchesa* who worked as a personal motivation coach, and a sixty-six-year-old Milanese businessman. They'd begun trickling in around 9 am, grumbling about being deprived of their morning coffee and cigarettes, which are forbidden before a tasting because they dull the senses; now they sat silently in their cubicles in attitudes of attention and reflection, like chemists in a lab, or scholars in a library. On shelves around the walls were several hundred bottles of olive oil, as well as sixteen brown laboratory bottles with neat white labels on which were printed "musty," "fusty," "rancid," "winey/vinegary," "cucumber," "grubby," and other unpleasant smells—the official taste flaws in olive oil, which these eight people had trained their senses to detect in the faintest degree.

The panel tasted the six oil samples according to a strict protocol, which, like each feature of the panel test room itself, was prescribed by Italian and European law. Cradling the glasses in their palms like brandy snifters to keep the oil warm, they smelled it carefully, jotting down the fragrances they perceived. They took a mouthful of oil. And then, as if they'd all been stricken by an oil-induced seizure, they began sucking in air violently at the corners of their months, a technique known as *strip-paggio*, which coats the taste buds in an emulsion of oil and saliva, and wafts the oil's aromas up into the nasal passages. After the first volcanic slurps, the *strippaggi* grew softer and more meditative and took on personal notes, the *marchesa*'s wheezy and almost wistful, the businessman's deep and wet, as if he were gargling Epsom salts. After tasting and retasting each oil for ten to fifteen minutes, and periodically cleansing their palates with mineral water, they recorded its flavor, aroma, intensity, texture, and other characteristics on a scoring sheet.

The tasters pottered in their cubicles for the next ninety minutes, snuffling and slurping and musing over the oils. Finally, after evaluating the last of the samples, they stood and stretched like people rising from sleep, and moved to the conference table in the middle of the room. Here they enjoyed their long-awaited cigarettes and coffee, while the panel leader, Alfredo Mancianti, collated their scoring sheets. "The tasters themselves don't score an oil," Flavio Zaramella, the Milanese businessman and president of the Mastri Oleari, told me. "They just identify and quantify the sensations they perceive in it. It's the panel leader who actually assigns a score to the oil, by making a composite of their eight assessments using robust statistical methods."

Looking over the panel leader's shoulder as he worked, I saw that the eight tasters had been remarkably consistent in their appraisals, describing the texture and personality of each oil in similar ways, and identifying the same subtle flavors and fragrances in each—artichoke, fresh-cut grass, green tomato, kiwi.

"The *tonda iblea* from southern Sicily was memorable, with those afternotes of artichoke and green tomato," Zaramella told the other tasters. "But all in all, I think the best full-bodied oil was the Marcinase DOP Terra di Bari from Puglia." The others nodded, though one taster said she preferred the Villa Magra Gran Cru from Tuscany because it was more balanced and harmonious.

By now I found it hard to sit still. Artichoke? Fresh-cut grass? They hadn't been tasting first-growth Bordeaux, for heaven's sake, but liquid fat. No doubt these oils had been made with great skill, "cold-pressed" and all that, but artichoke? Green tomato? Kiwi?

Something in my face must have alerted Zaramella to my skepticism. He stubbed out his cigarette, hopped to his feet, took my arm, and steered me into one of the tasting cubicles. "Oil talk sounds like effete nonsense, until you actually put a good oil in your mouth," he said. He began pouring samples of oil into tulip glasses and placing them on the warmer beside me, capping each with a glass wafer to hold in the aromas. When the thermostat light went out, indicating that the oil had reached twenty-eight degrees, Zaramella showed me the approved oil-tasting technique: how to smell the sample deeply several times, trying to clear the mind between sniffs; how to take a small sip and to roll the oil around with my tongue to coat the inside of my mouth; and how to perform the loud, slurpy *strippaggio*. From time to time he reminded me to clean my palate with mineral water, or with a bite of a Granny Smith apple.

For the next hour, under Zaramella's direction, like someone beginning to study ballet or yoga or violin with a master, I made my first brief foray into the vast, largely uncharted continent of extra virgin olive oil. I learned that oils made from different olive varieties, or from the same varieties grown in different places, can be every bit as diverse as wine from different grape varietals: the straw-colored *casaliva* oil from Lake Garda was almost sweet, with hints of pine nuts and almonds, while the emerald green *moraiolo* from central Tuscany was so peppery it left tears in my eyes and a lovely sear at the back of my throat. And sure enough, the *tonda iblea* from the hills of southeastern

Sicily had distinct green tomato and artichoke overtones, just as Zaramella and his colleagues had said. Tasting these oils was like strolling through a botanic garden, touring a perfume factory, and taking a long drive through spring meadows with the windows down, all at the same time—equal parts scientific analysis and lingering, attentive hedonism.

I raised the last sample Zaramella had poured for me, sniffed it perfunctorily, and sipped. Then, after a swirling moment of bewilderment and dawning disgust, I spat it into the sink. Something was wrong with this oil: after the tart, intensely fresh-tasting essences I'd been trying until now, it felt flabby and coarse in my mouth, and tasted like spoiled fruit.

Zaramella laughed his gruff laugh. "I brought the supermarket oil last," he said, "because it would have ruined your palate for the good ones, as surely as if you'd gargled cat piss."

He pulled down the brown lab bottles from the shelf on the wall, and set them in a row on the conference table. "Now comes the fun part," he told me. "You have to figure out precisely what's wrong with this last oil. It's like being a detective. Or a coroner."

He opened the bottles one by one and handed them to me, telling me to try to memorize each scent. The bottles contained a stunning range of reeks, stenches, and pongs, to which their labels—"rancid," "fusty," "winey/vinegary," "muddy sediment," "metallic," "esparto," "grubby"— hardly did justice. Then, after several bites of the apple and a lot of deep breathing to cleanse my palate, I sampled the oil again, sniffing and tasting and trying to put names to its flaws. I thought I recognized several, and jotted them down on a profile sheet.

When I'd finished, Zaramella drew me out of the cubicle and sat me down at the conference table, seated himself across from me, lit another cigarette, and took a voluptuous drag. He scanned my sheet. "Pretty good," he grunted, exhaling a cloud of smoke that briefly darkened the room. "'Rancid' and 'fusty' are both there. But you missed a few. The winey/vinegary is strong, and there's noticeable muddy sediment, too." He picked up the bottle of supermarket oil I'd been tasting. "You know, according to the law, if an oil contains just one of these defects—one hint of fusty, a trace of brine—it's not extra virgin grade. *Basta*, end of story. In fact, with the flaws this oil has, it's classed as *lampante:* 'lamp oil.' Which can only be legally sold as fuel: it's only fit for burning, not eating. Trouble is, the law is never enforced."

Suddenly he banged the bottle down on the tabletop, making coffee cups and ashtrays hop and rattle. "*This* is what nearly everyone in the world thinks is extra virgin olive oil! *This* stuff is killing quality oil, and putting honest oil-makers out of business. In wine, you can trust the label: if it says 'Dom Pérignon 1964' then that's what's in the bottle, not last month's Beaujolais Nouveau. In fact, champagne and Beaujolais support each other, spreading the prestige and brand recognition of French wine up and down the quality scale. But olive oil labels all say the same thing, whether the bottle contains a magnificent oil or this *schifezza* . . ." He pointed the neck of the bottle at me like a gun, then lifted his glasses to read the label. "It says what every olive oil says: 100 percent Italian, cold-pressed, stone-ground, extra virgin . . ."

He shook his head, as if unable to believe his eyes. "*Extra virgin?* What's this oil got to do with virginity? This is a whore."

Then, with the same precision he'd shown in the taste test, Zaramella catalogued the crimes widely practiced in the oil business. He described the deodorizing equipment he'd seen in Spanish mills, particularly in Andalucía, where it is illegally used to remove the bad flavors and aromas of inferior oils in order to sell them as extra virgin. He condemned the widespread practice of labeling heavily refined oils "pure" even though the refining process had stripped them of nearly all of their health benefits and sensory qualities, "light" although they contained the same number of calories per gram as other oils, and "organic"—from olives grown without pesticides or other chemicals—when in reality they were made from ordinary olives. Small-time oil crooks colored cheap soybean or canola oil with industrial chlorophyll, dumped in beta-carotene as a flavoring, and sold the mixture as extra virgin olive oil, in bottles adorned with Italian flags and the names of imaginary producers in famed olive-growing regions like Puglia or Tuscany. More sophisticated, large-scale frauds, he explained, required skilled chemists and multimillion-dollar laboratory facilities, and involved networks of conniving customs agents, businessmen, and government officials. Zaramella identified the headquarters of oil fraud throughout the Mediterranean, naming refineries and factories in Lugano, Switzerland; Málaga, Spain; Sfax in Tunisia; and elsewhere throughout the Mediterranean, where bogus extra virgins were fabricated. He reviewed the countries throughout the world where fake extra virgins were sold, and explained why the US was the best place on earth to sell adulterated oil.

In the coming year I spent considerable time with Zaramella, at the Milan offices of the Mastri Oleari and at oil tastings and conferences throughout Italy. I learned of his penchant for big, creative schemes and long odds: at different times in his career, he'd founded a thriving high-fashion firm in Milan and traded petroleum futures through an offshore company registered in Wyoming. On a wall in his office was a map of Somalia, where, in 1987, as the head of a humanitarian aid project, he supervised the construction of a high-tech hospital in Baraawe, a city on the Indian Ocean. "I got everyone working together: Communists, Catholic priests, Muslims, professors, illiterates, anyone with the will to get things done," he recalled. Two months after the hospital was completed, it was destroyed in the civil war. "Generosity is the purest form of egotism," he said with a shrug. Zaramella spoke of his abdominal cancer, for which he'd undergone four operations, and of the remarkable therapeutic properties of extra virgin olive oil against numerous conditions, including cancer; his illness, he said, had given him a special sensitivity to the healing qualities of oil. And he described how he'd first become interested in olive oil fraud twenty years earlier, after he started making oil from the trees on a small farm he'd bought in Umbria, and found that the farmer who tended them had been swindling him by cutting his olive oil with cheaper sunflower-seed oil. He said he was devoting the remaining years of his life to his biggest, most difficult scheme of all: redeeming the olive oil business from fraud.

Though his operations had left him gaunt, Zaramella still had the mellow baritone and plump, animated face of the 120-kilo epicurean he'd been before his illness. "My fight is a civic responsibility," he once told me, "to the thousands of honest oil-makers who can hardly make a living in this distorted market, and to millions of consumers who are being deprived of the therapeutic properties of quality oil. Real extra virgin olive oil contains powerful antioxidants and anti-inflammatories which help to prevent degenerative conditions—like my cancer. Fake extra virgin has next to none of them. Great oil is the essence of the Mediterranean diet. Bad oil isn't just a deception, it's a crime against public health." Zaramella's dedication to olive oil went beyond a sense of justice or the desire for a cure. Once we stood in his grove near Assisi in springtime, when yellow lilies were blooming among the trees, and looked out over one of those hillsides where Saint Francis had once sung odes to the birds and the sun and the sky. "Since ancient times, olive oil has stood for purity, health, holiness," Zaramella said softly, almost to himself, in a voice resonant with emotion. "I'm not a religious man, but for me, olive oil is sacred."

Here was Flavio Zaramella, a merry atheist, speaking of olive oil's sacredness, a *viveur* with a terminal disease dedicating his last energies to oil's healthfulness. Standing with him among the olives and lilies of Saint Francis, I first realized that olive oil did something special to people. Just as oil, a powerful solvent, brings out essential, sometimes unexpected flavors in food, it also reveals the essence of certain people: their hidden contradictions, their secret passions and dreams. It gets under their skin, seeps into their minds, and colors their thoughts, like no other food I know. As I went deeper into oil, I began to see this condition in many places. I recognized its symptoms in octogenarian olive farmers and nonagenarian millers, as well as eager young oil executives at multinational food companies. I saw it in the head of a food cooperative who made oil, at enormous risk, from olive groves confiscated from the mafia, and in monks who made oil from the thousand-year-old trees on their monastery grounds. I met politicians, union leaders, European

Union regulators, historians, archaeologists, chemists, agronomists, and botanists, all of whose faces lit up when the conversation turned to oil, and who always had a story to tell, funny or shocking or sad. Even shady characters who'd grown rich making fake oil by the tanker-load spoke wistfully of their childhoods spent at the olive mill, and of the life lessons they learned there. In every eye was the same oily glint of unfeigned fascination with a substance they'd do things for that they'd do for nothing else on earth. All these people suffered from the same condition. They were obsessed by oil.

I began to pay closer attention to this rich, slippery, subtly mysterious substance, a vegetable oil made from a fruit, a fresh fruit juice with the ideal blend of fats for the human body, a fat that slims the arteries and nourishes the mind, an age-old food with space-age qualities that medical science is just beginning to understand. I started visiting different producers, first in Liguria where I live, then in neighboring Lombardy, Piedmont, Tuscany. I bought a bottle of oil from each producer, and compared two or three at a time back home, sipping from tablespoons and little shot glasses at first, then buying tulip-shaped tasting glasses for more precision. My eight- and ten-year-old sons, Jeremy and Nicholas, began tasting with me. As we sipped, I told them about the people who had made each oil, where they lived, how they talked and carried themselves. I showed them pictures, and the boys studied the faces of these oil women and oil men, noticed their weather-creased faces and large, strong-looking hands. They began to point out when certain characteristics in an oil resembled its maker—the big-bodied gruffness of Flavio Zaramella's Flos Viridis oil, the sunny joie de vivre of a pale golden extra virgin made by a woman on Lake Garda with laughing blue eyes and blonde tresses. Before long they were holding forth about the tomato and artichoke highlights in certain oils, and even seemed to like the peppery bite of the bigger Tuscan and Pugliese cultivars, as if their young bodies sensed that the harshness was doing them good. Now and then I brought home bad oils from a discount supermarket or a well-meaning but maladroit farmer, and watched the boys sniff, wince, and hiss *"lampante!"* with the same righteous anger as Flavio Zaramella.

The first time my wife, Francesca, saw us sipping olive oil, her expression slid slowly from disbelief to disgust. "I'd rather eat butter cubes," she said. My wife is from Milan, where the traditional cuisine is based on butter and lard, not oil. But I persisted. I showed her articles from the *Lancet*, the *New England Journal of Medicine*, and other prominent journals about recently discovered health benefits in olive oil, against pathologies as diverse as heart disease, breast cancer, and Alzheimer's. I dressed our salads with splendid and exotic oils—one night a *biancolilla* that brought out the bitterness of arugula, the next a *nocellara del Belice* that inexplicably muted it. Gradually, my wife relented. Though she still wouldn't drink olive oil neat, she did start trying different oils on raw vegetables, salads, and in sauces. She substituted oil for butter in croissants, muffins, and cakes, which sometimes had a faint greenish tinge, as if they'd come from the garden rather than the oven, but were crusty and flavorful. These days she keeps several different olive oils in the kitchen, using them like different spices depending on the foods she cooks, and makes sure we all eat two tablespoons of top-quality oil every day, following the advice of leading medical researchers. She too is becoming one of the oil-obsessed.

Oil obsession is an ancient condition. Rereading poems and sacred texts I thought I knew well, I caught glints and scents I'd never noticed before, of a time when olive oil was not only an essential food, but a catalyst of civilized life and a vital link between people and the divine. Odysseus, haggard and salt-crusted after a shipwreck, spreads his body with oil and suddenly appears as handsome as a god. Mary Magdalene, the repentant prostitute, anoints Christ's feet with an aromatic oil that fills the house with its fragrance, then wipes them clean with her hair. The Prophet Mohammed, peace be upon him, uses so much olive oil on his skin that his shawl is often drenched with it. I read of Egyptian pharaohs who made thank-offerings of the finest olive oil to the sun god Ra, and of the meager ration of lamp oil in the sacred Menorah, only enough for one day, that lit the Temple of Jerusalem for eight full days during its dedication until more oil could be obtained, a miracle that Jews still celebrate at Hanukkah. The dove returning to Noah's Ark with an olive branch in its beak meant not only God's forgiveness after the flood—the olive branch had been carried by supplicants since ancient Greek times—but that Noah had come to a land of peace: olives are slow-growing trees that require regular tending, which can only happen in peacetime.

Here and there were hints of oil's darker side. Medieval sorcerers and Renaissance witches used olive oil in their spells and unguents, and *unguentarii* were said to spread the plague with tainted oil. Crime has been part of the oil trade for at least 5,000 years: the earliest known documents to mention olive oil, cuneiform tablets written at Ebla in the twenty-fourth century BC, refer to teams of inspectors who checked olive growers and millers for fraudulent practices. The warm glow of Hanukkah conceals a bloody civil war fought in 168 BC, the year of the famous miracle of the Menorah, when two Jewish factions battled for control over the Temple and over Hebrew religious practice. Olive trees themselves can be ominous. Sophocles described the unearthly, almost menacing power of a tree "not planted by men's hands, but self-created," and an ancient Christian legend relates that an olive tree sprouted from Adam's grave, rooted in his skull. Some modern poets have also felt the tree's cold shadow. Shortly before Federico García Lorca was shot by a Nationalist firing squad during the Spanish Civil War, he wrote of the Guardia Civil marching implacably through olive groves in Andalucía toward the scene of a murder, as black angels "with hearts of olive oil" watched from the western sky—as if in premonition of his own death. In the age-twisted olives of Provence, Richard Wilbur saw the privation just beneath the bounty of the Mediterranean landscape:

> Even when seen from near, the olive shows
> A hue of far away. Perhaps for this
> The dove brought olive back, a tree which grows
> Unearthly pale, which ever dims and dries,

> And whose great thirst, exceeding all excess,
> Teaches the South it is not paradise.

The fruit and fragrance of good oil are tempered with bitterness, as life's beauty is.

Why, I wondered, are olive branches and trees such enduring symbols, even in places where they aren't native? What is it about oil itself that has made it a universal liquid for millennia, seeping into every aspect of human life? And how did life in this oil-soaked world look, smell, and feel—the temples and bedchambers and bathhouses in the clear yellow light of oil lamps, the people dosing themselves with vast quantities of oil? For me, the anointing is the hardest of all to imagine. How did it feel when your entire body glistened and slithered with scented oil? When, like the high priest Aaron, anointing oil dripped from your hair into your beard, soaking your robes down to their hems? Or when a prostitute smoothed your feet with shining oil, then wiped them with her hair? It's hard to imagine, as I say, but tempting to try.

I began a series of experiments. I bought several oil lamps, replicas of medieval and Roman models, and lit them throughout the house, their flames floating above dark pools of oil and emanating a faint sweetness, bathing familiar scenes in the tremulous amber light of the past. I tried olive oil as a skin lotion: it softened chapped lips and soothed sunburn, and healed my baby daughter's diaper rash with one application. I made a batch of soap on the stovetop, mixing olive oil with tallow and lye, and pouring the resulting paste into molds I'd cut from blocks of olive wood. The soap produced a pinkish, faintly slimy lather which left the skin wonderfully soft, but was too slippery for washing dishes (as we decided after several broken plates). I tested olive oil's qualities as a solvent and lubricant, polishing mirrored surfaces on an old toaster and chrome trim, revealing new depths of grain in a battered walnut tabletop, silencing squeaky windows and doors throughout the house. I poured out little jars of oil and dropped in garlic cloves, rosemary sprigs, orange rind, and boiled eggs, and found within days that their olfactory essences had leached into the oil and now lingered there, magically imprisoned, like genies in a bottle. I jury-rigged a still from a pressure cooker and a coil of copper tubing, used it to extract essential oils from lavender, wisteria, jasmine, and bergamot, then stirred these essences into an olive oil base, creating vividly scented oils which I rubbed on my face, and furtively into my hair, thinking how it would be to play the Old Testament priest and pour the entire jar over my head, drenching my beard and dripping from my clothes.

The origins of olive oil's universal appeal are being uncovered today, by scientists in a range of fields with whom I consulted, each opening another doorway on this wide new world. With nutritionists and lipid chemists I peered into the molecular structure of olive oil, glimpsing the natural antioxidants and fatty acids which once induced people to anoint their heads and smear their faces with oil, following some obscure instinct to health. They used it to cleanse and beautify their skin because the primary lipid component of oil, oleic acid, is a powerful solvent which also enables oil to extract flavors in cooking and hold fragrances in perfume. Both the practical and the mythical popularity of oil derive, at least partly, from the almost miraculous agronomic characteristics of the olive tree, which thrives even in desert conditions and, when destroyed by fire or frost, sends up green shoots from the root ball through which the tree is reborn. The olive tree's crop is itself a minor miracle. As one agronomist told me, "The yield of an olive tree is an upward curve, tending towards infinity." There was a hint of wonder in his voice.

Continuing my search for answers about olive oil, I began to travel to places where great oil is made, and where it remains in some way central to daily life. Eventually I circled the Mediterranean, from southern Spain and North Africa to the West Bank and the eastern coast of Crete, seeing landscapes shaped by ancient groves, getting to know lifeways and folklore and religious rites steeped in their oil. Later I traveled even farther afield, meeting oil-makers in California and Chile, on the slopes of Table Mountain in South Africa and the Wheatbelt of far western Australia—places where olive trees and Mediterranean ways were oddly transmuted by the distance, yet fundamentally familiar.

But the first stage of my olive oil journey, and in many ways the most important, was to Puglia, the heel of the Italian boot. This region produces a large part of Italy's oil, as it has for thousands of years, back when the hillsides of famous oil areas like Tuscany and Liguria, Spain and North Africa were bare of groves, and oliviculture in America and Australia were millennia away. Wild olives, or *termiti*, have thrived in Puglia's hot, dry climate since the last ice age, providing sturdy rootstock on which farmers grafted the domestic olive trees brought there by Phoenician traders and Greek colonists. Many *pugliesi* still pour a cross of olive oil on their soup, and pause at midday by the hearth to drink a little cup of warmed oil, daily rituals of health and propitiation. Olive oil has been a staple here forever, and its beauty and ugliness come through with singular clarity.

OLIVES AND LIVES

On this the maids came to a halt and began calling one another back. They made Odysseus sit down in the shelter as Nausicaa had told them, and brought him a shirt and cloak. They also brought him the little golden flask of olive oil, and told him to go wash in the stream. But Odysseus said, "Young women, please to stand a good way off, so I may wash the brine from my shoulders and anoint myself with oil, for it has been a long time since my skin has had a drop of oil upon it. I cannot wash as long as you all are standing there. I am ashamed to strip stark naked before good-looking young women."

Then they stood aside and went to tell their mistress, while Odysseus washed himself in the stream and scrubbed the brine from his back and broad shoulders. When he had thoroughly bathed all over, and had got the brine out of his hair, he anointed himself with oil, and put on the clothes which the young woman had given him, Athena made him look taller and stronger than before, she also made the hair grow thick on the top of his head, and flow down in curls like hyacinth blossoms; she glorified him about the head and shoulders as a skilful workman who has studied art of all kinds under Hephaestus and Athena enriches a piece of silver plate by gilding it—and his work is full of beauty. He went down to the beach and sat a little way off glistening in his glory, breathtakingly handsome, and the young woman gazed on him with admiration. Then she said to her maids:

"Hush, my dears, for I want to say something. I believe the gods of Olympus have sent this man to the Phaeacians. When I first saw him I thought him plain, but now his appearance is like that of the gods who dwell in heaven. I should like my future husband to be just such a man as he is."

—Homer, *Odyssey*, Book VI

From 30,000 feet, the landscape of Puglia scrolling by below is a vast patchwork quilt of irregularly-shaped fields, each decorated with green polka dots of varying sizes: some as small as pinpricks and arranged in neat grids, others larger and irregularly scattered across the fields. As the plane descends through 5,000 feet toward a landing at Bari airport, and the aquamarine band of the Mediterranean comes into view, you see that the polka dots are olive trees: the small ones are young trees planted in neat ranks and files, according to modern agronomic practice, while the larger dots are ancient trees with huge, cloudlike crowns growing more or less randomly across the fields, where they were growing when the Crusaders rode through Puglia on their way to the Holy Land.

Olive trees grow close to the runway, and line the road on either side into town; many are ancient, corkscrew-trunked giants right out of the forests of fairy tale, with long limbs reaching horizontally and ending in drooping, witchlike fingers, a pruning method called "the chandelier." On and on the olive groves go as you drive south, and as far as you can see in every direction, toward the low sandy coastline and the limestone plateau inland. Puglia's sixty million olive trees are owned by 250,000 *pugliesi*—an average of 240 trees per person—in groves that have grown gradually smaller and more jagged as they've been passed down through the generations. Here and there is a bench in the shade of a big tree, or a tiny cottage of whitewashed stone that serves as both garden shed and vacation home, with an open-air oven for pizza or bread. The red soil is full of pale yellow fieldstones, which have been gathered and stacked to make dry-wall fences between the fields: olives, with their low, broad root systems, thrive in rocky, well-drained, calcareous soil. In sunny patches along the walls grow masses of climbing jasmine, and tall, flourishing Indian figs, also called the prickly pear, whose flat, oblong leaves give the scene a pinch of desert grit.

Six large swatches of Puglia's patchwork quilt belong to the De Carlo family, who since the year 1600 have made oil from their groves in the flat limestone lowlands of Bitritto, just southeast of Bari. Today the family business is led by Grazia and Saverio, the matriarch and patriarch of the De Carlo clan. They are an unlikely pair, the Lady and the Farmer. She is dark and plump and pretty, immaculate in her pleated skirts, cashmere cardigans, gold bracelets, and a string of fat pearls. He is rawboned and slope-shouldered, with the windburned face and layered flannel and polar fleece clothes of a man who spends most of his time outdoors, in all weather. Grazia fixes you with dark brown eyes that are warm yet penetrating, like a hawk's, and speaks eagerly and eloquently, her tanned hands fanning and fisting. Saverio speaks softly, with lowered eyes, as if shy, or weary. Often he'll sketch out a thought with a few words, as terse and weighty as a poem, then fall silent and let Grazia fill it in. "A good oil-maker needs technology and the hoe," he says, and then makes a little motion of entreaty to his wife, who amplifies: "To make the best oils, we combine the latest milling machinery with a mastery of traditional agricultural methods."

Spend a day with them, though, and you see that despite their differences—or perhaps because of them—Grazia and Saverio are a perfect pair. You sense this by the way their children, Marina and Francesco, in their mid-twenties, fall silent and listen when either of them speaks, with brief glances of affection and complicity. You know by the way they'll be good-naturedly poking fun at each other one moment, and the next, without really meaning to, bragging about each other. "Just look at how healthy he is," Grazia says, jabbing her finger into her husband's thick forearm, knotty as cordwood. "He's spent his life hefting hundred-kilo bags of olives out of the back of trucks, and eating ridiculous quantities of olive oil. By now he's indestructible." Saverio says of Grazia: "At first she hated the olive oil business, but her courage and new ideas have made us a success—and right now they're what's keeping us afloat."

Grazia comes from a wealthy merchant family, and had no experience in the oil business until she married Saverio. Yet, like many *pugliesi*, her earliest childhood memory involves olives. She remembers a misty December morning when she was three or four, walking with her mother at the beginning of the harvest into the olive groves that surrounded Bitritto. The pickers, all from local families, celebrated this momentous day with an annual rite, toasting bread slices over an olive-wood fire, pouring new oil over them, and sharing them around with the measured seriousness of a sacrament. Saverio's first memory, instead, is set in his father's mill: he's a small boy sitting with the workmen beside the millstone after a day's picking, while the mule that had been turning the stone munches in its nosebag nearby, and the men cook a vegetable stew they call *la bomba* ("the bomb") in a clay pot, singing folk songs whose words and tunes Saverio still remembers, though he hasn't heard them for a half-century.

I first visited the De Carlo mill at the height of another harvest sixty-odd years later, in late November, a time of year when their machines run day and night. Crates of *coratina* and *ogliarola* olives, hand-picked just as they'd begun to turn color from green to pale purple, were arriving on tractors and three-wheeled *Api* and being stacked outside the mill, in columns thirty feet high. Grazia walked me through the extraction process. A workman dumped crates of olives into a stainless steel bin, where spinning tines and a jet of warm air removed leaves and stems, after which they slid into another steel tank where they were washed.

Finally, sleek and shiny as pellets of fresh-blown glass, they slithered down a chute into the mill itself, where three granite grindstones as big as truck wheels, rolling in a circle one after another on a plate of granite, crushed them, pits and flesh and all, into a plum-colored paste. Saverio, who was supervising the milling process, waited until the pulp was the right consistency—he says he judges this mainly by the sound that the grindstones make—and then piped it into a malaxer, a vat with a fan screw turning along the bottom that stirs the pulp continuously, coaxing microdroplets of oil out of the cell membranes of the olives, and helping them to coalesce into larger drops which are easier to extract; the skilled oil-maker mixes the paste just long enough to concentrate its oil without exposing it to the air for too long, which would degrade its aromas and accelerate spoilage. After twenty minutes, Saverio sent the paste into a centrifuge, a steel canister resembling a small jet engine, inside which a drum was spinning at 3,000 revolutions per minute, separating the oil from the olive skins, pits, and flesh. Finally the oil went into a smaller, vertical centrifuge, which removed the remaining water.

Olive oil is the only commercially significant vegetable oil sold retail to be extracted from a fruit rather than from seeds, like sunflower, canola, and soy oil. Since the fruit contains considerable water, extraction can be done by mechanical methods alone, with a centrifuge or a press, whereas extracting seed oils generally requires the use of industrial solvents, typically hexane. To remove this solvent from seed oils, as well as to eliminate the unpleasant tastes and odors they normally have, they must be processed in a refinery, where they undergo high-temperature desolventization, neutralization, deodorization, bleaching, and degumming. The end result is a tasteless, odorless, colorless liquid fat. Olive oil, instead, can simply be pressed or spun out of the olive pulp, yielding a fresh-squeezed fruit juice with all of its natural tastes, aromas, and health-enhancing ingredients intact. By the same token, olive oil is the only oil for which the quality of the raw materials—the olive fruit—is of fundamental importance to the quality of the oil. You need prime olives to make extra virgin oil, but you can extract industry-standard seed oil from low-grade seeds.

A narrow tube at one end of the centrifuge emitted a slender, emerald arc of oil. Grazia caught some in a clear plastic cup, handed it to me, then filled another cup for herself. She sipped the oil, frowning slightly, completely absorbed, as if she no longer heard the rumble of the stones and the roar of the motors around us. Gradually her face relaxed in a guarded happiness. She raised her glass to study the oil in the sunlight lancing down from a high window, as if proposing a toast. The oil was a deep, pea-soup green, cloudy with suspended microparticles of olive pulp, invigoratingly bitter. It was warm, and tasted—*felt*—like pure nourishment, like liquid health. "This makes all the sacrifices worthwhile," Grazia said. Then her dreaminess faded, and she made a wry face. "Well, *some* of the sacrifices."

Though the De Carlo family has made oil for four centuries, the largest of their sacrifices have come in the last three decades. In 1972 they spent a small fortune to drill an artesian well 3,000 meters into the rocky soil, and built the first irrigation system for olive trees in Puglia, substantially improving their olive yield and quality. (Other local producers quickly followed suit.) Seven years later, they were among the first oil-makers in Italy to use a centrifuge to extract oil from their olives, while other producers were still using hydraulic presses not too different from those once employed by the Romans. Again, most oil-makers in Italy who are serious about quality have since switched to the centrifuge system, which not only is more efficient but yields better oil. At the time, though, people told Saverio that he was crazy for risking the family name on newfangled technology—particularly when the first batches of oil he made with the centrifuge turned out to be awful.

"The first year was a disaster," he remembers. "We couldn't get the centrifuge adjusted right. The oil was perfect in chemical terms, except that it had too much chlorophyll, and was horribly bitter. It was inedible." Farmers who had brought their crop to the De Carlo mill each year for generations dismissed Saverio as a hopeless eccentric, and began to mill their fruit elsewhere. The Alfa Laval technician who had designed the centrifuge, mortified by the apparent failure of his machine, com-

mitted suicide. But Saverio persisted. He worked day and night with
other Alfa Laval engineers, milling crate after crate of olives as they
searched for the correct settings for the equipment. Meanwhile he
coaxed some of his clients back by reinstalling the presses. "It was tough
to swallow my pride and bring the old gear back. But we had no choice.
We were going broke."

By harvest time the following year, Saverio had finally fine-tuned his
centrifuge, and he began to make the best oil his family had ever produced. "Our clients started the year using the presses, but they'd stop
by and taste my oil from the centrifuge," Saverio said. "They wouldn't
say anything. Their faces wouldn't change expression. They'd just taste
the oil and walk away. But the next time they came in with a batch of
olives, they'd want to use the centrifuge instead. These were the very
same people who the previous year had accused me of trying to ruin my
family and my father's good name, with my newfangled contraptions
and crazy ideas!"

At the time, the De Carlos were one of a handful of *pugliesi* to make
extra virgin oil. The vast majority of producers in the region were turning out *lampante* oil, which they made from overripe, windfall olives
gathered up off the ground. *Lampante* oil was sold to refineries, where
its unpleasant flavors and odors were removed with heat treatments,
activated carbon, and other processes, yielding "refined olive oil," a clear,
tasteless, odorless liquid fat which, with the addition of a small amount
of extra virgin oil, is sold in stores as "olive oil." Saverio De Carlo's use of
the centrifuge helped to begin a technology boom in olive oil production, during which Italian engineering firms like Pieralisi and Alfa Laval
invented new systems for olive crushing and malaxing and oil extraction, making quality olive oil progressively easier to produce. The De
Carlo family tried them all. Some, like the centrifuge, they adopted.
Other systems, like the stainless steel hammer and disk mills now used
by many modern producers instead of millstones, proved less suitable:
the De Carlos found that the old-fashioned millstones made more delicate oils from their strongly-flavored local *coratina* olives.

The De Carlos were pioneers in what has become an authentic renaissance in extra virgin olive oil in Italy. Over the last three decades, new oil-making technologies, together with advances in olive botany and agronomy, have enabled skilled Italian producers to make some of the best and healthiest oils in history. Italy is a long, narrow, mountainous peninsula that stretches from the Alps almost to Africa, and contains a remarkable variety of microclimates and soil types, as well as more olive cultivars than any other country—an estimated five hundred of the seven hundred cultivars recognized worldwide. Oil-makers are now using this rich botanical patrimony much as enologists use grape varietals, to create oils with a new subtlety of flavor, aroma, texture, and local personality. Italians are appreciating these brave new oils as never before: public oil tastings and training courses for oil sommeliers are becoming popular, "oil bars" on the model of wine bars are proliferating, and a growing number of restaurants offer an oil list as well as a wine list, that proposes oils of different characteristics to suit various dishes. Elsewhere the olive oil boom is even bigger: during the last fifteen years, consumption more than doubled in North America, trebled in northern Europe, and grew sixfold in parts of Asia.

Despite this flourishing market, however, the De Carlos and nearly all other producers of quality olive oil, large and small, are struggling. Over the last decade, the wholesale price of Italian extra virgin oil—or what is classified as such—has plunged; on the Bari commodities market it currently runs at €2 per kilo, a historic low. The olive-pickers employed by the De Carlos, members of local families whose ancestors have harvested the family's fruit for generations, are growing too old to work in the trees, and the job is too strenuous to attract their children. The rare art of the olive pruner, whom Grazia calls "the tailor of the countryside, the artist who determines whether you'll harvest this year or just stand by the window and watch," is being forgotten. Hundreds of olive oil producers have gone out of business, and unless the prices for quality olive oil improve, many more will follow. Francesco and Marina De Carlo are the only young people they know in this part of Puglia to follow their parents into the olive oil business. "Again and again you run into brick walls—injustices, distortions, and dirty dealing that don't exist in other industries," says Marina, whose plump round face and the gap between her incisors gives her an air of childish naïveté, until you hear her on the phone with a client. "I talk with my business school classmates who are working in other professions, and they can't understand why I stay. Sometimes I can't either." The time is ripe to make the best oils in Italian history, but few Italian producers can afford to make them.

Grazia and Saverio, like Flavio Zaramella, blame this contradictory situation on the dubious virginity of most olive oil, in Italy and abroad. To meet the legal requirements for taste and chemical properties of the extra virgin grade, an oil must be made from healthy, expertly picked olives, milled within twenty-four hours of the harvest to preserve their flavors and avoid spoilage. So it's far more difficult, expensive, and labor-intensive to produce than *lampante* oil from windfall olives. Yet if law enforcement is lax, extra virgin oil can easily be cut with cheaper oils, made with inferior olives or other substances entirely, creating unfair competition for honest producers. "Some of my customers see that I charge €8 for a liter of oil, a price that barely covers my costs, and they call me a thief," Grazia said with a bitter smile. "They tell me they've just bought a 100 percent Italian, extra virgin oil at the supermarket for €1.90. But behind the fancy label, I want to see what's really in that bottle, when even lousy, fake extra virgin oil sells wholesale for €2 a liter!"

After our visit to the mill, Grazia and Saverio drove me through their groves in a battered four-wheel-drive Fiat Panda, to show me what it takes—and costs—to make top-quality oil. A gravel road wound among fields ringed with low walls of yellow limestone. The De Carlo lands, which are scattered over an area of ten square miles, are divided into *tenute*, which in turn are made up of smaller *contrade*, each with its own distinct appearance and history, its own unique oil. Some groves consist of slender twenty-year-old trees in neat seven-by-seven-meter grids, while in others, like the Tenuta Arcamone, hoary grandfather trees grow far apart and are interspersed with other species: almonds, figs with low, reaching branches, grape vines of the local *primitivo* and *aleatico* varieties, white and black mulberry bushes, and umbrella-shaped carobs with their long brown seedpods, which produce a sweet, chocolatey paste used in confections. Saverio identified several different olive cultivars, which were hard for me to distinguish by looking at the trees, but easy when I got close enough to see the fruit, which varied considerably in shape and color. These trees included *coratina*, a popular variety in Puglia, which makes a bitter, peppery oil; the more mellow *ogliarola* and *termite di Bitetto* cultivars; and *peranzana*, originally from Provence, whose fruit can be used for oil and table olives alike. Some trees were hybrids, consisting of a meter-tall trunk of *cima di Mola*, which is highly resistant to pests and disease, onto which a sprig of *coratina*, one of the more productive cultivars in fruit and oil, had been grafted a century before and had since grown into a flourishing canopy.

This generous, mixed style of cultivation, which agronomists term "promiscuous," has been practiced here since classical times. According to Saverio, growing olives from ancient trees in these conditions isn't just picturesque, but makes distinctive oil; he said that some of the subtle flavors and scents of his oils derive from the pollens which almond trees, mulberry bushes, and other vegetation set adrift in the air, and the substances which they release into the soil. Yet it's far more expensive to make oil here than in orchards of young trees planted in orderly rows. We parked in the shade of a giant carob, and watched a team of five workers harvesting the last few olive trees at the far end of a field. Two operated a tractor with a vibrating arm clamped to an upper limb of one tree, which shook the olives loose onto a groundcloth spread below. Saverio explained that the trunk and the larger branches were too stiff and fragile to use this method without damaging them, so the rest of the tree had to be harvested using slower manual techniques; since labor costs account for most of the overall expense of the harvest, older orchards are more time-consuming and costly to work. The other three workers were standing on tall ladders propped against the far side of the tree, combing out the olives with hard plastic hooks strapped to their wrists, and with hydraulic whisks with vibrating rubber fingers shaped like large hands. To complicate matters, different cultivars ripen at different times; the De Carlos often pick them separately, and store the oil in individual tanks. Each of these details increases the cost of making fine oil, and reduces the De Carlo bottom line.

As we watched, Saverio analyzed the scene in wages, weights, and yields, showing a number-sense I've since seen in many oil-makers. One skilled olive-picker, who earns €100 a day, can harvest about six big trees, he said. Each tree produces between forty and fifty kilos of olives per harvest, which in turn yields about 15 percent by weight in oil—6 to 7.5 kilos per tree, or 6.6 to 8.2 liters of oil (one liter of oil weighs 0.91 kilos). So just to harvest this *tenuta* of ancient trees costs up to €2.50 per liter bottle of oil. Then there's the expense of milling the olives and bottling, marketing, and shipping the oil, as well as of caring for the trees throughout the year—pruning, fertilizing, irrigation, pest control. Add in taxes, permits, and chemical exams required by various government agencies that test oil quality, and each bottle of oil ends up costing the De Carlo family about €6 to produce.

Admittedly, he said, costs are lower in their younger groves, where the trees are short and neatly spaced with no foreign vegetation in the way, and each worker can harvest four times as many olives. They'd be lower still if the trees were planted in tight four-by-twelve foot grids and came to a point like Christmas trees, as they are in the so-called super-high-density groves of Spain, Portugal, and California, where the olives of a few specialized cultivars are picked with over-the-top harvesters like those used in the wine industry, and the trees are heavily fertilized and irrigated. Yet, given the high price of land, labor, and materials in Italy, even with the highest level of automation it's expensive to make extra virgin olive oil on Italian soil. And according to many experts, including the De Carlos, mechanizing the process beyond a certain point reduces oil quality. "What would happen to the complex aromas and flavors of our oils," Saverio asks, "if we made them with disposable trees, in an olive grove run like a factory?" Old trees aren't simply agricultural idealism.

For the De Carlos, making great oil requires hard work, determination, and a sharp number-sense, but also a dose of poetry.

Light filtered through the canopy of the carob tree over our heads. In the grove beyond, in the surreally bright sun of the Italian deep south, men on ladders leaned against the giant olive trees, hollowed by the seasons and twisting in the slow dance of growth and gravity. This scene of beauty and fecundity had been reenacted here every year down through the centuries, as the heavy pull of these trees shaped the lives of generation after generation. Seeing all this, I knew, would enhance the De Carlo oil when I tasted it, adding the richness of this place and its past to the perceptible tastes of the oil.

Flavio Zaramella had told me of fleets of eighteen-wheelers filled with olives from Puglia being unloaded in the night in mills throughout the north. I asked if the De Carlos knew any local growers who sold their olives like this. Grazia nodded. "Sure. Every year at the beginning of the harvest, the trucks park in front of the mills, load up with *coratina* olives, and head north to Tuscany, Umbria, Liguria." She grinned, her teeth white and even in her tanned face. "You know, those famous oil-making regions, where they grow so few olives."

FIVE YEARS AGO, in a grove of ancient olive trees in southwest Cyprus, archaeologists discovered the scene of a catastrophe. A large workshop had been destroyed by a powerful earthquake about 1850 BC and, as at Pompeii, time had stopped. Excavators found every object just as the terror-stricken workers had left it: distilling equipment and maceration dishes containing essences of lavender, coriander, laurel, and rosemary; smelting furnaces that still held traces of copper ore and bronze of the kind used to make statuettes; and looms for weaving linen and wool fabrics. At the center of the complex, they unearthed grindstones and a massive press for making olive oil, along with twelve enormous *pithoi* capable of holding a total of 3,000 liters of oil.

The significance of the mill at the heart of this seemingly haphazard agglomeration of industries gradually dawned on the excavators. Olive oil, they saw, was the common denominator for the entire complex: it was the solvent and base for perfume-making, the hot-burning fuel for the smelting furnaces, the fabric softener and lubricant for the looms in the textile mill. Workers in the mill also decanted olive oil into terra-cotta urns and sold it to local people, who would have used it as food, skin lotion, medicine, and lamp fuel. Worshippers in a triangular temple on the site even offered sacrifices of oil on a high stone altar to a mysterious god embodied as the skull of a bull with curving stone horns. "Olive oil was the greatest renewable energy source in antiquity, which burned as hot as benzene, and had twice the caloric content of carbon," says Maria Rosaria Belgiorno, lead archaeologist for the project. "At Pyrgos we find it playing a central role in a number of industries, including three—perfumes, textiles, and metallurgy—which were the central pillars of the Cypriot economy, and the main goods for long-distance trade via shipping routes and caravans. No wonder olive oil was considered sacred from the earliest times, together with the tree that produced it." Four thousand years ago, olive oil was already a driving force in the Mediterranean world: for machines, people, and the imagination.

The olive tree, *Olea Europea L. sativa*, is the domesticated cousin of the wild oleaster, *Olea Europea L. oleaster*, a hardy evergreen shrub with thorns and narrow, lanceolate leaves that is native to the Mediterranean basin and much of the Middle East. Olives are a member of the Oleaceae family, which contains some nine hundred species of trees, shrubs, and woody climbers distributed throughout the world, primarily in forested regions. Some members of the family, such as jasmines and lilacs, are famous for their flowers, while others, such as the ashes, are known for their fine-grained hardwood. *Osmanthus fragrans*, the tea olive, has sweet-smelling petals that are much prized in Japan and China as flavorings for tea, but only the olive tree produces economically important fruit.

The oleaster is extremely hardy, and thrives even in hot, near-drought conditions, producing generous vegetative wood each year as well as numerous suckers, or green shoots, that sprout from its root ball and, if not pruned back, rapidly create a dense growth at the foot of the tree. Its olives are drupes, or stone fruit, like cherries, peaches, and plums; the olive flesh contains mesocarp cells which produce tiny droplets of oil. The end product of photosynthesis, olive oil is a highly efficient energy storage medium for arid climates. The oil nourishes the olive seedling when it germinates from the stone, and helps to regulate the seedling's growth and development. As soon as an olive is separated from the mother tree, in fact, enzymes are released inside it which rapidly break the oil down into a kind of watery, microorganism-rich compost around the seed, an ideal microenvironment in which to germinate a seed in the desert.

Still, the olive's bounty remains something of a puzzle. An olive tree produces far more oil than its seeds appear to require, and the vast majority of oil contained in an olive is lost long before its seed germinates. Some biologists suggest that oil may aid in plant distribution, by making the fruit more appetizing with a dash of sweet, rich oil. A number of animal and bird species consume olive seeds together with the fruit and deposit them in their droppings, thus sowing olive seeds far and wide in rich dabs of manure. The dove of biblical fame is one species. Another is man.

Hints of the first human uses of the oleaster are scattered throughout the archaeological strata of the Paleolithic and Neolithic across the Mediterranean. From Spain and the French Riviera to North Africa, the Greek islands, and Israel, archaeologists have discovered heaps of oleaster pits which suggest they were being collected. Mysterious 7,000-year-old petroglyphs in the barren Ahaggar Mountains, deep in the Sahara, show dancing men with crowns of olive leaves, showing the importance of olives at a time when a milder climate permitted them to grow there. People gathered wild olives for food, and at some point began to press them for oil. Or perhaps the reverse: some scholars, noting the extreme bitterness of uncured olives, suggest that people first made oil for use as a skin lotion, and only later started eating it. The earliest known apparatus for extracting oil from wild olives was a stone grinder, similar to a mortar and pestle, which made a pulp that was subsequently placed in a stone basin and pressed for oil under a flat rock. Other early oil-makers may have obtained oil by putting pulped olives in a cloth bag and wringing it.

The oleaster was probably first domesticated in Palestine in the fourth millennium BC. By selecting and grafting oleasters with the best fruit, growth characteristics, and hardiness, and by pruning back excess green wood to concentrate their vegetative energies on fruit production, early farmers gradually turned the bush into a tree which bore larger, fleshier olives that contained more oil. But inside every domestic tree lurks a wild olive, which reasserts itself if the tree is abandoned: suckers sprout in a dense underbrush, the central trunk withers, and the tree reverts to the bush-like primordial olive.

By the late Bronze Age, olive trees were being cultivated systematically in the eastern Mediterranean, and oil was being extracted from their fruit with large presses, sometimes operated by several people at once. At Ekron in Palestine, a 2,800-year-old olive mill was found, with a battery of one hundred massive presses which used logs for lever arms and were capable of producing about 500,000 liters a year. In the third millennium BC, earnings from the sale of olive oil were already the lifeblood of several Mediterranean economies. Olive oil was an important part of the king's treasury in Ebla, Mari, Ugarit, and Minoan Crete, where it was stored in huge quantities in earthenware jars in the royal cellars. Cuneiform tablets at Ebla and Mycenaean Greek Linear B writings on Crete describe broad olive plantations, large-scale mills, and an extensive trade in oil with peoples throughout the Mediterranean. Olive oil helped not only to fund the rise of these civilizations but to preserve their histories as well: during the invasions or natural disasters that brought each culture to an abrupt end, the highly flammable oil stocks beneath the royal palaces caught fire, and baked the clay tablets stored in nearby archives as if in an enormous kiln, preserving them for discovery thousands of years later.

As the size and sophistication of the Pyrgos factory suggests, olive-oil-based perfumes were already a major industry in Cyprus by 1850 BC, which the island exported throughout the Mediterranean. Perhaps because of the miraculous way that perfumes capture the ephemeral

scents of spring flowers and aromatic herbs, or because of the mild eupho-
ria they can produce, the first mentions of oil-based perfumes occur in
religious contexts such as sacrifices and burials. Already in 3500 BC, at
Abydos in Upper Egypt, jars of scented oils and unguents appear in a
predynastic tomb. In the *Epic of Gilgamesh*, composed starting around
three thousand years ago, perfumes and oils appear as metaphors for
civilization. By the third millennium BC, perfumes were so widely used
in the Near East that specific styles of perfume-holder, made in alabas-
ter and later known in Greek as *aryballoi*, were mass-produced, and are
frequently found by archaeologists. Perfumes had other, less hallowed
uses as well. Since their base was an edible oil, perfumes were added
to foods and drunk in wine, either to enhance their flavors or to mask
their pong. They were used in massage and beautification, and some
were considered aphrodisiacs. After all, Aphrodite, goddess of love and
desire, was thought to be the inventor of perfumes; myths said she rose
from the sea near Cyprus, an island known for millennia as the center
of perfume production.

The Cretans also exported large quantities of oil to Egypt, where it
was used to make unguents and cosmetics as well as to embalm mum-
mies. By the Middle Kingdom, the Egyptians were producing their own
oil, olive trees had become an important motif in Egyptian art, and
amphorae of oil were a common grave good (the tomb of Tutankhamen
was amply supplied). For the Egyptians, the clear, strong light of burning
oil had sacred resonance. In a papyrus from about 1000 BC, the pharaoh
Ramses II expresses his devotion to the sun god Ra: "I made olive groves
in your city of Heliopolis, supplied with gardeners and numerous workers charged with extracting pure Egyptian oil of the first quality, to keep
alive the lamps in your sumptuous holy palace." In this life and the next,
olive oil was a sacred substance.

FOR THE DE CARLO family olives mean home, not only because
their family tree has intertwined with their groves and with oil-making

for the last four centuries, but literally as well: their house is perched atop their mill like the keep of a castle. The impression of defensiveness at casa De Carlo is accentuated by the imposing security wall which rings the property, as well as the surveillance cameras which film everyone who approaches the main gate and project them on screens inside the house. Local producers are periodically held up by armed oil bandits, who drive tanker trucks with high-pressure pumps to siphon oil out of storage silos. "After a certain hour we don't open the gates," Saverio said as we returned to the house for lunch, after touring the De Carlo groves. Francesco and Marina were waiting for us beside a large olive-wood fire, Francesco resting his head in his sister's lap as they ate pickled *cima di Mola* olives from a small porcelain bowl and tossed the pits onto the coals. (Olive pits are an excellent fuel, and oil-makers often sell their olive pomace—the solid residue from oil extraction, consisting mostly of crushed pits—to electric companies and other industries, to be burned in furnaces.)

Grazia knelt on the hearth beside them, and set several pounds of suckling lamb on a grill over the coals to cook. While the meat sizzled and popped and we watched the little eruptions of flame from each drip of fat, she told a true story of poisoning, blindness, and death, and said she half wished it would happen again.

In March 1986, she said, hospitals in northwest Italy began to admit dozens of people suffering from acute nausea, lack of coordination, fainting spells, and blurred vision. Twenty-six died, and twenty more went blind. Investigators eventually discovered that each victim had recently drunk a local white wine; several producers, they found, had been raising the alcohol levels of their wines by cutting them with methanol, a highly toxic substance also called wood alcohol. The scandal, and the resulting government crackdown, devastated the Italian wine industry. Consumption plummeted, and hundreds of producers, most of them honest, went bankrupt. Ultimately, however, the crisis radically improved Italian wine-making, and forced a generalized shift from quantity to quality.

"Before the methanol scandal, people around here didn't make wine like this," Grazia said, pouring glasses of Rivera Il Falcone 2004, a garnet-red wine made from a local grape variety, *nero di Troia*, by a producer at Castel del Monte, a nearby medieval castle. "And even if they had, nobody would have bought it. Most people just bought their wine in big jugs without labels. You'd see them on tables in restaurants, where they'd been sitting open for days. Most people wouldn't dream of buying a bottle of wine with a label on it."

After the methanol crisis, consumers grew more particular, and the producers who survived the market consolidation learned to use techniques and technology pioneered by French enologists. "After the scandal, producers started creating brand names they were proud of and wanted to defend. Only after methanol did people start thinking about what they were buying and drinking, and become willing to pay for the good stuff. And only after methanol did the government get really serious about checking quality, and making sure that the bottle contained just what the label said." During the 1990s, dozens of premier Italian wines emerged and wine became a major export product (wine recently topped $1 billion in annual sales in Italy).

Grazia brought the wine to her lips, then stopped and put it down without tasting it. "In olive oil, we're where the wine-makers were before methanol," she said. "We're stuck in the dark ages." She shook her head disconsolately. "It would be awful to see my children's livelihood damaged, even destroyed. And I'd certainly never want to see anyone hurt. But sometimes I wish there could be a methanol scandal in olive oil, which would obliterate this corrupt industry completely, and rebuild it in a healthy way. It's been Babylon around here for far too long."

Our lunch began with a succession of seasonal vegetables, mostly from the De Carlos' own garden: *lampascioni*, a small wild hyacinth bulb marinated in oil and vinegar; meaty, densely-flavored cherry tomatoes; *puntarelle*, the tender tips of a local chicory; and flat little artichokes as big around as a pound coin or a quarter, lightly fried. "*Pugliesi* eat an incredible amount of vegetables—we're like goats," said Francesco, a rangy twenty-four-year-old with a crew cut and large, dark, serious eyes that watch you unblinkingly, though their intensity is softened by a faint, unsarcastic smile that never leaves his lips. He holds a degree in food quality and a diploma in olive oil tasting from the University of Naples, and recently launched a De Carlo line of vegetables in extra virgin olive oil: mushrooms, artichokes, peppers, and other produce grown on their lands, as well as green table olives of the *picholine* and *cima di Mola* cultivars. "I introduced them to broaden our product offering so that our facilities would remain active throughout the year," he explained. "But given the sorry state of oil prices nowadays, they're a much higher-margin business and help us stay profitable." His modern financial jargon was so different from his father's homespun way of talking about the oil business that I instinctively asked if he and Saverio worked well together.

Francesco didn't miss a beat. "No. We argue every day," he said. "Every single day!" And when the laughter, a shade nervous, subsided, he added, with a quick, testing look at Saverio: "Disagreeing, sharing different opinions, deciding together the best way forward—that's the best way to collaborate, no?"

For all his university training, Francesco clearly shares his father's visceral enthusiasm for olive oil. His earliest memories also concern the family mill—such as the time, as a three-year-old, when he fell asleep in a little nest between sacks of olives, and slept through the increasingly despairing cries of his family as they searched for him amid the whirring blades and grinding wheels.

"If you'd come a couple of weeks earlier, or later, you'd be eating a completely different meal," Francesco said, looping a green ribbon of Arcamone oil over a big bowl of a half-dozen different wild-looking greens, most of which I'd never seen before, and whose names he knew only in the local dialect, not in Italian: *cuolacidd, spunzál, sevón, cicuredd.* "We *pugliesi* are demanding about these things," he continued as he stirred the glistening leaves. "We try to eat only vegetables and fruits that are in season. Many Italians are the same. They prefer fresh things from local gardens to the brown, tired-looking produce in supermarkets, even when local crops cost more. So why don't they buy their oil the same way? Olives are a seasonal fruit, and olive oil is a fresh-pressed fruit juice—it's best shortly after it's made, and goes downhill from there. Why on earth do people buy expensive vegetables like these, and dress them with the cheapest oil they can find?"

De Carlo oil flowed for the rest of the meal, gushing over the *burrata*, a rich, curdy cousin of mozzarella, and pooling in the little cups of the *orecchiette* pasta with *boragine*, a wild herb. At first I thought the De Carlos were showing off for me, but I soon saw that they used olive oil this way every day, choosing from the four different oils on the table the one that best fit each dish they were dressing. Saverio sloshed so much Tenuta Torre di Mossa, the family's pepperiest oil, over his grilled lamb that the others giggled and pointed. He bobbed his head and smiled happily, the first smile I'd seen from him. "I've spent my whole life making oil, but I can never eat enough of it. What other job gives you this?"

He handed me the oil, and I poured some over my lamb. As if it had catalyzed subtle chemical reactions in the meat, I tasted dense new flavors which I hadn't noticed in my previous, unoiled bites: the rosemary and *santoregia* Grazia had used to season it, the browned fat, the light charring from the olive-wood grill—each flavor had a new depth and intensity. The meat even felt different, more supple and juicy. This oil wasn't just a condiment, but had entered into the dish.

When I observed this, Francesco snorted. "Try telling that to a chef!" He explained that he'd recently given an oil-tasting course in Naples to twenty head chefs of prominent restaurants, most of whom had shown the most abject ignorance about olive oil. "Each of these guys ran a top-flight restaurant, right? Some had Michelin stars. They had highly developed palates for wine and for foods of all kinds. But every last one of them was using a refined olive oil or a cut-rate extra virgin in their kitchens, and even on their tables. They'd been using bad oils so long that they didn't even know what a good oil tasted like."

Grazia, who had been silent for some time, spoke with sudden force. "Then we've got to teach them. The road we've got to follow is *la cultura:*

educating people about good oil is the only way out of this crisis. Because once someone tries a real extra virgin—an adult or a child, anybody with taste buds—they'll never go back to the fake kind. It's distinctive, complex, the freshest thing you've ever eaten. It makes you realize how rotten the other stuff is, literally *rotten*. But there has to be a first time. Somehow we have to get those first drops of real extra virgin oil into their mouths, to break them free from the habituation to bad oil, and from the brainwashing of advertising. There has to be some good oil left in the world for people to taste."

She stood and went into the kitchen to get dessert, leaving a sudden silence in the room. Everyone seemed to be thinking about what she'd said, and what she'd omitted: that if the economics of oil-making don't change soon, no one will be left to make real extra virgin oil. Not even the De Carlos.

WRITING AROUND A THOUSAND years after the perfume factory on Pyrgos was destroyed, Homer tells of Odysseus's hair-raising nighttime shipwreck off the island of Scheria. The hero manages to swim ashore, and drags himself up the shingle in the dark, taking shelter in a thicket of olive trees where he is safe from bandits and wild beasts. Next morning he wakes to the sound of Nausicaa and her handmaidens playing ball on the beach, and asks them for help. They give him a jar of olive oil, which he spreads over his naked, salt-encrusted body, while they stand at a distance, trying not to stare. Then Athena, goddess of olive oil, makes the man who had seemed to them plain and somewhat scruffy appear as tall and handsome as a god, with sleek, sculpted shoulders and glistening ringlets. Nausicaa starts plotting to marry him.

Olive oil entered its golden age with the Greeks, who held the olive tree sacred and used the miracle of its oil in an almost incredible variety of ways: as food, fuel, skin lotion, contraceptive, detergent, preservative, pesticide, perfume, and adornment, as well as a cure for heart ailments, stomach aches, hair loss, flatulence, and excessive perspiration. One of olive oil's most conspicuous uses in antiquity was to make the skin softer and more sensual. Greek hosts gave their dinner guests a supply of oil, scented with pressed flowers and aromatic roots, which slaves rubbed into their feet, bodies, and hair; glistening faces and hair were images of conviviality and high spirits. The gods themselves demanded similar pampering. Cult statues like the enormous bronze and ivory effigy of Zeus at Olympia were regularly anointed with oil, not only out of reverence but, as Pliny the Elder says, to protect their metal parts from corrosion.

Oil was the economic lifeblood of many Greek city-states. "People were prepared to spend the same amount of money on olive oil back then as they do on petroleum today," Nigel Kennell, a specialist in ancient history at the American School of Classical Studies at Athens, says. "And governments went to great lengths to ensure a steady supply of it." The histories of Athens and Sparta, those famous enemies and polar opposites, are interwoven with the olive tree. The Athenians put themselves under the protection of Athena, goddess of the olive, and jealously guarded the ancient olive tree which, they claimed, she had planted on the Acropolis, and which they saw as a totem of their city: in 480 BC it was burned by the invading Persians, yet green shoots soon sprang from the charred stump, reassuring the Athenians that their city was destined to flourish again. Cuttings from this tree, planted nearby, grew into the *moriai*, a sacred olive grove tended by a special caste of priests and harvested by virgin boys. Plato held his famed Academy in their shade, and the Athenian playwright Sophocles praised the mysterious, almost supernatural quality of the olive tree as "not planted by human hands, but self-created"; none could destroy it without divine punishment, Sophocles wrote, "for it is watched upon by the all-seeing eye of Zeus Morios, and by Athena of the shimmering blue-gray eyes."

These mystical images reflect more pragmatic realities in Athenian society. Olive oil commerce helped build the world in which the plays of Sophocles, the philosophy of Plato, and the other artistic and intellectual triumphs of Periclean Athens took shape. Solon passed laws encouraging the cultivation of olives as well as the production and export of oil, and outlawed the felling of more than two trees per year. Aristotle, in the *Constitution of the Athenians*, went further, declaring that anyone who was convicted of cutting down an olive tree should be put to death. The winners at the Panathenaic Games, the athletic festival held every four years in Athens in honor of Athena, received as their prize not only enormous quantities of oil (up to five tons), but a tax exemption on oil exportation as well. Top Panathenaic prizes represented considerable fortunes, because the oil trade was lucrative. Plato himself financed a journey to Egypt by selling a batch of oil, probably made from his own trees.

Oil was likewise a vital economic resource in Laconia, land of the Spartans, whose fearsome war machine was bankrolled largely by oil revenues. Olive oil brought out the less spartan and laconic sides of their character. In the seventh century BC, the Spartans introduced the first organized sports culture in Greek society, systematically training their young men in competition, physical activity, and same-sex segregation in order to make them better warriors. The Spartans were also the first to perform sport in the nude and to anoint their naked bodies with olive oil, customs which were soon adopted in other parts of Greece. Some scholars, like Nigel Kennell, link them with the rise of bronze statuary in the sixth century BC. "A tanned athlete, shining in the summer sun, covered with oil, would really resemble a statue of the gods," Kennell says. Other researchers believe that this ritualized anointing, with its overt celebration of the male body in glistening nudity, contributed to the spread of homosexual love in the Greek world. "The oil on a gleaming, tanned, healthy body was a literally 'flashy' adornment," says Tom Scanlon, a professor of classics at the University of California, Riverside. "Oil heightened the body's erotic charge, and encouraged male same-sex desire and pederasty, first in Sparta, then throughout the Greek world."

For all their differences, by the fifth century BC the Athenians and the Spartans agreed on one thing: the generous use of olive oil in those cornerstones of classical society, the baths and the gymnasium. "The Greeks could not conceive of bathing or having athletic activity without olive oil," says Nigel Kennell. "It was not a luxury, it was a necessity." So much so, in fact, that when supplies of olive oil were cut off by barbarian raiders at the end of the empire, the baths and gymnasia closed. The Greeks used oil as fuel to heat water and light the gyms and bathhouses themselves, and as an essential ingredient of certain sports, like wrestling and gladiatorial combat (the classical Greek verb *aleiphein*, "to anoint with oil," also meant "to exercise in the gymnasium"). Above all, bathers and athletes, often assisted by slaves called *unctores* ("oilers"), slathered their bodies with ample quantities of oil; after exercising, they used thin metal blades called *strigiles* to scrape away the oil, together with a residue of dirt and perspiration. Perfumed oils were considered so precious and curative that bath and gym attendants even collected these scrapings, called *gloios*, and sold them to patrons as medicine. This oily residue was also scraped from the bronze and marble statues that adorned the baths, and from the walls and floors as well, suggesting both the quantities of oil thrown around by the bathers, and the sensory density of a day in the ancient world. "I think any Greek or Roman town of the time would have been olfactorily challenging for us," Kennell remarks.

Just how challenging? What did all this smell like? What scent wafted from Odysseus's shoulders and hair that Nausicaa found so irresistible, as he walked toward her down the beach, as handsome as a god (or as a bronze statue in the baths)? We now have fairly reliable answers to these questions, thanks to some archaeological sleuthing by Maria Rosaria Belgiorno and her colleagues at Pyrgos. Using chemical and toxological tests including the Halphen–Grimaldi method, Liebermann's reaction, and Bloor's mixture, they analyzed the dense, viscous residues stuck to the bottom of the pottery receptacles in the perfume factory. What emerged was a rich bouquet of aromatic substances that had been used in the perfumes, which included rosemary, anise, coriander, bitter almonds, bergamot, essence of terebinth, pine resin, laurel, myrtle, marjoram, sage, lavender, chamomile, and parsley.

Having identified the active ingredients of ancient perfumes, Belgiorno decided to recreate them, using the same tools and materials as in Bronze Age Cyprus. Working with Angelo Bartoli of the Antiquitates Center for Experimental Archaeology, a research institute near Rome, she made exact replicas of the terra-cotta amphorae, alembics, and other equipment found during the excavations. Aided by a Cypriot pharmacist with a passion for local wildflowers, Belgiorno obtained some of the same natural aromatics she had detected on pottery at the dig, including rosemary, lavender, and wild rose. She studied perfume recipes in works by the classical authors Dioscorides, Pliny, and Theophrastus, collected several liters of rainwater, and persuaded the Pandolfi, a noble family from Perugia who own large olive groves, to make some *onfacium*, an olive oil which the Romans pressed in August from green olives, whose extremely low free acidity and high natural antioxidants provided the ideal base for perfumes.

Then Belgiorno and Bartoli set to work. They filled a number of potbellied amphorae with olive oil and rainwater in equal parts, added one of the aromatics Belgiorno had identified to each container, and set them to decoct on a low fire. Gradually the essential oils steamed out of the plants and entered the oil. After five days the water had evaporated, leaving little pools of pure, scented oil.

Belgiorno, who often uses her own Iron Age perfumes, says that their olive oil base melts into the skin and leaves a lush, healthy gloss, unlike the drying and tightening sensations caused by the alcohol-based perfumes of today. (Alcohol-based perfumes, with their greater sterility and longer shelf life, replaced oil-based scents in the late nineteenth century, and natural perfume aromas were supplanted by cheaper synthetic scents made in laboratories.) She laments the loss of an entire world of natural fragrances, and continues to hunt the forests and upland meadows of Cyprus for more of the plants used by ancient perfumers at Pyrgos. And she remembers the strange sense of déjà vu the first time she and her Italian and Cypriot colleagues dabbed their new wild lavender oil on their wrists and throats. "It had a clean, fresh, slightly masculine fragrance, very different from the fruity aromas of today's perfumes," she says. "It was a scent we all recognized—an ancestral perfume that was a part of all of us. It was like the scent of the Mediterranean."

Odysseus smelled like this.

2

. . . .

OIL BOSSES

Olea prima omnium arborum est. [The olive tree is first of all the trees.]
—Columella, Roman agronomist, *De Re Rustica*, Book V

The olive tree, what a beast! You can't imagine how many problems it has caused me. A tree full of color, not too big, and its little leaves, how they've made me sweat! A breath of wind, and the whole tree changes its tonality, because the color isn't in the leaves, but in the space between them. An artist can't be great unless he understands the landscape."
—Pierre-Auguste Renoir, letter to Paul Durand-Ruel, 1889

*O*n the left bank of the Tiber, not far downriver from Rome's seven more famous hills, is an untidy knoll 150 feet tall and over half a mile around at the base, covered with a thin pelt of grass and a few trees, one of those odd bucolic relicts that give much of Rome a countryside feel even in the heart of town. During the Middle Ages this hill, called Monte Testaccio, was the scene of riotous banquets, and a carnival ritual in which a cartload of pigs was driven off the mountaintop and crashed to the ground below, where hungry, knife-wielding locals fell upon the unfortunate beasts. Nowadays it is lively only at night, thanks to the trendy restaurants, sushi bars, gay nightspots, and bleeding-edge dance clubs dug into its base around the perimeter. While I was in Rome to interview the Italian agriculture minister about olive oil imports, I visited Monte Testaccio, which is a testament to olive oil importations on a vast scale. As I climbed the steep upper slope, something crunched now and then underfoot, like thick seashells at the beach.

"Testaccio" derives from the Latin word *testa*, meaning potsherd, and the hill crunches when you climb it because it is composed of 25 million amphorae, dumped here by the Romans between the first and third centuries AD: Monte Testaccio is the classical world's biggest midden. Each amphora held about seventy liters of olive oil, imported from southern Spain or North Africa—in all, Monte Testaccio represents something like 1.75 billion liters of olive oil, which was distributed free to Roman citizens as part of a food subsidy known as the *annona*. Monte Testaccio is the largest known olive oil dump, but every other city, town, and army camp in the empire had a smaller version of its own. Standing at the summit of this mountain of olive oil bottles and looking out over Rome's rooftops, you understand that olive oil was every bit as vital to the ancient economy as petroleum is today. "Petroleum" is from *petra* and *oleum*, Latin for "olive oil from a stone."

If the Greeks celebrated the aesthetic and spiritual aspects of olive oil, the Romans, as Monte Testaccio suggests, concentrated on its commercial possibilities. In parts of the empire, per capita consumption was as high as fifty liters a year, and the Romans turned olive oil into an international cash crop. Agronomists like Cato and Columella codified the practice of olive cultivation. They identified twenty different olive cultivars, and distinguished several quality grades of oil; the best, they agreed, was *oleum viride* ("green oil") made from half-ripe olives, while *oleum maturum* (from mature fruit) was less desirable, and *oleum cibarium* ("fodder oil," the Roman version of *lampante*) from spoiled olives was suitable only for slaves. The Romans planted large groves in North Africa, southern Italy, and Andalucía, the source of most of Monte Testaccio's amphorae, and built huge, high-throughput mills with batteries of a dozen or more enormous lever presses. (The tall masonry housings of these presses, which still dot certain areas of the Maghreb like megaliths, are so stately and tall that early British explorers in the region mistook them for religious monuments.) The Romans set up commodity markets in oil prices in major ports, and formed specialized guilds in the oil trade, ranging from *olearii*, small retailers in olive oil, to progressively larger-scale *diffusores* and *mercatores*, to *negotiatores* who sold oil in bulk throughout the empire. Roman cargo ships crisscrossed the Mediterranean loaded with oil.

A commodity of this importance became a vital bargaining chip in the politics of empire, and was sometimes preferred to cash. Julius Caesar, wanting to punish Leptis Magna for taking part in the resistance to his invasion of Africa, fined the town fathers three million Roman pounds, or 1,067,800 liters, of olive oil. Olive oil could smooth the path to power in the empire. Emperors Marcus Aurelius and Hadrian were scions of olive oil clans in Baetica (today Andalucía), and Septimius Severus was born in Leptis Magna, capital of the famous oil-producing region of Tripolitana (modern-day Libya), where his family had grown rich making oil and the amphorae to ship it. "I've always thought of [Septimius Severus] as somewhat parallel to an oil sheikh," says David Mattingly, a professor of Roman archaeology at the University of Leicester and an authority on Roman olive cultivation. "Olive oil was the source of fabulous wealth and power."

Having obtained his authority through oil, Septimius Severus used oil to keep it. Shortly after his accession, he asked the citizens of Leptis for a "voluntary" donation of one million pounds of olive oil per year—the mafia-style offer they couldn't refuse—and distributed it free to the Roman populace. (The amphorae it arrived in, naturally, were dumped on Monte Testaccio.) His strategy, which might be called the "bread, circuses, and olive oil" approach to boosting his approval rating, worked: Severus ruled successfully for nearly two decades, and transferred his power to his two degenerate sons, Caracalla and Geta, murmuring to them on his deathbed, "Get along with each other, give piles of money to the soldiers, and forget about everybody else." (His sons, lacking his oil man's savvy, paid no attention, and ended badly.)

Since the Roman legions frequently planted olive trees where they were stationed, for food and fuel, the gnarled trunks and gray-green leaves of the olive became symbols of conquest and cultural ascendancy. As Aldous Huxley observed, "The crown of olive was originally worn by Roman conquerors at ovation; the peace it proclaimed was the peace of victory, the peace which is too often only the tranquillity of exhaustion or complete annihilation." A jug of olive oil on the dinner table likewise marked the triumph of Roman cuisine over barbarian beer and lard. "The inhabitants lead the most miserable existence of all mankind," wrote a homesick Roman senator of the second century AD posted to a settlement on the Danube, deep in the beer and pork fat forests of the barbarian north. "For they cultivate no olives, and they drink no wine." Culinary historian Massimo Montanari claims that the Romans considered oil, like wine and bread, to be "symbols of their own identity" that demonstrated the Roman ability to shape nature itself, since none of these foods exists in nature. "They become material and mental markers, in the sociological sense, of *romanitas*," Montanari says.

A substance of such prestige and volume, the ancient world's answer to sweet light crude, naturally attracted criminals. In fact, oil fraud is far older than the Romans. The five-millennia-old cuneiform tablets from Ebla describe investigators charged with combating oil fraud, naming the "olive oil surveillance team at Nuzar," near modern-day Aleppo in Syria, and a certain Ingar, head of the royal anti-fraud brigades. Oil fraud appears to have been widespread in Ptolemaic Egypt. The Romans, too, experienced a measure of it. The physician Galen mentions oil traders who cut high-quality olive oil with cheaper substances like liquefied lard. Among the many oil-drenched recipes of Apicius, the wealthy merchant and bon vivant whose cookbook was a bestseller in antiquity, is a proce-dure for doctoring cheap, smelly Spanish oil—the kind whose amphorae built Monte Testaccio—with minced herbs and roots, to make it taste and smell like prized oil from Istria.

Yet in preventing oil fraud, as in so many other areas of life, the Romans had a system. Many amphora fragments bear *tituli picti*, stamped inscriptions or handwritten notes in black or red ink that record information such as the locality where the oil was produced, the name of the producer, the weight and quality of the oil when the amphora was sealed, and the name of the merchant who imported it. Other annotations record the name of the imperial functionary who confirmed this information when the amphora was reopened at its destination in Rome. The purpose of this vast bureaucratic apparatus and of the detailed, explicit labeling of each amphora was to ensure that none of the middlemen in the long supply chain linking the olive groves in Spain and Africa to the imperial oil warehouses in Rome siphoned off oil, or substituted an inferior product. Monte Testaccio is a monument to the fight against international food fraud.

That fight continues in Italy today, though the methods and results are less impressive. The enormous popularity of the "Made in Italy" label worldwide makes it an appetizing target for food fraudsters, who earn an estimated €60 billion a year selling counterfeit or adulterated faux-Italian foods. In some of these crimes, mafia syndicates and other criminal networks sell substandard or unsafe products at huge prof-its. In the so-called Italburro scandal, for example, several dairies near Naples controlled by the Camorra blended up fake butter from vegetable oils, lard, petrochemicals, and animal carcasses (some possibly infected with BSE, or mad cow disease), and sold 22,000 tons of their product throughout the EU. Other cases involve "legal frauds," which, though seemingly unethical, are nevertheless permitted under Italian and EU law and are not mentioned on labels. Four "Italian" products in ten are actually foreign imports relabeled as Italian, often with false certificates of authenticity: over a third of pasta manufactured in Italy is made from imported wheat, half of mozzarella is produced with German milk and curds, and two-thirds of prosciutto comes from foreign hogs.

Many more cases fall somewhere in between, linking large, outwardly reputable companies with criminals, either directly or through a series of trading companies and intermediaries. Since price competition in the food industry is fierce, companies are often willing to buy their raw materials from dubious sources, even at prices so low they suggest that the foods may be fake. The Camorra-made butter in the Italburro scandal was bought up by major food companies in Belgium, France, and Germany, some of which were household names, and resold to consumers as butter and in ice cream and sweets. Regarding these high-profile companies, Paulo Casaca, former EU parliamentarian and head of the European Commission's Budget Committee, who followed the case on behalf of the EU, observes: "I'm not sure which is worse—that these companies knowingly bought tainted butter and resold it to consumers, or that, as they claim, they didn't know what they were buying, meaning that they weren't competent to distinguish between real and fake butter." (Italburro's clients also collected generous EU subsidies for the production and sale of their "butter.")

In another case dating from 2005, prosecutors alleged that Francesco Casillo, head of Europe's leading producer of semolina for pasta, brought a transport ship into Bari harbor loaded with Canadian wheat infected with a carcinogenic mold, whisked it through customs using false analytical results prepared by a complicit food chemist, then sold it to a number of major pasta manufacturers, who used it to make *fusilli* and *rigatoni* subsequently bought by consumers throughout Italy. The prosecuting magistrate, Antonio Savasta, explains that Casillo initially offered to plea-bargain a charge of selling substances not adulterated but dangerous to public health, but that the judge at the initial hearings held that the penalty for this crime was insufficient for the incident in question. In July 2012, after a long trial during which they maintained their innocence, Casillo and the chemist were acquitted for lack of evidence, among other reasons, because the EU regulations on the sampling of grain had been modified to require a larger number of samples per shipment. Antonio Savasta will await the official judgment before deciding whether to appeal, but says he is disappointed that the EU regulations have become so permissive, to the point where it has become nearly impossible to take suitable samples of quantities of grain as large as a transport ship. More recently, in November 2010, a biodiesel company delivered three batches of fatty acids intended for industrial uses, such as paper production, to a German manufacturer of vegetable feed fat. These fatty acids were contaminated with dioxin, an industrial by-product and potent carcinogen; nevertheless, they were blended into the feed fat, yielding as much as 2,256 tons of tainted feed fat, which was sold to twenty-five compound feed manufacturers. They, in turn, used it in their animal feeds, which they supplied to thousands of poultry, pig, dairy cattle, beef, rabbit, and goose farms in Germany, France, and Denmark. European health officials continue to analyze potentially affected foods, but have ordered extensive farm blockages and product recalls.

More disturbing than these individual cases of food contamination, however, is the likelihood that, for each case which comes to light, many more occur without ever being detected by authorities. Speaking of the tainted semolina incident, Antonio Barile, president of the Puglia chapter of Confederazione Italiana Agricoltori (CIA), a major farmers' union, says that these cases "open a terrifying window on what for years we have defined as 'the economy of deceit' practiced by a part of the Italian food industry. We suspect that the arrival of contaminated shipments is a regular feature of the grain imports into our country." In Italy, a range of enforcement agencies works to protect the food industry, including military police forces like the Carabinieri and the Guardia di Finanza, the agriculture ministry's Fraud Repression Unit, customs and public health offices, even the forestry service. Despite their collective efforts—2009 saw some 600,000 inspections, over 66,000 irregularities detected, and seized goods valued at about €160 million—food fraud is rising steeply. The trend is the same worldwide. OLAF, the anti-fraud agency of the European Union, reports the rapid spread of food adulteration and counterfeiting. In 2009, a new Food Fraud Advisory Unit was formed in the United Kingdom to meet the rising pressure of food crime. In the US, where retail sales of foods and beverages were worth $560 billion in 2010, several major academic institutes including Michigan State University have recently established food fraud centers, and President Barack Obama has created a presidential task force that is discussing steps to radically improve testing and enforcement by official agencies (at present the FDA only tests 0.3 percent of the total American food supply).

Admittedly, the size and far-flung internationalization of the food and agriculture sector, which has been estimated to be worth something like $5 trillion per year worldwide, makes policing it very difficult. But the reasons food fraud is on the rise go well beyond size and globalism. Some frauds are committed by companies whose chemical knowledge and expertise far outstrip those of the investigators. The enormous profits associated with food allow unscrupulous businessmen to bribe often low-paid customs agents and law enforcers. This is all the more true when the companies cooperating in the fraud are multinational concerns, who thanks to their deep pockets can influence legislators, pay for powerful advertising campaigns, and employ legal action to silence individuals and media who question their practices. Ultimately, however, the central reason fraud is on the rise is that most governments lack the political will to confront it. In an age of laissez-faire economics and blind faith in the free market, companies are often given a free hand, even at the expense of consumers.

The Romans, who created and ran one of the largest and longest-lived international empires in history, largely thanks to their immense pragmatism, even cynicism, knew this attitude, and had a phrase for it: *caveat emptor*, "let the buyer beware." But Monte Testaccio proves that the Romans sometimes took better care of the buyer than they let on. When you purchased an amphora of oil in the Roman world, you knew from the label exactly what you were getting.

DOMENICO RIBATTI, former olive oil tycoon, greets me at the door of his apartment in the center of Andria, a town forty kilometers northwest of Bari that is one of centers of olive oil production in Puglia. He is a small, slender man of seventy, with large amber eyes and thick, arched, salt-and-pepper eyebrows which give him a knowing look. His voice is surprisingly deep for someone his size, but soft and slightly reedy. This wasn't the voice I imagined as I'd read the court sentences against him, which contained numerous police intercepts of his phone calls, where he'd spoken as a man used to success, to power, to giving orders and seeing them carried out swiftly. The rough, reddish, slightly puffy texture to the skin, the careful way he walks as he leads the way across the apartment to his office, suggests he's been unwell. "This whole business has ruined my health," he says wearily. "They dragged out one trial into thirteen separate trials."

The blinds are drawn; the spacious apartment is filled with a blue-green, almost undersea twilight. We pass a low, broad, pale divan with a side table on which is a framed photograph of two young girls in ballet costumes—his daughters, he says, now in their thirties. There are several glass cases containing little boxes and animal figurines, inlaid with ivory and rare hardwoods, which glint in the low light, like a museum at closing time. His office, however, is bright and tidy. A shelf along one wall contains sheaves of documents in blue folders. "These are all of my trials," Ribatti tells me, resting his hand on one of the folders like a farmer with a prize bull, familiar but dangerous.

On the walls are photographs and documents. There is a photo of Lumière, Ribatti's foster daughter from the Congo, to whom he sends €40 each month. There is also a long, typewritten letter from one of his daughters, which she sent him while he was in prison. "Thirteen months and two days," he says with a slight quaver in his voice, looking at the letter. "I'm very Christian—profoundly so—and I've had a family who has supported me throughout. Which helped me to survive." And there is Ribatti in 1990, just before the troubles began, receiving the award for Best Extra Virgin Olive Oil Supplier from a Unilever representative: suntanned, handsome, with a suave smile of success. He is a changed man today.

Ribatti was the third son of four sons and four daughters of Giuseppe Ribatti, a classic example of a self-made man of the early years of the twentieth century, when so many southern Italians were escaping the grim poverty of their homeland and emigrating to the United States, Australia, and South America. Ribatti, who spent much of his childhood in a Benevento boarding school run by a local religious order, speaks of his father with pride and perhaps an edge of fear: an intensely hardworking, parsimonious, and unselfish man, who learned the oil trade by doing odd jobs in local mills until 1920, when he'd amassed enough cash and experience to open his own. "He started with nothing and worked his way up," Ribatti said. "He earned and invested, earned and invested, never taking big risks—he was a very prudent man. . . . Everyone says that I took after *papà*."

Ribatti's father continued to expand his mill, and eventually bought a second one. By 1963, the two facilities together were capable of milling 30,000 kilograms of olives a day. In that year, just as Domenico was about to complete his university degree in Parma, his father summoned him back home to join the family business. "I was only missing five exams and two reports, and had already started my thesis, on olive oil," Ribatti says with a touch of regret. His life had taken a fundamental turn. By the time his father died, in 1971, Domenico and his brothers were running a flourishing oil business, which, he says, sold about 75 percent of its product in bulk to major olive oil companies like Bertolli, Sasso, Filippo Berio, and Carapelli, and the remainder to consumers under their own label.

Three years later, in 1974, Domenico Ribatti went into business for himself, founding a new company, Riolio S.p.A. Instead of the conservative approach of his father, he earned a reputation for making big, bold decisions. In the late 1950s, a number of vegetable oil refineries opened in Puglia, where *lampante* oil was purified of its unpleasant tastes and odors; Ribatti bought a small refinery near Andria, and rapidly expanded it into a production center of 55,000 square meters. "I set a goal, which I later achieved, to be the leader in the international market," he says. By 1985, in fact, Ribatti was the world's foremost dealer in bulk olive oil. "First and foremost I was a speculator: I'd guess which way the market was going, and jump in with purchases five or six months in advance. I always nailed it—I always read the market right. I'd buy up ten, twenty, thirty thousand tons of oil that I knew would come in handy to Bertolli, Sasso, Carapelli, Unilever." His company remained in constant contact with its larger clients, and sometimes sent them entire tanker ships of oil. "We were expert tasters. We knew the companies well, and what standard of oil they wanted. We'd prepare and ship them lots of one thousand, two thousand tons." He says that he and a few other large companies helped to set the market price of olive oil. "We'd talk on the phone each morning, according to the deals we had to make. It's not that we'd created a cartel; we were just doing well by the producers and the millers, and doing well by ourselves, too."

Ribatti employed sales agents in Tunisia, Turkey, and Spain to make purchases of oil on his behalf, and traveled incessantly: throughout the Mediterranean to monitor the yearly olive crop and maintain contacts with oil dealers; to Switzerland to manage the intricate financial structure he had set up to handle his oil transactions; and to Rome, where he sat on the board of directors of ASSITOL, the powerful Italian trade association of oil producers, and of several other national oil associations. He was on the road so much that he missed the birth of his children. "The people at ASSITOL used to say, 'Domenico Ribatti has oil in his veins instead of blood,'" he remarks.

Ribatti turns to look at the photograph on the wall, of himself receiving the extra virgin award from the Unilever executive. He says he recently visited the ASSITOL offices in Rome. "They got all choked up when they saw me, they had tears in their eyes. 'Since you've left the business, it has gone to shit. We can't understand a thing anymore.'" He shakes his head, still looking at the photograph, as if struggling to recognize himself, to remember his earlier life, and how things were before. "From December 17, 1991, when a former friend turned against me, I've battled for eighteen years—for a lifetime." His voice has dropped to a murmur. He claims that investigative magistrate Domenico Seccia, a friend with whom he formerly used to go to dinner, suddenly subjected him to a species of judicial persecution. "I paid for the others," he says. "I was a scapegoat."

According to Ribatti, the charges made against him that he sold fake extra virgin olive oil made with hazelnut oil and other cheap vegetable oils were completely false. He says the authorities "seized about 5,500 samples of 100 grams each, and they never found a gram of this goddamn hazelnut oil! . . . Analyses, laboratories—the companies I delivered the oil to, they weren't stupid, eh? Bertolli, Unilever, they analyzed [it]! Do you think they took seed oil for olive oil?" He claims that ignorant investigators and farm union leaders attacked him because they wrongly believed the collapse of olive oil prices was due to adulteration, rather than to natural fluctuations in the oil market. He describes the incursions of military police investigators in his oil facility, the seizure of documents, his eventual arrest. "This song and dance went on for a year and a half, but they never found a fucking thing." Even before that time, he says, he knew that he was under surveillance by the authorities, both at home and when he traveled. "But I'm used to it, I'm coolheaded. I'm very human and affectionate, but I have that sixth sense that the Lord gave me, the good fortune to have a firm wrist."

He looks at me, his eyes sharp with challenge. "Since Mimmo Ribatti left the business, olive oil has gone deeper and deeper into the shit, right?" he repeats. "Why has it gone to shit? Today the price of olive oil is at €2, €2.20—these are prices from twenty-five or thirty years ago, from 1980! Was it Ribatti with hazelnut oil?"

By now he is shouting, red in the face. "That's something done by traveling salesmen, at the neighborhood market! We're talking here about the international olive oil trade!"

His voice has grown deep and gravelly and powerful, and he's breathing openmouthed, sending a dense breeze of coffee and cigarette smoke across the desk to me.

"They should have come here to talk to me! But they're afraid to talk to me."

ITALIAN INVESTIGATORS tell Domenico Ribatti's story differently. According to them, Ribatti's fall began on August 10, 1991, when a rusty tanker called the *Mazal II* docked at the industrial port of Ordu, in Turkey, and pumped 2,200 tons of hazelnut oil into its hold. The ship then embarked on a meandering voyage through the Mediterranean and the North Sea. By September 21, when the *Mazal II* reached Barletta, a port in northeast Puglia, its cargo had become, on the ship's official documents, Greek olive oil. It slipped through customs, possibly with the connivance of an official, was piped into tanker trucks, and was delivered to the refinery of Riolio, Ribatti's company. There it was sold—in some instances blended with real olive oil—to Riolio customers.

Between August and November of 1991, the *Mazal II* and another tanker, the *Katerina T.*, delivered nearly 10,000 tons of Turkish hazelnut oil and Argentinean sunflower-seed oil to Riolio, all identified as Greek olive oil. Domenico Ribatti grew rich, assembling substantial real-estate holdings, including a former department store in Bari. According to Italian court documents, he bribed two officials, one with cash, the other with cartons of olive oil, and made trips to Rome, where he stayed at the Grand Hotel, and met with other unscrupulous olive oil producers from Italy and abroad.

However, by early 1992 Ribatti and his associates were under investigation by the Guardia di Finanza, the finance ministry's military police force. One officer, wearing a miniature video camera on his tie, posed as a waiter at a lunch hosted by Ribatti at the Grand Hotel. Others, eavesdropping on telephone calls among Riolio executives, heard the rustle of bribe money being counted out. During the next two years, the Guardia di Finanza team, working closely with agents of the European Union's anti-fraud office, pieced together the details of Ribatti's crime. They identified Swiss bank accounts and Caribbean shell companies that Ribatti had used to buy the ersatz olive oil, and deciphered code names and aliases in company records: "O.T." for *olio turco* ("Turkish oil," which investigators say meant hazelnut oil), and "Nicola da Bari" for his co-conspirator Nicola Scirone (a play on Saint Nicholas, the patron saint of Bari, whose bones are said to exude a holy oil). The investigators discovered that seed and hazelnut oil had reached Riolio's refinery by tanker truck and by train, as well as by ship, and they found stocks of hazelnut oil waiting in Rotterdam for delivery to Riolio and other olive oil companies.

The investigators also discovered where Ribatti's adulterated oil had gone: to some of the largest producers of Italian olive oil, among them Nestlé, Unilever, Bertolli, and Oleifici Fasanesi, who sold it to consumers as olive oil and collected the equivalent of about $12 million in European subsidies intended to support the olive oil industry. (These companies claimed that they had been swindled by Ribatti, and prosecutors were unable to prove complicity on their part.) Yet this incident was only a drop in the dark sea of counterfeit oil. "We managed to catch wind of these two ships, but there have been hundreds of others we know nothing about," Domenico Seccia, the prosecutor in the case, told me. "It's a traffic of colossal proportions."

In March 1993, Domenico Ribatti was arrested, along with his chief chemist and three other accomplices, and charged with contraband, fraud against the European Union, operating a criminal network, and other crimes. During an extended legal battle, he insisted that he had been defrauded by his suppliers—Caribbean shell companies that had sold Riolio hazelnut oil instead of olive oil. But when Pascal Brugger, a Swiss financier who handled financial transactions for these companies, turned state's evidence and revealed that Ribatti himself controlled them, his defense collapsed. In the end, Ribatti plea-bargained a thirteen-month prison term.

Leonardo Colavita, former president of ASSITOL, the olive oil trade association of which Domenico Ribatti was a leading member, and the owner of the Italian olive oil company Colavita, told me that the group's policy is to expel member companies which are accused of illegal activity, so that, as he put it, "no one can attack us, no one can say, 'You have criminals in your organization!'" According to Colavita, when Ribatti resigned from the organization he said, "If I leave, everybody's got to leave." (No other company left ASSITOL at the time, however.) "Mimmo Ribatti was a gentleman, because he didn't name names," Colavita said. "If he had named names, a lot of folks would have gone to jail." He claims that many oil firms, including major Italian brands, knew that Ribatti was selling them adulterated oil (Colavita said his firm did not buy oil from Ribatti). "They say they didn't, but they knew. If they didn't know, then they were incompetent—just as I knew, they had to know, too. And since they aren't incompetent, it means that they knew."

OLIVE OIL is one of the most frequently adulterated food products in the EU; within Europe, the problem is particularly acute in Italy, the leading importer, consumer, and exporter of olive oil and the hub of the world olive oil trade. (For the past twenty years, Spain has produced more oil than Italy, but much of it is shipped to Italy for packaging and is sold, legally, as Italian oil.) "The vast majority of frauds uncovered in the food-and-beverage sector involve this product," Colonel Leopoldo Maria De Filippi, the commander for the northern half of Italy of the NAS Carabinieri, an anti-adulteration group run under the auspices of the Ministry of Health, told me.

Many olive oil scams involve straightforward mixing of low-grade vegetable oils, flavored and colored with plant extracts and sold in tins and bottles emblazoned with Italian flags or paintings of Mount Vesuvius, together with the folksy names of imaginary producers. More sophisticated scams, like Domenico Ribatti's, typically take place in high-tech laboratories, where cheaper oils of various kinds, made from olives but also from seeds and nuts, are processed and blended in ways that are extremely difficult to detect with chemical tests. One popular technique is "mild deodorization," by which cheap *lampante* oil is cleansed of its unpleasant tastes and odors by heat-treating it at 40–60 degrees Celsius. (Alfa Laval, the leading manufacturer of extraction equipment for olive oil and other vegetable oils, produces the SoftColumn refining system, a low-temperature deodorizer which the company markets for seed oils but which is reportedly used to deodorize large quantities of olive oil as well.) Deodorized oil, though unnaturally bland and devoid of the fruitiness required by law in extra virgin olive oil, is also largely free of defects, and lacks the telltale chemical signatures left by conventional refining.

Deodorized olive oil appears to play a role in another recent case involving the Azienda Olearia Valpesana, one of the biggest oil traders in Italy. Between May and June 2012, four executives of the company, including its president, Francesco Fusi, and the head of the chemical analysis laboratory, Davide Passerini, were arrested on charges including fraud and forming a criminal network. Investigators impounded almost 8,000 tons of the company's oil as physical evidence. In the Valpesana chemical laboratory, agents of the Guardia di Finanza found notebooks with handwritten notes explaining how to mix oils of various qualities and origins, including lampante oil and oil from Spain and Tunisia, to produce oils apparently extra virgin and entirely Italian. In addition, they found numerous sales contracts for Spanish extra virgin oil on which, alongside the officially declared characteristics of the oil consistent with the extra virgin grade, different chemical characteristics had been added by hand: alchyl esters, peroxides, and free fatty acidity below EU requirements for extra virgin olive oil, and which investigators say indicate the actual chemical characteristics of the oil.

Using phone and wire taps, detailed analysis of the flows of olive oil through Italian customs, and other techniques, investigators assembled a picture of what they call "a sophisticated mechanism of fraud" by which "extra virgin" oils were assembled using inferior oils, including *deodorato*. A document of the Guardia di Finanza notes that some of Italy's leading olive oil companies are clients of the Azienda Olearia Valpesana and observes that "the prosecuting district attorney does not exclude the possibility that the investigation will spread to involve numerous [other] companies in the [olive oil] business, both national and foreign."

The Azienda Olearia Valpesana maintains its innocence. It states that chemical analysis of the oil in question by leading oil chemists working as consultants for the company have demonstrated that it does, in fact, meet EU norms. Whatever testing ultimately shows, it seems unlikely to explain the apparent double notation system that the investigators say they found. It also raises a more fundamental question: Are EU norms, formulated in part by chemists working for big oil companies, sufficient to guarantee the quality of the olive oil that we eat?

Other large-scale frauds appear to succeed thanks to the powerlessness, acquiescence, or even complicity of officials responsible for detecting oil crime. In April 2008, for example, investigators in Puglia confiscated nearly three million liters of olive oil from the Azienda Olearia Basile, which according to the investigative magistrate in the case, Michele Ruggiero, was falsely marked as organic, or as "100% Italian" when the company had actually imported it from North Africa. Among the suspects in the case was Tonino Zelinotti, head of the chemical analysis laboratory and taste panel of the Italian customs agency and a central figure in the creation of olive oil laws and authenticity tests in Rome and Brussels. Prosecutors accused Zelinotti of wrongly certifying oil from Azienda Olearia Basile as extra virgin grade when it was in fact virgin or worse, and falsifying chemical analyses to throw off investigators. (Zelinotti died a short time later and is no longer a suspect in the case, for which a decision is expected in October 2012. Members of Azienda Olearia Basile maintain their innocence.) Complicity exists at the highest levels of the Italian administration. In 2007, an EU investigation determined that 95 percent of detected misappropriations of European agricultural subsidies, a large portion of which had occurred in the olive oil sector, had taken place in Italy. Brussels has charged Italy with negligence in recovering these funds, and is suing the Italian government for €311 million in unrecovered subsidies. Sometimes, in fact, the deck seems intentionally stacked against investigators in olive oil crime, who are hampered by bureaucratic delays, legal cavils, low sanctions, and the fact that producers fined for infractions can postpone payment for years. Colonel De Filippi acknowledged that some companies are essentially immune to investigation. "Unfortunately, there are big producers who have strong political ties," he said.

Certainly ASSITOL and its member companies have considerable influence both in Rome and in Brussels. The heads of the oil laboratories of several ASSITOL member companies sit on the Italian government's Technical Commission on Oils and Fats, which helps draft olive oil regulations. (Domenico Ribatti's chief chemist, Gioacchino De Marco, was a member of the commission until his involvement in the Riolio case.) Senior members of the commission, and of the analogous EU olive oil technical commission in Brussels, have also served ASSITOL as scientific consultants. ASSITOL enjoys close ties with the Italian ministry of agriculture, as is clear from joint projects such as the plan to form a "Mediterranean Axis of Olive Oil," described in a 2004 government document as "an informal cartel of international dimensions among olive oil producers." According to Leonardo Colavita, ASSITOL's former president, the project was initiated by Giovanni Alemanno, the agriculture minister from 2001 to 2006, and would be financed by the Italian government. The goal, he said, was to expand olive oil production in Syria, Morocco, Turkey, and other southern Mediterranean countries outside the EU and to facilitate the sale of the oil in Italy, using a duty-free storage facility in a southern Italian port.

Paolo De Castro, who replaced Alemanno as agriculture minister, told me that he was unfamiliar with the project, and there is no evidence that it was ever implemented. But when I described it to him he said that he supported its aims. "We have to avoid distortions, not place limits on business," he told me. "The important thing is that people don't act like wise guys, and that this Tunisian oil doesn't become extra virgin olive oil from Puglia. Now, this is quite a little problem, eh?" However, any plan to create a cartel among olive oil producers violates Article 101 of the European Union Treaty, which specifically prohibits cartels as harmful to free trade and consumer choice. If carried out, such a scheme would also appear to facilitate the evasion of duties on oil imported from outside the European Union. A plan like the Mediterranean Axis of Olive Oil would seal the fate of small Italian oil-makers like the De Carlos, who, betrayed by the agriculture ministry that should be defending their interests, would be swamped by cheap imported oil.

WHILE INVESTIGATING Domenico Ribatti, the European anti-fraud team discovered that the two tanker ships he had used to import hazelnut oil had also transported further contraband oil to Monopoli, another port in Puglia. The team traced this oil to an acquaintance of Ribatti's named Leonardo Marseglia, the managing director of Oleifici Italiani, an olive oil and vegetable oil company in Monopoli. This company, now called Casa Olearia Italiana, became one of the leading olive oil importers in Europe, and owns one of the largest edible-oil refineries in the world.

Even his enemies speak of Leonardo Marseglia as a man of unique talents. An officer in the Guardia di Finanza who spent years investigating him and his associates for allegedly importing contraband, misappropriating EU funds, forming a criminal network, and committing other offenses—charges later dismissed on statute of limitations—described him as "a person of great astuteness, with an exceptional business mind." An elderly resident in Marseglia's nearby hometown of Ostuni, who had known him since childhood, said he was widely admired in the area, where he was nicknamed "Onassis" for his flamboyant lifestyle. "He's audacious, hardworking, courageous as a lion, utterly unscrupulous," the man told me.

Not long ago I traveled to Monopoli to visit Marseglia at Casa Ole-aria. The coastal highway ran through a series of ancient olive groves, trees of the local *ogliarola* cultivar with huge barrel-shaped trunks and short branches, some of which were a thousand years old. Through occa-sional gaps in the trees, the Adriatic shone pale green, bordered by low dunes and broad yellow-sand beaches. Puglia's flat, sandy coastline and numerous small bays, together with its proximity to the Balkans and North Africa, has long made the region a haven for smugglers. Before a sweeping government crackdown in 2000 disrupted the trade, cigarette smugglers ran nighttime convoys of custom-armored SUVs through the back roads of the region, with front bumpers made from railroad iron to act as battering rams and tires filled with silicone to prevent them from being shot out by police. "Criminal organizations large and small tend to divide up the coast of Puglia into little fiefdoms, each specializing in its own illegal trade," says Pasquale Drago, an investigative magistrate in Bari who has been a leader in fighting contraband in cigarettes, mari-juana, and heroin, and has successfully prosecuted prominent mafia figures. Puglia remains a primary doorway into the EU for illegal immi-grants, drugs, and, as in the Riolio case, illicit olive oil and other veg-etable oils from Turkey and the Maghreb, much of which is resold as Italian extra virgin oil.

Since 1994, Antonio Barile, the farm union president in Puglia, has led tens of thousands of olive farmers in blockades of the ports of Monopoli, Bari, and Barletta, where many tankers carrying foreign oil arrive. Some oil shipments are outright contraband, he says, but oth-ers enter the country with government approval, though in violation of European law, which allows oil to be imported from countries outside the EU only when local supplies cannot meet demand. He denounces "the shameful silence of the port authorities and the customs office," who fail to report how much foreign oil arrives in Puglia, and has repeat-edly criticized the Italian agriculture ministry, particularly under the former minister Giovanni Alemanno, for authorizing illegitimate importations, which undercut local producers and benefit only the olive

oil industry. "He must revoke the authorizations, because they are killing Puglia's olive oil," Barile said of Alemanno in an interview in 2004,
another crisis year for local olive farmers. So much of this cheaper foreign oil enters the local market that, for example, according to investigators at the Guardia di Finanza, only 1 per cent of the oil made in Puglia
during the 2003–4 harvest and intended for sale in Italy actually sold at
a profit for local producers. "Thousands of olive oil producers are victims
of this 'drugged' market," Barile told me.

At Monopoli, the highway skirts the Casa Olearia plant, a gleaming
expanse of stainless steel silos, office buildings, smokestacks, and warehouses set, incongruously, in a grove of massive olive trees, like a space
station that has just touched down. Since Leonardo Marseglia bought
the complex in 1981, it has grown fifteenfold; in 2005 the company,
which also operates in energy, tourism, construction, real estate, and
finance, processed about a million tons of olive oil and vegetable oils.
The Italian press has called Marseglia, who began his career driving a
delivery truck for his family's olive oil company, "the emperor of Italian oil" and the "baron of extra-virgin." Nonetheless, Marseglia says
he recently decided to leave the olive oil business because of incessant
attacks by local authorities, who for years have accused him of a range
of olive oil crimes. Instead, he is using oils to make biofuel and generate
electricity, because, as he told me, in these fields (which also happen to
be subsidized by the EU), the authorities "break your balls less."

On a wall in the reception area at Casa Olearia was a gaudy, expres-
sionistic oil painting of three peasant women gathering olives from the
ground beneath a gnarled olive tree—a tree that resembled those visible through the window. Marseglia, who is sixty-five, has the powerful
frame, thick neck, and heavy-lidded eyes of an aging prizefighter, and
the ready, raffish grin of a fighter still game to go a few more rounds.
Despite a habit of referring to himself in the first person plural, he is
disarmingly informal, and he prodded my arm companionably from
time to time to emphasize a point. I asked him whether he was guilty
of olive oil adulteration, contraband, or the other crimes with which he

had been charged. "We have never been convicted of anything up to this point," he replied. "Therefore we don't think there's anything to add. We have suffered trials, and we have been acquitted because the events did not take place." He said that he knew Domenico Ribatti but had never done business with him. "He was convicted, and ended up in prison. To us this didn't happen."

Regarding the idea that major oil companies had known that some of the oil they bought from Ribatti was adulterated, he made no comment, but later observed that *caveat emptor* was the golden rule in the olive oil trade, even when it came to chemical testing. "You don't pay anything up front. Test first, then pay—otherwise you don't pay. And if everything turns out all right, that means that you"—here Marseglia paused and raised his eyebrows significantly, then laughed—"that you were in on the scam! Pure logic, see?" He winked and said, "You'll get the 100 percent truth only from us, because we're out of the [olive oil] business."

Marseglia is another oilman who grew up in the olive oil culture of southern Puglia, buzzing like an eager bee around his father's small mill in Ostuni, where there were 108 such mills when he was a child. "When nobody knew where I was, because I wasn't at home, they could always find me at the mill—it was a sure thing." He remembers his father bending down to pick up an olive that had fallen to the ground, which otherwise would have been lost—much like the women in the painting in the foyer of Casa Olearia. "Which taught me that from little drops you could even make the sea. . . . I also learned the drive to make quality oil, which was my father's obsession. In fact, we were the first to produce edible olive oils, at a time when everyone else in the area made lamp oil, *lampante*."

He said that most Italians still know surprisingly little about olive oil quality. "There's a lot of mystification, of outright ignorance. Even many producers can't tell you if their oil is good or bad: it's good because it comes from their olives, because they harvested at the right time, blah blah blah. And they say that folks should eat stuff which comes from the countryside, that there's no need to taste the oil or test it—no, this isn't right. Here tradition is clouding the facts, how things really are."

Marseglia told me that he came into conflict with the local oil culture when he began to import olive oil from abroad, to improve the quality of low-grade local oils. Here he began writing figures on a pad in front of him, in a large, slanting, but legible hand. "Italy produces 300,000 tons of oil. 300,000 tons more [of imported oil] are required to satisfy internal demand, and an additional 400,000 for exports, more or less. So you have to import 600,000 to 700,000 tons per year. In Puglia this oil has a very high value. If you import into Tuscany or Molise, where people are selling extra virgin olive oil at €10, €15, nobody pays any attention, but in Puglia, the ship arrives and people say, 'Fuck!' And since we imported a lot, to make blends to save many bad, smelly local oils, people basically saw it as an affont. As if we were stealing income from poor folks."

Marseglia estimated that 98 percent of olive oil sold in Italy as extra virgin isn't actually top-grade oil. "The law says up to 0.8 percent [free acidity] and no taste defects, that's it. I think that's how it should be. How it *should* be, but not how things are." He drew a pie chart showing what he considered the real quality of olive oil in the world: 2 percent excellent oil; 8 percent second-tier oil, good but not exceptional; and the remaining 90 percent what he called "so-so oil." Since excellent oil was far too scarce to meet consumer demand, he explained, olive oil companies sold second- and third-tier oil as extra virgin. "It's anything but extra virgin, the oil we have here," he said, indicating the second- and third-tier oils in his diagram. "It's decent oil, sure, but, if we want to talk about 'excellent,' it's not."

He didn't seem to think that this was a problem. "First of all, let's give people good oil," he said. "Then the excellent—all the extraordinary stuff at €40 or €50 a kilo, which a few idiots in the world can afford—we'll think about that later, no?" He told me that his family uses ordinary oil: "For us, the concept of 'good' is enough. We want to be average folks."

Over lunch in the Casa Olearia canteen, Marseglia showed me what he meant by good oil. The *strippaggio* and other elaborate taste-testing methods used by olive oil sommeliers were "all hot air," he said. "Tasting a plate of pasta is easy. Tasting a glass of wine is easy. Tasting a piece of fruit is easy. Tasting oil is the same. It has to have the same pleasurable tastes. If it has an unpleasant one, it's not good—that's pretty simple. They say you need a lot of knowledge to understand it, because they want to make the subject seem more intellectual."

He reached across the table for a bottle of Giusto, his company's supermarket label, unscrewed the cap, and pointed it at me. "Smell this. Does it smell good, or stink?" It smelled good: a tart, intensely fresh fragrance that I'd come to associate with *coratina* olives.

Marseglia brought the bottle to his lips and tipped in two big glugs. "So you put it in your mouth, right?" he said thickly, through the oil. "Either it's disgusting, and you spit it in somebody's face, or it's good." The sign of a good oil, he went on, is the *bocca bella* ("pretty mouth"), the pleasant taste and clean sensation that remain in the mouth after you've swallowed the oil.

Marseglia passed me the bottle. "Now you taste it, without doing what those other guys do," he said. "Pretend you're eating a candy, something good. Then we'll see how it leaves your mouth." He watched my face intently as I swallowed the oil, then nodded, satisfied. "Tasting things is simple," he said.

IN 1994, eighty agents from the Guardia di Finanza raided Casa Olearia and seized documents detailing four illegal shipments of oil involving the *Mazal II* and the *Katerina T.* In July 1996, an arrest warrant was issued for Marseglia and sixteen business associates, on charges that included contraband, European Community tax fraud, and operating a criminal network. Three weeks later, Marseglia, accompanied by his lawyer, surrendered to the authorities and was jailed. Prosecutors accused him of importing Tunisian olive oil falsely identified as a product of Europe, thus evading the duty imposed on non-European goods, and of illegally receiving European olive oil subsidies when, later, he sold the oil. Domenico Seccia, the prosecutor in the case, who also prosecuted Ribatti, believes that Marseglia taught Ribatti the criminal techniques for which Ribatti was eventually convicted. "Ribatti inherited from Marseglia all the methods and procedures of the fraud," Seccia told me. "The Marseglia case is identical to Ribatti's."

In a ruling on January 13, 1997, Italy's Supreme Court noted that the magistrate who authorized the arrests of Marseglia and his associates had "amply demonstrated, with documentary evidence, that the product unloaded in Monopoli was extra-EC olive oil from Tunisia, free from import tariffs, which was subsequently made to appear to be Italian olive oil using false sales transactions, resulting in serious EC fraud." The court also noted that the magistrate had ordered the men's arrests because of what he considered "the concrete risk that similar activities would be repeated," and because of the "criminal character of the defendants." Nonetheless, after years of judicial wrangling, the prosecutors were unable to win convictions, and the charges against Marseglia and his associates were dismissed in 2004, when the statute of limitations expired.

Leonardo Marseglia's problems with the law continue, however. In late 2010, he and five associates were tried at a closed hearing in Bari on charges relating to another olive oil crime, this one involving the United States. According to documents compiled by investigators of the Guardia di Finanza, between 1998 and 2004 Casa Olearia evaded more than €22 million (about $30 million) in EU duties by illegally importing 17,000 tons of Turkish and Tunisian olive oil, apparently with the cooperation of Italian customs officials. EU law allows non-European companies to ship oil duty-free to Italy for processing by an Italian company; however, investigators say that AgriAmerica, the American firm that Casa Olearia says imported the oil, was a shell company created by Marseglia in order to evade customs duties. The oil was processed in the Casa Olearia laboratories, where investigators suspect that it was mixed with vegetable oils, though they have been unable to prove this. Some of the oil was bought by Italian companies, but the bulk was shipped to distributors in the United States, who sold it as Italian olive oil. According to Guardia di Finanza investigators, AgriAmerica customers included some of the largest olive oil distributors in America, including East Coast Olive Oil (now part of the Portuguese food giant Sovena), America's leading olive oil importer and private label bottler; the supermarket group Wakefern Food; and Sysco, the biggest food service distributor in North America. (There is no evidence that these companies knew the origin of the oil they bought from Marseglia.) The fact that most people don't associate these names with olive oil shows how completely the business is in the hands of intermediaries, and how many middlemen stand between the consumer and the groves.

Marseglia and his co-defendants were charged with forming a criminal network and other crimes; an investigator familiar with the case told me that Marseglia was unlikely to be convicted. "He has protection at the highest levels, from right to left across the political spectrum," the investigator told me. Marseglia, citing the ongoing nature of the case, declined to comment on the charges against him but said that he expected to be found innocent, as he had been in previous investigations. In fact, in May 2012 he and his codefendants were acquitted on all charges; the prosecuting magistrate in the case, Isabella Ginefra, is awaiting the official judgment before deciding whether to appeal. Despite ASSITOL's policy of expelling members that are undergoing legal proceedings, Casa Olearia has remained a member in good standing of the organization, which has considerable influence in both Rome and Brussels. The head of the Casa Olearia oil laboratory, Mario Renna, like the lab heads of several other ASSITOL members, belongs to the Italian government's Technical Commission on Oils and Fats, a group that helps draft olive oil regulations.

ASSITOL seems unconcerned about the past legal troubles of Leonardo Marseglia's company Casa Olearia. "It's true, fifteen years ago they did some big frauds," Colavita told me in 2006. "They imported extra [virgin olive oil] calling it seed [oil], and vice versa." But according to Colavita, those days are over. "For the last ten years he's 100 percent clean," Colavita said of Marseglia. "He wasn't before, but a lot [of companies] weren't, starting with the big ones."

3

· ·

OLIVES SACRED AND
PROFANE

Silently, the olive is reading within itself the Scriptures of the stone.

           —Yannis Ritsos, "Lady of the Vines"

While European horizons darken under the haze of uncertainty and disorder, Italy offers the world a marvellous spectacle of composure and discipline, of civic and Roman strength. Nations who do not know us, or who know us merely through literature, are today amazed by our economic, political and military presence.... It is, therefore, a great olive branch that I hold high, between the end of the fourteenth and the fifteenth years of the Fascist Era. But beware, this olive tree grows in a vast forest: a forest of eight million well-sharpened bayonets, held by men who are young, intrepid, and strong.

           —Benito Mussolini, speech of October 24, 1936

A path runs past my house, angling up the steep slope between dry-wall terraces faced with granite and pink limestone, where grape vines climb trellises of wild chestnut branches bleached by the sun to the color of bone. On a map of the area drawn by French surveyors at the beginning of the nineteenth century, after Napoleon had pocketed Liguria during his conquest of Italy, it appears as an "ancient roadway." It's at least as old as the Middle Ages, and a local historian believes it dates to Roman times, perhaps even to the Iron Age. These days it's only traveled by a few elderly farmers; the earth is soft underfoot between the uneven cobbles, and large stretches of its course are overgrown in summertime by clover and thyme and wild mint. Yet the landscape still respects this ancient route: the terraces defer to its straight, sharp vector, and the medieval farmhouses on either side face toward it like people around a campfire, glad for its company and movement and clatter of trade, its news from the wider world. The path was here before every other thing in this landscape, and everything is oriented to it.

Everything except one. As the path crosses a saddle on the hillside a hundred meters above my house, a charmed spot where the sunlight lingers in the afternoons and spring violets bloom weeks earlier than in the valley below, it makes a small horseshoe bend, where centuries of travelers have taken five extra steps to avoid something in their way. This ancient obstacle is an olive tree, squat and thick-trunked like the local farmers, its partially exposed roots gripping the soil like a pair of old hands. The bark is pierced with holes made by woodworms, birds, nails, and what may have been bullets (during World War II, partisans sometimes hid from the Fascists and Nazis inside the hollow trunks of giant olive trees). Inside the trunk there's a patch of charred wood from some wildfire beyond living memory, which must have devastated the tree. But in the fiercely patient way of olives, green shoots grew up from the charred remains and the tree was reborn. Like the mythic olive tree on the Acropolis cherished by the Athenians as the talisman of their city, which burned in the Persian sack of 480 BC but sprouted anew the next day from its smoking stump, a sign that the city would survive and prosper despite the disaster. Or like the olive tree at the head of the bay in Ithaca, which Odysseus sees when he finally returns there after his epic voyage, the one fixed point in a landscape altered by long absence, which tells him that he's home.

Until I moved here ten years ago, this detail made no sense to me: why would Homer have chosen an olive tree to make Odysseus realize he's back in Ithaca, and not, say, the generous curve of the bay, or the familiar silhouette of the surrounding hills? Then I began to notice the olive tree on the hill behind my house as I returned each day from my own modest odysseys. Somehow it was that tree, and not the old stone path or the shape of the horizon or even the roofline of my house, that I looked for. It seemed natural to think of the tree in mythic terms. It has watched a procession of peasants, priests, Napoleonic soldiers and Renaissance mercenaries, highwaymen and barefoot saints walk down this roadway and vanish into the sandstorm of time. It seems as permanent a part of this landscape as the hillside itself, the pink limestone cliffs across the valley, or the bright blue ribbon of sea beyond them, where Corsica floats like a dream on clear mornings. Yet despite the tree's mass and hoary tenacity, you know it's mortal: it can be killed back by drought or poison, or cut off tomorrow by frost or a saw. The rings in its trunk mean more than a geologic record, the neat strata on a canyon wall: their lean and fat years capture the history of this community, the hardships and plenty of people who have tended this tree for generations, and in turn have been fostered by it. Until recently its oil lit every home in the village, made machines run smoothly, cured the villagers' ailments. Its oil still feeds them, and its branches hang in their houses throughout the year, distributed at Eastertime by the parish priest as reminders of patience, courage, strength. This olive tree stands for our community, and its oil is the essence of this place.

That a tree can live so long, and spin its wondrous juice from photosynthesized sunlight and a little rainwater sucked from the rocky soil, is itself miraculous. No wonder the ancients held this lifegiving, wondrously tenacious tree to be sacred, and its oil to be the gift of Athena, Aristaeus, and Hercules. And no wonder this vital active ingredient of the classical world seeped deeply into the three great monotheistic religions which arose there, giving the rites of the Hebrews, Christians, and Muslims the luster of oil and filling their sacred texts with images of gnarled, gray-green trees.

COOKBOOKS, LIKE HISTORIES, are written by the victors. When the Germanic tribes of northern and eastern Europe overran the Roman Empire in the fourth and fifth centuries, they revolutionized its culinary fashions and brought the revenge of animal fat on imperial oil. These woodland hunters and pastoralists, who dressed in skins and furs instead of linen togas and silken tunics, introduced a Germanic *nouvelle cuisine* based not on the Greco-Roman triad of bread, wine, and olive oil but on meat, beer, and animal fat. The tastes of the new masters of empire soon caught on. Pork was included together with oil in the *annona*, the distribution of free food made to Roman citizens living in the capital. Forests came to be measured not in hectares but in hogs— the space that a pig grazed in a day. On illustrated calendars, December scenes of the olive harvest familiar to the Greeks and Romans gave way to pigs battening on woodland acorns, and the hog slaughter. Classical authors, who had formerly described the barbarian predilection for animal fat with bewilderment or disgust, now celebrated it: Anthimus, a learned philosopher and physician at the court of Theodoric the Great, king of the Ostrogoths, described the wondrous qualities of lard, which he said the northlanders used as a dressing for vegetables and every other sort of food, and even ate raw as a kind of cure-all: "For them it is such a remedy that they have no need for other medicines."

In the sea of barbarian beer, butter, and lard that washed over the ancient empire, Christian monasteries and cathedrals formed isolated islands of old-fashioned oil expertise. Olive oil remained a vital ingredient in the worship, economy, health, and daily diet of the Christian clergy, and through them, in the lives of the faithful. To make their holy oils and light their churches, monks and priests needed steady supplies of olive oil. To this end, church councils decreed the protection of olive groves, sometimes prohibiting the cutting of even a single tree. Olive oil was often used as an alternative currency, and commanded a premium price: in high medieval contracts, three to five liters of oil had the same value as a fat hog. Monk-agronomists tended the olive groves and made oil on their communal lands according to the advice of Cato, Columella, and other classical authorities, whose tracts they could consult in their monastic libraries. As the Germanic tribes converted to Christianity, their national diets entered into tension with the dictates of the Church, especially during fast days, when Christians were forbidden to eat meat and animal fat. For 100 to 150 days each year—Fridays, the forty days of Lent, and a range of other holidays and vigils that were determined by local custom—good Christians used olive oil instead of suet or lard to cook and season their food.

Making olive oil required some old-time Greco-Roman skill, which the barbarians often lacked. In his *Dialogues*, Gregory the Great tells a story from the life of Sanctulus of Norcia, a sixth-century priest who lived in what is now Umbria shortly after the area was conquered by Lombard war bands. Sanctulus arrived at an olive mill one day and asked its pagan Lombard owners to fill his oilskin. These rough men, who had struggled all day at their press without obtaining so much as a drop of oil, thought Sanctulus was mocking them and cursed him loudly. The imperturbable saint merely smiled and said cheerfully, "Is this how you pray for me? Come, fill my skin and I will leave you." As the Lombards renewed their insults, Sanctulus glanced at the press and saw that no oil was coming out. He asked for a bucket of water, blessed it, and then, with all eyes on him, threw it over the press. "And such an abundance of oil ran forth," the hagiographer concludes, "that the Lombards, who before had long labored in vain, now had enough oil to fill not only their own vessels, but also his skin. Their hearts were filled with gratitude, because the holy man, who had come to them begging for oil, was now, through his blessings, supplying in great abundance that which he himself had come to find."

Sanctulus's help was probably more technical than celestial: experienced millers commonly threw hot water on their presses to increase yields, especially during the second pressing, when they coaxed a few last drops of oil from the nearly spent pomace. (The expressions "first pressed" and "cold pressed" once distinguished high-quality oil extracted from fresh olives from oil made with the overheated dregs. Nowadays these terms are largely obsolete, because all true extra virgin oil is made from fresh olives milled at low temperatures, and most of it isn't pressed at all, but centrifuged.)

Olive oil was also an essential fuel in churches, burning in lamps at altars and saintly shrines. Some large churches consumed huge quantities: in the Lateran basilica during the fifth century, 8,730 oil lamps burned around the clock, all year long. Olive oil was preferred to other fuels because it was long-lasting, gave off a clear, brilliant light, and was odorless—the pork fat customarily burned in the lanterns at the ninth-century abbey of Fulda smelled so foul that its studious abbot Rabanus Maurus, who certainly burned much midnight fat himself, begged the Carolingian king Louis the Pious for an olive grove in Italy, to light his church in a more seemly and fragrant way. No doubt agreeing with Rabanus, well-to-do worshippers throughout Europe willed money gifts or supplies of oil to churches, to fuel lamps that would burn perpetually for the salvation of their souls. Sailors and traders who arrived in the port of Venice, following an ancient tradition, left money or oil to fuel the altar lamps of the Basilica of San Marco. Elsewhere the faithful bequeathed olive trees or entire groves to a church, to supply oil for its lamps. When a group of knights rode through Puglia in 1147 on their way to the Holy Land during the Second Crusade, they stopped at the Bari cathedral to pay their respects to Saint Nicholas, patron saint of the city, to whom they deeded the oil of forty olive trees in perpetuity, on the condition that a lamp with their oil be kept burning continuously until their safe return. Such bequests often stipulated that the gift be void if oil were used that had not come from the deeded groves—evidence of a brisk trade in ersatz lamp oil, perhaps cut with liquefied pork fat.

While in the Bari cathedral, the knights no doubt collected some oil as well, to preserve them during their upcoming ordeal in the Holy Land. The bones of Saint Nicholas, which had been transferred there from Turkey sixty years earlier, were celebrated throughout Europe for the miraculous oil they exuded, said to cure countless diseases. Nicholas's grave was one of many sites in Europe and the Middle East where the relics of a saint gave off a holy oil, as sweet-smelling as the flowers of Paradise, which might spring up like a holy gusher at the anniversary of the saint's death. Even the oil that burned in the lamps beside saintly shrines frequently had sacred power. Perhaps because of olive oil's well-known tendency to absorb tastes and fragrances, as well as its time-honored associations with divinity, lamp oil was believed to soak up the sanctity of the shrines where it burned, becoming the essence of holiness. Medieval pilgrims eagerly collected this substance, known as "the oil of the saints" or "the oil of prayer," at holy places across the Christian world, and brought it home in small bottles of silver, lead, or terra-cotta known as *ampullae*, which are still found in the treasuries of many European churches, some containing traces of holy oil. This oil also made the ideal preservative for saintly relics; in eleventh century Rome, Christ's foreskin and umbilical cord (which He evidently left behind when He ascended bodily to heaven) were reverently stored under oil in the pope's private chapel. Saintly lamp oil was held in such regard that some Monophysite heretics drank it during the Mass instead of communion wine.

To this day, the bones of Saint Nicholas are still believed to exude a holy, healing oil, which the cathedral clergy collects each year in a solemn May ceremony. After the crypt in Bari was renovated in the 1990s, however, the quantity of liquid has dropped off sharply; today the priests only manage to sponge up a few precious glassfuls, which they dilute with several gallons of holy water and distribute to the faithful. Cutting Nicholas's holy oil doesn't seem to trouble the Catholic Church, which is less concerned about oil purity than in former times: Pope Paul VI ruled in 1973 that vegetable oil could be used instead of olive oil in the sacramental anointing of the sick.

Even in the Middle Ages, for all its holy resonance, olive oil remained a slippery substance, semantically and symbolically, and it was possible to have too much of a good thing. Because it had been widely used in Greco-Roman baths, gymnasia, amphitheaters, and temples, where it was a vital active ingredient in athletics, hedonism, flashy sexuality, and religious sacrifice, olive oil retained a whiff of paganism that Christians sometimes found offputting, even threatening. The Church attempted to coopt some of these symbolic valences, applying chrism and other holy oils to the bodies of the faithful at baptism, confirmation, exorcism, and extreme unction, which theologians were quick to point out made them athletes of Christ in the contest against sin and evil. However, uneasy memories remained trapped in olive oil, and the strict regulation of its use as a skin lotion in early monastic communities suggests its lasting heathen appeal. A monastic rule of the fifth century prescribes severe punishments for monks who cover themselves in oil after a bath, and enjoins, "Do not permit anyone to spread your body with oil, except in cases of grave illness." Ascetics like Saint Anthony, the formidable desert hermit, demonstrated their superiority to paganism and the wiles of the flesh by renouncing a well-oiled body forever: Anthony ostentatiously refrained from applying any oil to his limbs, much to the amazement of his contemporaries.

Though the people might renounce oil during their daily routines, their miracle stories, dreams, and fantasies suggest that they still yearned for a good oiling. In the sixth century *Life of Saint Radegund*, the saint appears in a dream to a nun dying of dropsy, and orders her to undress and climb into an empty washtub. Radegund pours oil on the dropsical nun's head, and dresses her in new clothes. The next morning the nun awakes, her hair still fragrant with Radegund's wondrous oil, to find she has been healed of her disease. The fourth-century Egyptian holy man Macarius, famed for his asceticism, cured a virgin who had been transformed into a mare by sorcery, by rubbing oil over her entire

body—a ticklish task even for a good ascetic to tackle without at least
a squirm of concupiscence. Perhaps the most vividly pagan oil miracle
appears in the *Passion of Saint Perpetua*, the strange, troubling tale said
to have been written in prison by Perpetua herself, just before she was
martyred by wild beasts in the arena in Carthage in 203 AD. One night,
the story relates, Perpetua dreamed that a Christian deacon named
Pomponius came to her cell, took her hand, and led her to the amphi-
theater, where a huge crowd of people were watching from the stands.
"And there came out against me a certain ill-favored Egyptian with his
helpers, to fight with me. Also there came to me comely young men, my
helpers and aides. And I was stripped naked, and I became a man. And
my helpers began to rub me with oil, as is their custom for a contest."
Perpetua defeats the Egyptian, tramples his head to signify her triumph,
and claims the victor's prize: a staff with golden apples attached to it.

Freud would have had a field day.

At any rate, the sacred role of olive oil in hagiography tracked the
widespread popular use of olive oil to cure a range of maladies. Medieval
pharmacists and apothecaries, following the advice of Hippocrates, prescribed olive oil against numerous ailments, from skin disease to digestive
disorders to gynecological complaints, and used it as a base for numerous
philters and unguents; medieval formularies mention oil-based extracts
of scorpion, viper, stork, bat, fox, and other medicinal creatures. Some
authorities prescribed a hot bath followed by a full-body rubdown with
olive oil to cure kidney stones and seizures, and recommended submerg-
ing the lower half of the body in oil as an antidote against certain poisons.
Olive oil, taken internally, was considered an effective cure for many ailments, including intestinal worms, snakebite, and even insanity, though
one medical writer cautioned that oil not be given to people of a choleric
disposition. Monastic cellarers believed olives and oil to be effective in
reestablishing a proper balance among bodily humors, and sometimes
prescribed olive oil to control violent impulses or sexual urges, which
were thought to result from an excess of hot and moist humors in the
blood. Doctors and holy men alike used oil against leprosy, blindness,

and demonic possession, wives fed it to their husbands to free them from the wiles and incantations of prostitutes. Occasionally, holy oil and oil of the saints could even resuscitate the dead.

Yet olive oil was also employed in evil spells and incantations. The Church issued frequent bans against the use of consecrated holy oils by sorcerers and magicians; in the year 810, for example, the chapter of the cathedral of Tours ordered priests to guard the holy chrism vigilantly, because of the widespread belief that any criminal who managed to anoint himself with it could never be brought to trial. And there was a fine line between holy oil and snake oil. In the 430s, a monk appeared in Carthage carrying a martyr's bone steeped in oil. Sick people and cripples that he dosed with the oil seemed to recover, at least as long as the monk was with them, but after he left they invariably relapsed. The citizens of Carthage eventually decided that his supposed cures were the result of demonic hallucinations rather than divine healing, and the monkish grifter skipped town.

I SAT WITH Ehud Netzer, archaeologist at Hebrew University in Jerusalem, on top of Herodium, the conical 300-foot hill where he had recently uncovered the tomb of Herod the Great. We were eating a lunch of olives, pita bread, and bitter onions, and looking toward the purplish haze of Jerusalem in the distance. Here and there in the lowlands rose the minarets of bedouin villages, surrounded by sandy sprawls of corrugated iron and raw concrete, while the neat ovals of tile-roofed houses in the Jewish settlements—Tekoa, Nokdim, and Eldar—occupied the nearby hilltops, like tiny fortifications. To the east and south, the naked folds of the Judean Hills rolled out toward the horizon, incandescent under the desert sun. Here and there were small olive groves, pale ridges of green on the sun-baked soil. That trees could survive in such fierce conditions seemed impossible.

Yet survived they had, and even thrived, since antiquity. Tekoa's olive oil was famous in Old Testament times; in a yearly ceremony after the olive harvest, it was sent in wagons to Jerusalem, where it was used in the Temple for ritual offerings and to light the great Menorah.

When I said this, Netzer grunted and tossed a handful of pits down the slope. "Olive trees are power," he said with surprising vehemence. "People here, both Palestinians and Israelis, grow them to control the land—to occupy it."

He said he'd been watching the groves grow up around Herodium for decades as he excavated the site, and their advance had become a constant reminder of the social turmoil and latent violence of this land. For years at a time the Israeli army had denied him access to the area, fearing Muslim attacks, and Netzer worried about losing access to it permanently, as had happened in Jericho, one of his most important archaeological excavations, when the Palestinian Authority assumed full control there after the Second Intifada in 2000. The risks of working here were real. On July 3, 1982, David Rosenfeld, an American-born Israeli settler, was murdered at Herodium. The killers, who stabbed Rosenfeld over one hundred times, were two local bedouins, one of whom worked in Netzer's excavation crew. "I was very close to the murderer's old father," Netzer said sadly. "Two days after David's death, a group of Israelis and Americans, Arabs and Jews, washed away the caked blood. We lit an oil lamp and said Kaddish, the Jewish prayer for the dead."

At the same time, Netzer also felt under pressure from Jews. The day after David Rosenfeld's funeral, Jewish activists occupied a new outpost, El-David, on a neighboring hilltop, in reprisal for the murder. (The community later changed its name to Nokdim.) "Instead of panic and fear on the part of Jews," the community's website stated, "the Arabs got a new settlement and new settlers." As if this wasn't enough, Netzer received a visit from another ultra-orthodox group, called Atra Kadisha, which defends Jewish graves, sometimes by force, against disturbance of any kind, by archaeologists and road-builders alike. In the back of his mind, he said, was the threat that Atra Kadisha might shut his excavations down.

Year after year, around Herodium and in other parts of the West Bank, Netzer had watched olive trees being planted by the opposing factions, until their beauty had become tainted in his mind. "Now I see their other side. I see power struggles, I see places where rock-throwers and killers can hide. In my mind, this universal symbol of peace, for Jews and Arabs alike, has become a picture of conflict, hatred, danger."

After the Six-Day War of 1967, Israel occupied most of the West Bank territory, which contained an estimated 10 million olive trees owned by Palestinian farmers. The Palestinians continued to tend their trees more or less undisturbed until in 2000, the year of the Second Intifada, when Israeli soldiers and Jewish settlers, citing security concerns, began to burn, cut down, and uproot olive trees in many parts of the region, particularly near roads and Jewish settlements, and along the borders with Jordan and Syria. Since then, hundreds of thousands of olive trees owned by Palestinians—some sources put the number as high as half a million—have been destroyed, in what the liberal Israeli press calls the Olive Wars.

The destruction has accelerated dramatically since October 2005, when Israel began building the West Bank barrier (which many Palestinians refer to as the "racial segregation wall"), more or less following the Green Line, the border between Israel proper and the West Bank territories. This network of walls, ditches, barbed wire, and other obstacles, which in places is sixty meters wide, eight meters tall, and resembles the Berlin Wall in all its Cold War grimness, has intensified the destruction, and put many other groves off limits to their Palestinian owners. Israeli settlers have been accused of stealing Palestinian olives, both already harvested and directly from the trees, sometimes with the tacit approval of the Israeli army.

Christians are caught up in the Olive Wars as well. Two days after speaking with Ehud Netzer in Herodium, I visited Aboud, a town northwest of Jerusalem, to meet Father Firas Nasib Aridah, a Jordanian-born Catholic who is the parish priest of Our Lady Mother of Sorrows, the town's church.

"So you actually did come!" he said when he saw me. On the phone he'd instructed me to visit Aboud with a Palestinian driver and by daylight, "to avoid any unpleasantness on the road," as he'd put it. Aridah has close-cropped reddish-brown hair, a booming voice, and moves like he talks, swiftly and decisively. Despite his cassock, he has the energetic air and upright carriage of an athlete, or a soldier.

After showing me around the small church, with its naïve stained glass windows and a lectern made from an ancient olive tree destroyed by Jewish settlers in 2000, he walked briskly toward the edge of town to show me the scene of his dramatic recent confrontation with the Israeli army. Along the way the townspeople, many wearing checked *keffiyeh* headdresses, called out to him, addressing him as *abuneh*, which in the local Arabic dialect means both "patriarch" and "man of God." He stopped to heft babies, pat shoulders, and distribute good-natured jibes in Arabic. He laughed frequently. "If I'm not laughing, I'm not a real priest," he told me. "Laughing trains many muscles that you don't train any other way."

Aridah explained that his town has 1,300 Muslims and 900 Christians, who for centuries have coexisted in tolerance and mutual respect. "They work and shop and travel together, send their children to the same schools. Muslims celebrate Christmas and Easter with us, in the multipurpose room of our parish, and Christians celebrate Ramadan and [Eid al-]Adha in a hall near the mosque. And Christians and Muslims harvest their olives side by side. Even the poorest people bring a bottle of their first olive oil to our church, to be used as a sacrament."

The West Bank barrier threatens to disrupt this ancient equilibrium. At the edge of town, the road we were walking on ended in a berm of raw earth, thrown up by Israeli bulldozers to block traffic into the area near the barrier. We climbed the berm and surveyed the terraced olive groves and pasturelands beyond. A reddish swath cleared by the dozers ran through them like a scar.

Aridah said that 5,100 of Aboud's trees had already been destroyed in the work so far, and that if the barrier were completed, Aboud's inhabitants would be cut off from a further 1,100 acres of village land, with 10,000 more trees.

"Some families lost everything to the barrier. Generations have supported their families from these groves. Many families eat between forty and sixty liters of oil per year. Now some have to buy their oil, or use cheap seed or palm oil instead because they can't afford olive oil. Plus there's the lost income. On a good harvest year, one olive tree can produce $200 in profit, through sales of the oil, table olives, and olive oil soap. For our families, the olive tree isn't just a symbol of life, it *is* life."

We descended the far side of the berm and walked into the groves between the village and the wall line. The trees were squat, healthy, thick-trunked, with reaching dark limbs that seemed blackened by the relentless sun. The prickly pear cacti and yellow fieldstone made me think of Puglia, until the muezzins of the area began the call to prayer.

Ever since the borders were closed to Palestinians, Aridah said, many people lost jobs they'd held in Israel, making the income from these trees all the more vital. "Without it, many young people can't get an education. A number of men in their twenties and thirties aren't able to marry, because they don't have enough money to ask for the bride's hand with pride. People can't build homes. This seems to be the Israeli strategy: to destroy the society from below, to cut it at the roots. They are killing us, indirectly, through our trees."

Aridah paused, as if sensing he'd gone too far. "Look, I have good relations with everyone. I have friends in Beit Aryeh and Ofarim, the nearest Jewish settlements, even though they were built on Aboud's land, I talk with generals in the Israeli army, and with common soldiers— I respect them, and they respect me. Soldiers have orders, and have to carry them out. We just want a basic level of justice and dignity."

We walked past the last trees, into the trough cleared by the dozers. Aridah stopped in the churned, reddish marl, where there was no sign that anything had ever grown, and pulled out a stack of photos, creased and blurry, taken the day the Israelis came. He flipped through them, showing me how the bulldozers had advanced, with the Israeli army in the lead. How the soldiers in riot gear with assault rifles at the ready had formed a line, here where we now stood, and paid out a coil of razor wire. And how he and the villagers had knelt before them, and planted a tiny olive sapling in front of the soldiers' steel-toed boots.

"We presented them with this peace offering, and said, 'All we ask is that you give us what we need to live.'"

Aridah's last photo showed the tiny tree, crushed under a solder's boot.

"Soldiers have their orders," he said, glaring at the image. "But I hope they didn't include this."

THE GREEKS EAT more oil than any other nationality, twenty-one liters per capita every year as compared with thirteen liters in Italy and Spain, one liter in Britain, and a little less than a liter in the United States. Among Greeks, the inhabitants of the island of Crete consume (and produce) the most oil. And among Cretans, the inhabitants of Kritsa, a village of 2,800 people in the southeastern part of the island, take the prize, eating about fifty liters per person per year. Kritsa can fairly claim to be a world capital of olive oil.

The king of Kritsa is Nikos Zachariádes, a pugnacious ex-policeman who returned to his native village after thirty years of service in the food fraud division in Athens, and threw himself body and soul into oil. Zachariádes is a fireplug of a man with a balding head, a pug nose, and slightly bulbous eyes that fixed me in a fierce glare, his forehead creased with concentration, when we met in Kritsa one bright January morning in 2011. For a moment, caught in that glare, I inadvertently pitied the food fraudsters who had run afoul of him in the past, and at the same time worried a little about his blood pressure. He asked me why I was interested in olive oil. As he listened to my answer, his worry beads clacking softly in his fingers, his brow smoothed, and his features relaxed into a knowing smile. And then Nikos Zachariádes gave me a resounding backslap, accepting me as one of the anointed.

For the next forty-eight hours, from early morning until very late in the night, he marched me with relentless kindness through the groves, mills, homes, offices, and workshops of Kritsa, and showed me the remarkably oleocentric lives these people lead. I met a few village notables—the mayor, the priest, the knife-maker, and the cobbler who still fashions traditional Cretan boots by hand with goatskins and wooden nails—but otherwise the town was empty, because the other villagers were out harvesting their olives. Everyone in town owns olive trees and makes oil; according to a local proverb, a person is truly poor only when "he doesn't have a single olive tree to hang himself on."

One of our first stops was at the modern mill of the Kritsa cooperative, where two big Alfa Laval centrifuges droned like twin jet engines. I watched farmers deliver hemp sacks of olives in trucks, utility vehicles, and on muleback. Each farmer dumped his fruit onto a large scale, collected a slip of paper with its weight, and departed, long before the oil was made—a radical difference from other communal mills I'd visited, where producers watched every stage of the oil-making process intently, and only left with their oil in hand. Zachariádes explained that, at his prompting, all of the 1,000 producers in the cooperative had agreed to make their oil collectively, treating the village lands as one big grove. "We all share the same beliefs about making excellent oil—grow good olives, process them quickly. Using this system, we can finish the day's deliveries by dinner, and minimize the time that the olives sit around before they're crushed." Farmers in neighboring cooperatives, by contrast, make their oil individually, and routinely wait in line at the mill until long past midnight. Kritsa's common pressing system not only makes better oil, but makes it in quantities that are ten, twenty, even fifty times greater than most Greek cooperatives, allowing them to sell to larger clients like supermarket chains.

Zachariádes instituted this revolutionary system, and made other important changes in the oil-making procedure, after he returned to Kritsa from Athens in 2006 and became president of the village cooperative. Six months later, Kritsa's oil won a bronze medal at the prestigious Mario Solinas Awards, the yearly contest sponsored by the International Olive Council. In 2008, Kritsa's oil won the gold medal at the same competition. Soon after, Zachariádes took another bold step by forming an alliance with Gaea, a private producer of high-quality olive oil and other Greek specialty foods, headed by prominent Greek businessman Aris Kefalogiannis. "Our partnership was an unprecedented move for Greek agricultural cooperatives, which are typically very political entities and regard private companies with suspicion," Kefalogiannis explains. "Here's yet another way that Nikos Zachariádes showed his innovative business sense, as well as his courage." Thanks to this partnership, Kritsa is able to sell its oil in the UK, Finland, Lithuania, and other distant places, finding wider and more profitable markets than other Greek cooperatives can on the domestic market, and to send a larger slice of earnings directly to the olive growers. At a time of crisis in the Greek economy, with oil prices at historic lows and many growers abandoning their trees, the farmers of Kritsa are earning 25–30 percent more for their oil than farmers in neighboring villages.

After touring the mill, we ate an impromptu meal on the mill floor, passing around plates of fresh-picked *stamnagathi*, a wild green something like spinach, and crusts of whole-wheat bread called *latherà*, over which Zachariádes gushed streams of tart, peppery oil made from local *koroneiki* olives, using a modified gas pump connected to one of the centrifuges. Nothing can prepare you for the amount of oil that the people of Kritsa eat, or the countless ways that oil and olives enter their daily lives. During my visit I thought often of Ancel Keys, a Minnesota epidemiologist and biochemist who in the 1950s laid the foundations of what is now called the Mediterranean diet, while studying the link between traditional diets and heart disease on Crete, in southern Italy, and elsewhere. Keys and his colleagues were impressed by the quantities of oil consumed on this island: "It was incredible to see an old farmer start the day by knocking back a jigger of olive oil," his close collaborator Henry Blackburn remembers. Experiences like this forced Keys to consider the potential health benefits of an olive-oil-rich regimen.

Every visit and house call I made during my time in Kritsa followed the same script: shortly after the introductions, my new host would pass around little shot glasses of raki, the potent local aquavit, and begin bringing plate after plate of local specialties cooked with, or swimming in, oil fresh from the village mill. In one corner of every kitchen stood a tall *pithari*, a terra-cotta urn for oil with a capacity of 100 liters, and a *muzuraki* sat by the stove, a metal oil can which held about a liter of oil and was usually empty by the end of the meal. We ate raw artichokes, white radishes, lupins, and a dozen other Cretan vegetables I never learned names for, all glossy with oil. There were pita-shaped cheese breads cooked in puddles of oil in a special little frying pan, wild rabbit stewed in oil and rosemary, pastry pockets stuffed with goat cheese and deep-fried in oil, and little fish called *barbugna* oil-fried and eaten whole, heads and all. For dessert we had macaroons and sesame cookies sprinkled with chopped hazelnuts and honey, whose telltale green color revealed the quantities of olive oil they contained.

Greek Orthodoxy is no less steeped in oil. During a baptism in Kritsa, as elsewhere in Crete, the godfather smears the baby's entire body with oil, which must according to religious custom be left on the child's skin for three days after the ceremony before the parents can wash it away. At marriage, couples exchange olive crowns, and a bride's dowry invariably contains holdings of olive trees. During funerals, after the deceased is lowered into the grave, the priest pours a cross of olive oil over the coffin, intoning, "Cleanse me with hyssop, and I will be clean; wash me, and I will be whiter than snow." And at harvest time, many of the faithful bring bottles of their new oil to the church, to be blessed by the priest and used in a range of cures and rituals. As in classical times, olive oil is burned in church lamps, as well as in the lamps that illumine the icons in family homes and the images of the saints in roadside shrines. (During a storm at sea, some of the older villagers drip a few drops of oil from lamps that light the icons of Saint Nicholas, the patron saint of sailors, which they believe will calm the waves.) Olive oil is considered an aphrodisiac; a local proverb, loosely translated, runs, "Eat olive oil to come at night, eat butter to sleep tight." Following ancient, semisacred rituals, oil is used to avert the evil eye and even to read the future: people eagerly observe the shapes made by the oil floating on the surface of the water in the baptismal font, which reputedly foretell the character—and financial success—of the child.

A reconstruction of the seventh century BC oil mill discovered at Ekron, Israel, which could produce about 500,000 liters of olive oil per year. *Courtesy of Jean-Pierre Brun*

Bas relief in the memorial temple of the pharaoh Seti I, in Abydos, Upper Egypt, showing the gods Thoth and Horus anointing Seti with scented oils.
Jim Henderson/Alamy

Greek athletes oil up before a competition, which made their skin more supple and enhanced their physical beauty, making them appear, as classical writers pointed out, like gleaming statues of the gods. *Bildarchiv Preussischer Kulturbesitz, Berlin/Art Resource, NY*

Olive oil was so vital to sports and bathing in the classical world that small containers for scented oil, called *aryballoi,* have been found in hundreds of archaeological sites throughout the Mediterranean.

Courtesy of Maria Rosaria Belgiorno

Greek women bathing and anointing themselves with oil (note the *aryballoi* suspended from the tree) on a vase from the fifth century BC, much as Homer described Nausicaa and her handmaidens four centuries earlier in the *Odyssey*.
Erich Lessing/Art Resource, NY

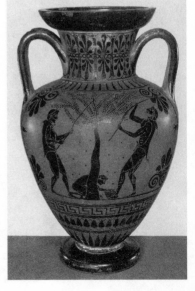

Greek men harvesting olives by beating the branches with canes, a technique condemned by Roman (and modern) agronomists because it bruises the fruit and damages the trees. *Bildarchiv Preussischer Kulturbesitz/Art Resource, NY*

Perhaps the earliest method for extracting olive oil, still being used by these women in Jerusalem in the early twentieth century, involved crushing olives by hand with a stone roller, placing the resulting paste in a bag, and twisting it to draw out the oil.

Courtesy of Jean-Pierre Brun

The olive harvest as depicted by Sano di Pietro, in a fourteenth-century monastic calendar from Siena called the *Codex of the Nuns* (under the month of October).

Scala/Art Resource, NY

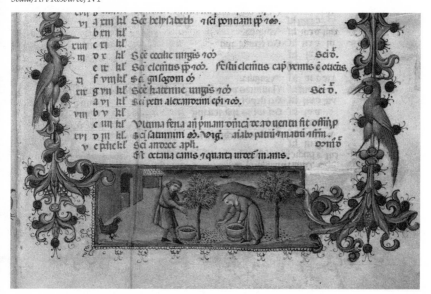

Renaissance apothecaries used olive oil in a wide range of salves, unguents, folk remedies, and nostrums. Note the amphora-like terracotta jars on shelves behind counter, and the young apothecary assistant seated in the lower right hand corner, blending up a new concoction with a mortar and pestle. *Scala/Art Resource, NY*

Pilgrims used *ampullae*, also called "pilgrim flasks," to collect lamp oil and holy oil at shrines around the Mediterranean, which were thought to heal illnesses and protect against demons. This Coptic ampulla shows Saint Menas, the fourth-century Egyptian martyr and wonder-worker, flanked by camels. *Réunion des Musées Nationaux/Art Resource, NY*

A state-of-the-art olive oil mill circa 1600, as depicted in an engraving after Jan van der Straet, which appeared in *Nova Reperta* ("New Discoveries"), a manual celebrating technological breakthroughs. *Nova Reperta, plate 13, engraved by Philip Galle*

Provençal oil production is limited today, but at the turn of the nineteenth century the region supplied oil to a number of foreign capitals, including the royal courts of Sweden, Luxembourg, and Russia, and to Vietnam, a former French colony. *Courtesy of Mark Wickens, http://pages.infinit.net/wickens/*

This skull of a Roman-era athlete on Crete, discovered in a tomb near the town of Hagios Nikolaus, wore a crown of golden olive leaves that had been set on the deceased's brow, which over the centuries became laminated to the skull. *Nikos Psilakis*

Some nineteenth-century explorers in North Africa believed that the remains of Roman olive presses were cultic structures from some lost pagan ritual. *Courtesy of Jean-Pierre Brun*

A range of amphora shapes catalogued by Heinrich Dressel, the
nineteenth-century German archaeologist and classicist who led the first
systematic study of Monte Testaccio
in Rome, a 150-foot hill composed
of broken olive oil amphorae. *Corpus
inscriptionum Latinarum, vol. 15*

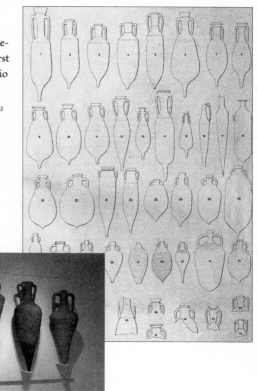

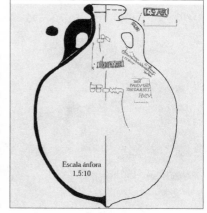

Amphorae in various forms used to transport olive oil and
other goods throughout the Roman world. Such amphorae
were carefully packed in the hulls of transport ships, and
have been found, still interlocked, on the sea floor, in the hulls
of Roman-era shipwrecks throughout the Mediterranean.
Metropolitan Museum of Art, NY

Roman olive oil amphorae
frequently bore inscriptions that
recorded where and when the
oil was produced, its weight and
quality at shipment, and the name
of the imperial functionary who
received it in Rome—all methods
for preventing olive oil fraud.
Courtesy of José Remesal Rodríguez

Oil has always been central to life in these lands. Nikos Zachariádes took me to the ruins of Lato, a pre-Minoan fortress on a hilltop near Kritsa overlooking the Aegean, where we saw magnificent cyclopean stonework and the remains of large oil presses and cisterns. In Dreros, another nearby site dating from the early Iron Age, archaeologists have unearthed an inscription describing a rite of passage performed by all young men of the city, which required them to plant and tend an olive tree and to ensure that it grew healthy and tall. Clay tablets found an hour's drive west of Kritsa, at Knossos, capital of a Minoan empire built largely on olive oil wealth, describe libations of oil that were offered to a range of deities during regular ceremonies; the frescoes, sculptures, and jewelry unearthed at the Minoan palace there are bushy with olive trees and studded with their fruit. Graves excavated near Kritsa, spanning the 3,000 years from pre-Minoan times to the present, routinely contain olive pits and oil containers among the bones, evidently considered vital provisions for the afterlife. A Roman-era grave found in the nearby town of Hagios Nikolaus, apparently belonging to an athlete, contained an *aryballos* to hold perfumed oil and a *strigil* to scrape it away after sports or bathing; a crown of golden olive leaves had been placed on the dead man's brow, evidently to honor his sporting skill, which over the centuries the damp earth had pressed into the skull, forming a permanent, gleaming veneer on the bone.

Near the end of my stay in Kritsa, we visited a grove in the highlands east of town, where five members of the Zacharia family—a young man and woman in their late twenties, their parents in their fifties, and a grandmother approaching ninety who wore a black headscarf and green wellies—were bringing in their crop of teardrop-shaped *koroneiki* olives. The parents and their son used hydraulic wands with vibrating fingers to rake down the olives, which they gathered up in tarps and carried to the leafing table, a four-legged platform with a metal screen over it, where the young woman and her grandmother separated the fruit from the leaves and twigs.

As she worked in the late afternoon sunshine, Georgia Zacharia, the young woman, spoke to me in a calm voice. She said that she looks forward to the harvest each year, because it brings her family together. "And in the evenings I have no time or energy to think about my problems and my worries. I'm too exhausted." She said that the olive harvest is a great comfort to her during the economic crisis that Greece is currently suffering. "Everyone has olive trees, a garden. Being self-sufficient is not that far away for us. Things are going to be all right."

AT DAWN one morning in April 2010, workers from the agricultural cooperative Terre di Puglia, walking into an olive grove they were to prune that day in Mesagne, near Brindisi, discovered a pipe bomb at the foot of a tree. This wasn't the first warning. Several months before, someone had broken into one of their cars and scrawled a death threat on the dashboard. Scraps of paper had appeared in their mailboxes from time to time, bearing thinly veiled threats: "Whoever goes to work today will pay the price for everybody." "Silence!" "Stop breaking our balls!" Arsonists had slipped into their lands by night and set groves, vineyards, and farm equipment alight.

A bomb was a new level of intimidation. "Of course, it wasn't meant to kill anybody," Alessandro Leo, president of Terre di Puglia, told me. "Like all the other messages we've received since we started cultivating these lands, it was put there to intimidate, to destabilize our cooperative."

Leo looked hard at me for a moment, as if trying to see whether I believed him—or to decide what he himself believed about the incident. Then he laughed, high-pitched and merrily, and shook his head. "At least, that's what I tell myself. After all, we know who these people are, what they've done in the past. We know they're capable of anything."

Leo and his colleagues at Terre di Puglia are cultivating lands that until recently belonged to the Sacra Corona Unita, the *pugliese* mafia. Their former owner, Cosimo Antonio Screti, known as Don Tonino, was a powerful member of the organization and greatly feared in the area. After Screti was convicted of crimes including drug trafficking and membership in a criminal organization, the Italian government confiscated much of his real estate holdings, including this grove, which investigators believe Screti bought with the proceeds of illegal activity, particularly the drug trade. In January 2008, the grove and several other vineyards and farmlands were given in usufruct to Terre di Puglia, a member of a nonprofit organization called Libera Terra ("Liberated Land") which fights mafia infiltration throughout Italy and cultivates farmlands taken from the mob. The workers in the cooperative are socially disadvantaged, and include several recovering drug addicts; these former victims of the narcotics trade work to regain their dignity and autonomy through hard labor on this land, which was once bought with drug money by a noted mobster.

Trouble was, the mobster hadn't left. After being released from prison for reasons of poor health, Don Tonino returned to his villa in the middle of the fields then being farmed by the cooperative. Neither he nor his former associates in the Sacra Corona Unita were pleased to see someone else harvesting olives and making oil on property they still considered to be theirs. "He walked around like he was still the boss here," Leo remembers, "with the patronizing attitude and the arrogance that are typical of this kind of character."

The year Terre di Puglia took over management of the lands, no farmers or laborers dared to work for them, despite chronic unemployment in the area. "People avoided us," Leo remembers. Not owning a tractor, he and his coworkers had to call the Italian forest service to plough their lands before they could sow the first wheat crop.

Nevertheless, the inaugural harvest was a modest success. Using a rare local species of wheat which they'd tracked down among elderly farmers in the area, they baked traditional *pugliese* crispbreads called *tarallini* and *friselle*. They grew local *fiaschetto* tomatoes, from which they made pasta sauces and sun-dried tomatoes. They pruned and tended the long-abandoned vines of the *negroamaro* grape varietal, which yielded an excellent red wine. And from their small grove of centuries-old olive trees, they made a few hundred bottles of oil.

As word of their work spread, local and national organizations lent a hand. Agronomists and enologists from Slow Food, the culinary and fair-trade NGO, began to advise them, and a few supermarkets, like COOP, a national chain, started selling their products. Libera Terra signed a collaborative agreement with a prominent institute of agronomy in nearby Ostuni, and with several local olive-growers and oil-makers. Finally, one by one, local farmhands began coming to work at the cooperative. "I never dreamed I'd set foot on Don Tonino's lands one day," one of them told Alessandro Leo. "Or see this soil, which was overgrown with brambles for so long, turn fertile again."

For Leo, the first taste of the *olio nuovo* produced powerful emotions. "I thought about the unique story of injustice and justice it contained. I thought about the people who used to taste this oil, and about the people who can taste it now."

Leo says the oil is emblematic of the kind of food Libera Terra grows. "Each of our products has a story to tell. We want to recover a sense of food as having not just material and commercial value, but a cultural value too. We do this by emphasizing the link between a particular food and the *territorio*, the landscape where it's grown and always has been. These ancient olive trees, in particular, are symbols of this *territorio*. They're a central part of this landscape, and have sustained its inhabitants for countless centuries. When you eat this oil, you're not just eating something made from an anonymous tree in some industrial grove. You're eating a food from one specific spot on the planet, with a unique history."

Leo and his colleages at the cooperative are using only approved, natural chemicals on their trees and, starting next year, their oil will be certified as *biologico*, or organic. "We're freeing the land from systematic poisoning by pesticides and other toxic agricultural products, which concentrate particularly in olive oil. Here's another kind of organized crime, another mafia that we all need to stand up to and speak out against. Or else they'll kill us just as sure as a hit man would."

4

THE LOVELY BURN

The olive tree is surely the richest gift of heaven.

—Thomas Jefferson, letter to James Ronaldson, 1813

Olio eta egia gaña dadukate. [Olive oil and truth come to the surface.]

—Basque proverb

"The universe is chiral!" announced Alissa Mattei as I entered her airy, sun-filled parlor, where a long oak table held tasting glasses, a laptop, a dozen bottles of olive oil, and molecular models of isoprene and other organic compounds, made from toothpicks and balls of colored clay. (Chirality, I soon learned, is the characteristic of structures that, like our right and left hands, can't be superimposed on their mirror images.) Mattei, who directed the Carapelli quality-control laboratories for almost three decades before leaving the company in 2008, when it was taken over by the Spanish food multinational Grupo SOS, is a striking figure: small, plump, with full reddish hair, and arresting scarves, and large, almond-shaped eyes that seem to look straight into your soul, with an intelligence and humor you can't mistake, and with something else, too, that might be cunning, though you don't really care since it's such pleasure just to stare into those eyes, deep green like newly pressed olive oil from her native Tuscany. Since leaving Carapelli she runs Casa Montecucco, a homey farmhouse turned *agriturismo*, and educates people on fine oil and fine living in the Maremma, the wild woodlands of the south Tuscan coast where some of Italy's best boar-hunting, horseback riding and Super Tuscan wines are to be had. The daughter of a Tuscan painter and a Neapolitan *baronessa* (you can bet her eyes are the *baronessa's*), she is satisfyingly down-to-earth when dealing with guests and organizing a meal, yet now and then makes sweeping, enigmatic, Neapolitan statements—"the universe is chiral," "everything in nature is the result of chance and necessity," "I am an extremely generous person." All of which, after spending a short time with her, you see are very likely to be true.

Mattei speaks matter-of-factly of fraud, which she says is endemic in the olive oil industry. "It always makes economic sense. Add 2 or 3 percent seed oil to your extra virgin olive oil, which sells for three times more, and you make money by the bucketful." She tells the modern history of oil fraud with an intimate knowledge of names, dates, and places—the company in Liguria that invented deodorized oil, and the companies in Puglia that perfected it—and observes that chemists who devise new methods of adulteration sometimes sit on the selfsame scientific committees that create the tests to detect adulteration. She says that major oil traders routinely quote a price for deodorized oil, although selling such oil as extra virgin is illegal: the "soft refining" of the deodorization process is forbidden in extra virgin oil, which can only be made with mechanical methods. She too is developing new deodorization techniques, she says—not for fraud, but simply for the chemical challenge of eliminating unpleasant odors and tastes from otherwise good olive oil.

As she speaks, you know that the olive oil world she is describing, with its industry chemists, traders, and deal-makers, its compromises and rationalizations, is a mortal threat to olive oil quality, steadily debasing the extra virgin grade and putting unsustainable price pressure on countless small producers of high-quality oil. Yet it's also quite clear that Alissa Mattei has a passion for fine olive oil. She has an exceptional palate, for which she's in great demand as a consultant for Slow Food and several major olive oil producers. She is one of the world's leading oil chemists, who knows the twists and turns of olive oil's molecular geometry as a farmer knows his fields. And after a career at an oil multinational where, as she says, she hardly saw an olive tree, for the first time in her life she owns her own grove, slender little five-year-olds which she cossets as if they were her children, and from which she makes a gorgeous oil. Alissa Mattei is another person olive oil has touched, bringing out her inner contradictions.

She also cares about spreading the message of great oil, and lectures frequently on its chemical and sensory properties to the general public. Today I'd come for her celebrated introduction to oleic acid, the main fatty acid in olive oil. First, however, she flashed through a series of bright molecular models on her laptop to illustrate her interest of the moment, the concept of chirality. "Chiral molecules exist throughout nature. Which is a mystery, since the simple molecules that were around when life began, like methane and ammonia, are symmetrical, not chiral. How did chirality start?" Olive oil too, she explained, has a number of chiral components, such as alpha-tocopherol and chlorophyll. "So olive oil contains at its heart one of the deepest mysteries of nature!" she said with a twinkle in her eye.

"Now let's make oil." She handed me toothpicks and chunks of clay, and I tried to follow along as her round, capable hands rolled a series of colored balls—blue for carbon atoms, red for oxygen, white for hydrogen—and used toothpicks, which represented chemical bonds, to link three carbon atoms together. She added oxygens and hydrogens branching off from the carbons, producing a molecule shaped roughly like a capital E. "This is glycerol, the core of olive oil, which is a triglyceride—a glycerol base with three fatty acids branching off of it." Then, to each horizontal bar of the glycerol E, she attached a fatty acid, which consisted of a long chain of carbon atoms, each carbon sporting a pair of hydrogens. Mattei explained that all fats and oils are composed of triglycerides, and differ in the length of their carbon chains. Oleic acid is eighteen carbon atoms long; lauric acid, found in human milk and coconut oil, has twelve carbons; while the erucic acid in rapeseed and mustard-seed oil has twenty-two. Like other lipids, olive oil is a cocktail of many different fatty acids, whose proportions change according to factors such as the cultivar of the olive, the climatic conditions it grows in, and the amount of water it receives. An oil's content of oleic acid, its primary fatty acid, can vary from 55 to 85 percent. (Olive oil also contains lesser amounts of eighteen other fatty acids.) Mattei reached down the table for a portly bottle of oil with a neck tag announcing its first-place finish at a recent olive oil competition and pronouncing it The Best Olive Oil in the World. "Different oils can have very different lipid characteristics, almost as though they came from different plants," she said. "How can there be one 'best oil'?"

Resuming her lesson, Mattei explained that fatty acids differ not only in the length of their carbon chains but in the type of bonds between the carbons. Most carbon atoms are joined to each other with single bonds, which she signified with one toothpick. Yet halfway down our chain, between the ninth and tenth carbons, she made a two-toothpick bond instead; at this point she also plucked away a hydrogen atom, and put a 30-degree kink in the chain. This missing hydrogen means that oleic acid is "unsaturated"—its carbon chain isn't fully saturated with hydrogen atoms. Oleic acid and other fatty acids with one double bond are called monounsaturated, while those with two or more double bonds are polyunsaturated; these two types of fatty acids are typically found in vegetable oils. Other fatty acids, whose carbon chains are filled to capacity with hydrogens, are saturated. (Butter, suet, lard, and other animal fats are made up largely of saturated fatty acids.) The numbers of kinks and missing hydrogen atoms in a fatty acid, determined by the number of double bonds it contains, have important biological implications. Saturated fats, with no bend-inducing double bonds, have straight carbon chains that pack neatly into tight crystal structures, and are usually solid at room temperature; monounsaturated and polyunsaturated fats, which are full of twists and don't pack so tidily, are typically liquid. What's more, at a site on a fatty acid chain where a carbon double bond exists, the missing hydrogen leaves a gap that makes the chain vulnerable to invasion by reactive molecules, like atmospheric oxygen. The more double bonds a fatty acid contains, the more easily it oxidizes, or turns rancid. Hence olive oil, which is largely monounsaturated, keeps fresh far longer than other vegetable oils, which are polyunsaturated.

Saturated animal fats, devoid of double bonds and chock full of hydrogens, keep best of all. Recognizing this, over a century ago food chemists devised a method of topping up the gaps in carbon chains with extra hydrogen atoms, thus increasing shelf life. This chemical process, known as hydrogenation, also straightens out double bonds, making hydrogenated fats lie straight and pack solid. In fact the body mistakes them for natural saturated fats and incorporates them in structures like cell membranes, where they can set off inflammatory reactions that promote atherosclerosis and heart disease.

"But enough oil theory, it's time for practice," she said abruptly, standing and walking into the kitchen nearby. "We have guests for dinner." She led the way into Casa Montecucco's professional-grade kitchen, a realm of marble and stainless steel where her husband, Luciano Cipriani, scion of a family of hoteliers and restaurateurs, was boning a Parma ham with a knife as big as a machete. For the next three hours I watched Mattei and her husband move swiftly and in perfect synchrony around the kitchen as they prepared a five-course meal for fifteen people, using impressive quantities of oil. As someone who grew up in 1970s and 1980s America with a steady anti-fat mantra, I found it liberating to see Alissa Mattei loop emerald festoons of the stuff over *acquacotta* soup, *árista* pork loin, potatoes and endives and hot peppers from her garden, with the practiced abandon of an orchestra conductor.

On a shelf in the kitchen I noticed a five-liter jug of Carapelli, which she said she used for cooking and frying—evidently she remained faithful to her former employer. Without thinking, I asked what oil she liked best of all. For a moment her jolliness faded, as if in disappointment, and I remembered what she'd said about the chemical differences in oils. Then she brightened, and reached for the award-winning oil we'd seen earlier. "The best in the world, of course," she laughed. Then she held the bottle up to the light and squinted, as if studying its contents. "Who knows what's really in there . . ."

"IF I WERE a king, I'd eat nothing but fat." Thus a seventeenth-century farmer expressed his longing for triglycerides, both saturated and unsaturated, five centuries before they fell from medical and culinary favor—and before hydrogenation made them dangerous. Fats and oils are a remarkably efficient fuel, not only for lamps and furnaces and the olive's germinating seed, but for people as well. In times of unrelenting manual labor and ever-present cold, when most people's main preoccupation was how to fill their bellies, fatty foods were associated with health and prosperity. In church, our fat-starved farmer would have heard the advice of Isaiah to the true believer: "Eat ye that which is good, and let your soul delight itself in fatness." He'd have heard the psalmist compare losing oneself in God to the bliss of a greasy meal: "My soul shall be satisfied as with marrow and fatness; and my mouth shall praise thee with joyful lips."

But which fat to choose—saturated or unsaturated? Animal fat or olive oil? By the late Middle Ages, the battle line between these ancient antagonists more or less followed the modern border between Tuscany to the south and Emilia-Romagna to the north. South of this line, despite some pockets of pork fat created by barbarian invaders, olive oil was the favored condiment for vegetables, soups, and fish both grilled and fried. To the north, in Italy and beyond the Alps, where olive trees didn't thrive because of the cold, a few olive oil aficionados existed among the upper classes, but animal fat held sway among the masses except during Lent and fast days. Northern Europeans had mixed emotions about olive oil. They prized it for its sacred symbolism and medicinal properties, yet disliked its bitterness and bite, so different from the sweet animal fats used to season their native comfort foods. If they ate olive oil at all, they preferred milder oils like those grown on the shores of Lake Garda, but often enough they simply kept the substance well away from their mouths. Hildegard of Bingen, the German abbess, mystic, poet, and polymath, spoke for many northerners when she concluded that olive oil was excellent medicine but miserable food, which "causes nausea when eaten, and ruins other foods when cooked together with them." Or perhaps Hildegard and her sisters were getting bad oil. Thomas Platter, a Swiss traveler of the late sixteenth century, observed that only low-grade olive oil reached northern Europe, pressed from the lees after the good oil had already been extracted. An expression current in England in his time, "as brown as oil," suggests this oil's appearance—and taste.

A new campaign in the enduring culinary war between olive oil and animal fat began in the fifteenth century, with the triumphant arrival of butter. This second invasion came about not, as at the end of the Roman Empire ten centuries earlier, in a rush of wild-haired, fat-eating Germans, but through subtle changes in dietary custom, and a gradual loosening of Rome's grip on food that occurred in the run-up to the Reformation. In certain areas of northern Europe, where no olives grew and residents had little taste for oil, modifications in canon law permitted the consumption of butter during Lent and fast days, opening the door to widespread substitution of butter for olive oil.

French and English cooks began to replace olive oil with this milder-tasting fat, long a part of their indigenous cuisine, and to weed out Mediterranean influences in their cooking. As far south as Sicily, certain gastronomes and gourmands sang the praises of this wondrously sweet new condiment. In his influential cookbook *Libro de Arte Coquinaria*, written about 1450, Maestro Martino, court chef to the patriarch of Aquileia, instructs his readers to prepare *maccaroni siciliani* with fresh butter and spices rather than with oil. A contemporary play has a group of Venetian gentlemen sitting down to plates of *maccaroni* covered with vast quantities of cheese, cinnamon, sugar, and "so much butter that they swam in it." Butter even worked its way into the dreams of the poor, like the family of sharecroppers in Modena who left their fields and moved across the Po River into Lombardy, "because there, it's said, you get gnocchi with plenty of cheese, spices, and butter." From the fifteenth century down through the nineteenth, the struggle between oil and butter was brought to life in European paintings, literature, and street dramas as the war between carnival and Lent, with butter marching into battle in full armor at the head of an army of animal fats and dairy products, as its archrival, olive oil, leads up a host of herrings, cabbage, bread, and other Lenten allies.

Still, most southern Europeans remained faithful to olive oil, not only because of their ancient devotion to Mediterranean fare but because butter struck many of them as unnatural, even dangerous. Nobles at the court of Mantua packed ample stores of *oleum bonum* for a journey to England, and the cardinal of Aragon, travelling in the Low Countries in 1517, brought along his personal cook and a generous supply of olive oil. "Due to the butter and dairy produce that is so widely used in Flanders and Germany," he observed, "these countries are overrun with lepers." If some chefs pushed butter, others championed oil: a new generation of cookbooks appeared in the fifteenth and sixteenth centuries, primarily in southern Italy, which proposed an exciting new multiethnic Mediterranean cuisine oozing with oil. The prominent humanist Bartolomeo Sacchi, better known as Platina, wrote *De honesta voluptate et valetudine* ("On Right Pleasure and Good Health"), a gastronomic treatise which provided some of the first detailed advice on the proper use of olive oil in Italian cuisine. Like modern-day Italian cooks, Platina recommended adding oil in abundance to fresh vegetables and legumes, and more sparingly with a range of fish dishes. The common folk, too, expected their daily dose; an English traveler in Tuscany remarked on the large quantities of olive oil consumed by the Tuscans, "the rich because they like to economize, the poor because they have no choice." In Tuscany, even humble sailors got their fix: daily rations included 28 grams of olive oil, dipped from earthenware jars stowed in the hold. Similar jars carried oil to the New World with the first Spanish and Portuguese explorers, and have been found in shipwrecked galleons and caravels on the Florida and Carolina coasts.

The Renaissance saw olive oil used in a wide, sometimes bizarre new range of ways, which made the most of its chemical properties and spiritual resonances, and boosted olive oil consumption. During outbreaks of the witch craze, judges and papal inquisitors learned that witches routinely covered themselves with secret salves and unguents, often made with olive oil, which supposedly allowed them to raise storms, destroy crops, and fly off to the Sabbath on their broomsticks, as well as numbing their limbs so they wouldn't shrink from Satan's touch. In some areas the mere possession of oil, together with "ointments, hurtful powders, pots with vermin or human bones," was sufficient to justify arrest for witchcraft. Though olive oil was considered beneficial in times of plague, *unctores* ("oilers") were thought to use oily substances to spread the plague. Inquisitors themselves loosened the tongues of accused sorcerers with applications of boiling oil, and sometimes executed them with still more generous doses of the stuff. Exorcists drove demons from the bodies of the possessed using holy oils and consecrated olive branches, as they intoned, "I anoint you with this blessed oil, and through this anointing free you of all curse, incantation, binding spell, written magic and charm that has been worked on you by the diabolic arts."

On a more luminous note, olive oil was also a favorite vehicle for the pharmacological and alchemical creativity of Renaissance protoscientists. The brilliant, fiery, and famously beautiful Caterina Sforza used it widely in her *Experimenti*, a collection of nearly five hundred medicines, scents, creams, and beauty cures. She derived several of her recipes from magical rituals, and wrote them in code to keep them secret; others were nothing less than X-rated aphrodisiacs and sexual aids, with which she carried on the proud tradition of oil-enhanced sex celebrated by the classical Greeks.

Apart from its use by witches and sexual adventurers, the biggest impetus to olive oil production came from several emerging industries, which exploited the chemical characteristics of olive oil as fatty acid, lubricant, and solvent. In soap-making centers like Marseille and Venice, olive oil was blended in great copper cauldrons with lye, soda ash, and seawater, and the resulting dense, porridgy mixture, a sodium fatty acid salt known in lay terms as soap, was poured into molds to harden. Every woolen mill from Flanders to Florence needed generous supplies of olive oil to soften the yarn before it was woven, since the carding and combing process had removed the lanolin, wool's natural lubricant. Olive oil was also widely employed in textile-dying and leatherworking.

The mounting demand for olive oil helped to advance olive-growing and oil-making expertise. In his *Tesoro dei Rustici* ("Treasure of Rustics"), fourteenth-century *bolognese* poet Paganino Bonafede elucidated the art of planting, grafting, pruning, and fertilizing olive trees in 143 hendecasyllables. Some authorities recommended beating the trees with canes to bring down the fruit, but Umbrian writer Corniolo Della Cornia, like Roman agronomists before him, favored hand-picking because it caused less damage to the branches and produced more oil. Treatises with titles like *Panoply of the Agricultural Arts* built on and improved the knowledge of the ancients, bringing a new scientific approach to olive oil by classifying cultivars and production regions, and perfecting methods of harvesting, milling, storage, and transportation. Clever engineers began to build olive mills along watercourses, using hydraulic power instead of mules and oxen to turn the millstones; sixteenth-century Tivoli, near Rome, had eighteen water-powered mills. Merchants like Francesco Balducci Pegolotti, a Florentine, helped standardize and regulate oil commerce. In his popular manual *Practico della Mercatura* ("The Practice of Trade"), Pegolotti describes the different weights and measures used for oil in each major Italian city, and the increasingly close supervision of oil production, quality, and shipping methods being performed in the ports of Puglia.

Puglia, in fact, was the world leader in oil production in the Renaissance as it had been in the Middle Ages, despite the rapid expansion of groves in southern Spain and Greece. *Pugliese* families like the Scoppa in Barletta and the Rufolo in Molfetta grew rich on the international oil trade, and the Scaraggi family of Bitonto became so wealthy shipping oil to Egypt and Byzantium that they could maintain sales agents in Venice, Alexandria, Constantinople, and other eastern Mediterranean ports. But the most successful merchants in Puglia were foreigners: the Lombards and especially the ever-present Venetians, active in Bari, Molfetta, Barletta, and other major cities in Puglia, whose ships carried *pugliese* oil throughout the Mediterranean, from Genoa and Mallorca in the west to Tunis, Alexandria, and Constantinople in the south and east.

The market for olive oil became increasingly discerning and sophisticated. Industrialists found they could use cheaper, lower-grade oils like those made from rotten olives, second-pressed from olive pomace with the help of hot water, or slurped out of the "inferno," a cave-like space beneath the press which caught the waste oil. Producers began to grade olive oils, distinguishing in their contracts and bills of sale between *oleo grosso* ("coarse oil") for factories and *oleo claro* ("fine oil") for food, the *claro* being worth twice as much as the *grosso*. Merchants differentiated among production areas according to the quality of the oils made there: oil from Lake Garda, Gaeta, Tuscany, and the Marche was generally of the highest quality; Puglia, Mallorca, Liguria, and Catalonia of middle grade; and oil from Calabria and Andalucía, though abundant, was widely called "soap-making oil." (Generally speaking, until the advent of modern oil-making technology and methods over the last four decades, the unrelenting heat of the southern Mediterranean made the production of flavorful, fault-free oil far more difficult than in cooler climes, and to this day the majority of oil made in Calabria and Andalucía is *lampante*.)

The emergence of industrial oil and a range of oil grades increased the ever-present risk of fraud. Many cities passed strict laws against mixing high-quality oils with lower-grade ones, which yielded inferior blends that might be passed off as higher-priced oil. The fifteenth-century statutes of the oil trade in Verona prescribe penalties for crooked olive millers, and denounce the "new and malicious fraud" of cutting high-grade oil with olive pomace oil, "a bitter, smoky and murky" substance which "even in small quantities utterly spoils a large amount of good oil." By now the *veronesi*, like other oil-makers in high-quality but small-scale production areas like Lake Garda and the Marche, were being steadily squeezed out of the business by less prized but high-volume oils from Puglia and Andalucia being marketed by the wily Venetians.

Even low-grade industrial olive oil was subject to fraud, through adulteration with cheaper vegetable oils. In 1618, authorities in London dispensed fines and prison sentences for soap-makers who used anything but pure olive oil. Two decades later, the Livorno-based sales agent of the English wool-weaving company Fairfax and Barnsley wrote to his London partner about the recurrent problem of worm infestation in wool cloth, which he blamed on adulteration. "There is no marvel why the worm breeds in cloths for, since the planting of rapeseed in England, the clothiers have got the trick to mix that oil with olive oil . . . which, lying long packed, breeds a worm."

As the liquid gold of olive oil flowed from port to port around the Mediterranean and the Levant, cities began to tax it, which in turn fostered tax evasion. In a fifteenth-century trial, oil merchants Alessandro Miniscalchi and Leonardo Pellegrini, scions of two illustrious Venetian families, were charged with systematically defrauding the fisc of La Serenissima. After years of deliberation, the court eventually cleared the accused of all charges, but it did strengthen anti-fraud measures, and authorized oil-crime investigators and customs officers to use "inquisitorial procedures," even torture, in future cases, "since many frauds are committed these days, following many different methods and routes, this territory being so broad and wide open to all." Modern oil criminals who evade EU taxes and embezzle EU subsidies are following a time-honored tradition.

Venice's hold on the olive groves and mills of Puglia began to loosen in the sixteenth century, as the growing Turkish power eclipsed Venetian trade in the Adriatic. As Venetian maritime dominion waned, French, English, and Dutch ships took over the job of carrying oil to the city. Then the city fathers levied a new tax on olive oil just as an outbreak of plague prevented oil ships from entering the port, which wrecked the Venetian oil business and decimated internal consumption. The French, English, and Dutch began to collect oil in *pugliese* ports themselves and, bypassing Venice, to deliver it directly to foreign manufacturing centers. Most of the profit from Italian olive oil—as well as from oil fraud and tax evasion—now fell into foreign hands. Multinationals which now dominate the olive oil market in Puglia, dictating prices and relabeling *pugliese* oil as they like, perpetuate a situation that arose in the Middle Ages and was consolidated in the Renaissance.

A SHARP SEAR came at the back of Gary Beauchamp's throat, together with an overwhelming sense of déjà vu. As his eyes filled with tears and he started coughing convulsively, a eureka moment came of the kind that scientists dream of, a chain reaction of interdisciplinary inspirations ricocheting through biochemistry, immunology, and human history. All triggered by one sip of extra virgin olive oil.

Beauchamp, who holds a PhD in biopsychology, directs the Monell Chemical Senses Center in Philadelphia, a nonprofit research institute that studies the chemical underpinnings of smell, taste, and other sensations. His epiphany—the insights of which he's been following up on ever since—took place in 1999 at Erice, a hill town in western Sicily that overlooks the brilliant blue Tyrrhenian Sea. There he took part in a symposium on a new field of study, termed "molecular gastronomy," at which chefs and scientists performed a number of culinary experiments, presenting a food or preparing a dish and asking the participants to work out its chemical significance. During one session, Italian physicist Ugo Palma brought out several plastic Coke bottles of olive oil, recently made at his family's grove outside of Palermo. He poured out three-finger doses of the dark green liquid into wineglasses, distributed them to the gathering, and demonstrated oil-tasting with the *strippaggio*, the slurp that draws the volatile components up into the nasal passages. After the first sips and slurps, the room erupted in coughs and tearful groans of admiration.

The instant Beauchamp felt that odd burn in the back of his throat, he thought of ibuprofen, a nonsteroidal anti-inflammatory. Back in Philadelphia, he'd recently spent several months chewing and swallowing doses of ibuprofen during a study commissioned by a pharmaceutical company, which hoped to substitute ibuprofen for acetaminophen, another analgesic drug which they were then using in one of their over-the-counter cough remedies. "Ibuprofen produced this very particular burn in the throat when swallowed," says Beauchamp. "It's not like hot peppers, which burn everywhere on your lips, mouth, throat. Ibuprofen produces an entirely different sensory percept, which is extremely localized in the throat, and only happens after you swallow it. Since the sensory qualities of a compound often tell you a lot about its pharmacology, when I felt that ibuprofen-like sensation with olive oil, I realized that they probably had a connection."

And here the avalanche of questions started. Ibuprofen's anti-inflammatory properties derive from its inhibition of COX-1 and COX-2 enzymes which cause swelling. Was olive oil also a COX-inhibiting anti-inflammatory? Ibuprofen and other COX inhibitors, in addition to pain relief, have been linked to reduced risk of heart disease and certain forms of cancer. Could olive oil's mysterious anti-inflammatory do this, too? Was olive oil the key to the Mediterranean diet?

To start answering these questions, Beauchamp brought a Coke bottle of oil back to the Monell lab, where he and his colleagues broke it down into its chemical components and tasted each one to see if that substance burned their throats. They eventually isolated one molecule that did; to ensure that no other chemicals were involved, they synthesized the molecule *de novo*, dissolved it in tasteless corn oil, and, after waiting many months for FDA authorization to ingest a novel man-made substance, finally swallowed it—and felt the same throaty bite. They named the substance "oleocanthal," a term they cobbled together from the Latin words for "oil", "sting," and "aldehyde" (an organic compound produced by oxidizing an alcohol). Further tests revealed that although oleocanthal had a completely different molecular structure from ibuprofen, it inhibited COX-1 and COX-2 enzymes in a strikingly similar way. Beauchamp and his colleagues later demonstrated that oleocanthal also reduces the adverse effects of ADDLs, highly toxic protein byproducts which are believed to contribute to the onset of Alzheimer's disease; what's more, the substance appeared to make ADDLs a better target for antibodies, thus enhancing the effects of immunological therapies for Alzheimer's.

This potent yet little-known remedy is part of extra virgin olive oil's "polar fraction," a delicate cocktail of over one hundred polyphenols, hydrocarbons, vitamins, and other perishable and often volatile compounds which vanish when the oil is treated with chemicals or heat. (They are also known as the "unsaponifiable fraction," because they are left over when oil is mixed with an alkali to form soap.) Though many of these compounds are poorly understood, they are coming under increasing scrutiny by medical researchers, who are revealing that they possess a wide range of therapeutic properties.

A number of substances in olive oil's polar fraction shield us from the far-reaching damage done by an essential part of our own body chemistry: oxygen. One of nature's great ironies is that this element, vital to creating and nourishing life, also accelerates aging and death. Oxygen is required for cell metabolism but produces certain highly reactive byproducts called free radicals, which damage cells, combine with LDL ("bad" cholesterol) to sludge up artery walls, degrade DNA strands leading to malignancies, and break down proteins in the body. By the age of eighty, the proteins in an average person's body are 80 percent oxidized; oxygen, in other words, is making us go bad. Polyphenols in olive oil such as hydroxytyrosol and secoiridoid aglycones, as well as hydrocarbons like squalene, are potent antioxidants, natural preservatives that protect olive oil from spoilage caused by oxidation, and also help shield tissues in various parts of the human body from the assault of free radicals. Clinical tests suggest that, thanks either to these antioxidant properties or their ability to inhibit cancer-cell proliferation, polyphenols in olive oil also help prevent cancers of the colon, breast, ovary, and prostate gland.

Polyphenols and other substances in olive oil also appear to have cardiovascular benefits, thanks to their anti-inflammatory properties and because they reduce the clotting action of red blood cells, diminishing the risk of thrombosis, stroke, and heart attack. Other compounds act as antibacterial agents, amplifying the immune system's response to infection. Still others block the sun's ultraviolet rays, and protect against skin cancer when the oil is spread on the skin. And others, like oleocanthal, appear to guard against neurological damage in degenerative conditions like Alzheimer's.

"A low incidence of cardiovascular disease, dementia, and certain kinds of cancer—these are among the central benefits attributed to the Mediterranean diet," says Gary Beauchamp. "Since the 1950s, people have accepted that olive oil, the main source of fat in this diet, is the keystone of this dietary regime." Some of olive oil's positive effects stem from its monounsaturated fat profile, but, more and more, medical research suggests that the polyphenols and the other "minor components" of olive oil, which constitute a scant 2 percent of its volume, are the main source of oil's health benefits. These same substances give a high-quality olive oil its pepperiness, bitterness, and other prized sensory properties; in fact, the oil's healthful properties are directly proportional to the strength of its flavors, aromas, and other sensory characteristics. If an oil doesn't sting at the back of the throat, it contains little or no oleocanthal. If it isn't bitter, it's low in tocopherol and squalene. If it isn't velvety in texture, then it's missing hydroxytyrosol. (Table olives, depending on their cultivar and how they've been cured, frequently contain high levels of oleic acid, as well as generous doses of polyphenols and the other precious minor components also found in extra virgin olive oil.)

The concentration of these beneficial substances varies widely among oils, from about 50 to 800 milligrams per kilo of oil, depending on factors such as the olive cultivar, where it's grown, how much water the trees receive, the ripeness of the fruit at harvest, and the milling and extraction methods used. Refined olive oils contain next to no polyphenols, because they and the rest of the polar fraction disappear during the refining process. Yet olive oil labels rarely communicate this crucial health data—most contain just a heart health message about the fatty acids in olive oil, which lumps extra virgin olive oil and refined oil together as one undifferentiated commodity. Gary Beauchamp points out that many health benefits only derive from first-rate oil. "Before researching olive oil, I used to buy any old oil in the supermarket. It was just something to dump over salad. Today, knowing what I know, I'm willing to spend $25 or more for a bottle of high-quality oil." In fact, it's the consumption of polyphenol-rich olive oil and the other elements of the Mediterranean diet over the long term that produces most of the diet's health benefits. "Many Italians at the Erice conference made their own oil from family trees," Beauchamp remembers. "Often when they were kids, their grandmothers had given them a little cup of oil each morning to drink, like a medicine."

Given the bitterness and astringency of some quality oils, Beauchamp wonders how people ever tumbled to the notion that olive oil was good to eat. "When I had that first taste of real extra virgin olive oil, the pungency, astringency, and bitterness were overwhelming. For a minute I felt as if I might have done myself harm. Bitterness, for example, usually signals the presence of a substance that's toxic to some part of our anatomy—medicines are bitter because they're killing something. So when people eat good olive oil and taste that bitterness, what they're experi-

encing is an interaction between a fruit that doesn't want to be eaten
and their organism, which doesn't want its tissue destroyed. Great olive
oil is decidedly an acquired taste. But it's one we'd all do well to acquire."

SHORTLY AFTER SPEAKING with Gary Beauchamp, I had dinner
with Lanfranco Conte, perhaps the world's leading authority on olive
oil chemistry. He holds the chair of food chemistry at the University of
Udine, and also serves as adviser to the International Olive Council in
Madrid, the agriculture department of the European Union in Brussels, and the Italian government's Technical Commission on Oils and
Fats in Rome. But among his favorite activities are the olive oil tastings
he holds in elementary and middle schools in the countryside around
Udine, where we met.

"Before we start tasting the oils," Conte told me, "I show the children
a picture of my cat. I tell them how acute her senses are, while ours have
grown dull and need to be trained and sharpened. That always breaks
the ice, and they start telling me about their own pets—their dog that
recognizes people by smell through closed doors, their grandfather's goat
that knows him by the sound of his footsteps. Then I give each child
two glasses of oil, one good and the other bad, and without explaining
anything about them, we begin."

Conte is an imposing figure, a tall, densely bearded man in his mid-
fifties, with a resonant basso voice smoothed by decades of lecturing and
a slight hump over his right shoulder, the result of a birth defect, which
give him the stage presence of a Shakespearean actor. But he knows how
to put the children at their ease.

"When I distribute the glasses of oil, I always say to smell them, but to
wait before sipping them. There's always a show-off, though, who gulps
both oils right down. So I point to him and say, 'You *drank* that? The bad
oil too? What a moron!' Which always gets a big laugh, and starts the
session off well."

Udine is in Friuli, at the northeastern tip of Italy. From the restaurant where we sat, the green fields and stone farmhouses just a few kilometers away were in Austria and Croatia. Conte joked that he'd been "posted to the outer limits of the empire," much like that forlorn Roman senator of the second century AD, deep in barbarian territory on the Danube. In fact, Udine is on the oil-and-lard watershed that once divided the lands of the Roman Empire from the barbarian backcountry, a border still marked to this day by church steeples: the sharp spires of churches built by the Republic of Venice rise in places where people habitually eat olive oil, while the onion domes of the Austro-Hungarian Empire mark the lands of the lard-eaters. Our restaurant was in the lard zone: my cabbage stew and *frico*, a cheese-and-potato pancake, had the dense tang of pork fat, and nothing on the menu contained olive oil. The country kids Lanfranco Conte teaches about oil come from both worlds: some are from oil-making regions like Istria, famous since Roman times, while others have never tried oil in their lives. "Whatever their background, though, it's nice to see the enthusiasm and freshness that they bring to the subject," Conte said. "They have no prejudices about what olive oil should taste like, much less the blind certainty of so many adults in Italy that the oil their grandfathers make is the best on earth."

During his olive oil lessons in schools, after distributing the first pair of oils Conte has the children smell them carefully, then taste them. "They quickly recognize the good and bad oils. Their senses are almost as sharp as my cat's, and they sometimes describe the oils with a chemist's insights." One boy sniffed an oil that had a flaw known as "fusty" and said, "This smells like cow." Puzzled, Lanfranco Conte asked what he meant, and the boy explained that the oil reminded him of the smell in his father's dairy barn when the milking machines needed washing. In fact, Conte said, this sour-milk scent was produced by the same lactic acid fermentation that causes fustiness.

Conte's occupation, which he calls "the best job in the world," is to teach at university and analyze foods, especially olive oil, in his laboratory, working out the biochemical causes of cow-smell, greasy mouthfeel, and the hundreds of other tastes, odors, and sensations produced by oil. "My wife knows when I've spent the day in the lab, because I come home as carefree as if I'd just taken a long motorcycle ride through the mountains." Conte loves nothing better than to peer into the deep chemistry of olive oil, scrutinizing the length and kinks in its fatty acid chains, the concentration of its phenols and configurations of its sterols and the degradation of its volatile compounds, which taken together document the life history of each oil. Some of his tests measure an oil's freshness, and may reveal errors made by the farmer or miller while making it. For example, a high level of free fatty acids, which are produced as oil decomposes, suggests that the oil was made from spoiled fruit or extracted using outdated methods. He measures the amount of peroxides in an oil, which rises as the oil combines with oxygen in the air and goes rancid; high peroxide levels indicate that an oil may have been exposed to the air for too long during milling, malaxing, or storage, or is simply old.

Sometimes Conte finds more sinister clues to an oil's past. Elevated levels of erythrodiol and uvaol, or more than 225 parts per million of waxes, indicate that an oil probably has been illegally blended with pomace oil, while unusually high levels of arachic or linolenic fatty acids suggest it has been cut with canola or soybean oil. Conte uses further tests to identify contaminants, such as polycyclic aromatic hydrocarbons (PAHs), chemical compounds formed during the incomplete combustion of organic substances which have been found in olive pomace oils (pomace is dried in furnaces before its oil is extracted) and have been shown to cause cancer as well as genetic and neurological damage. "My job isn't as easy as it looks on television shows like *CSI* or *Quincy*, where the hero puts a sample into the mass spectrometer, hits a few buttons, sees a peak as big as Mount Everest, and announces, 'This is cocaine!' But each transformation in the oil, whether natural or man-made, leaves traces that a good chemist can pick up."

The analogy with detective work is appropriate. Conte formerly headed a laboratory of the agriculture ministry's Fraud Repression Unit, which tested olive oil and other foods for contaminants, adulteration, and other irregularities. Today he uses his dual experience as chemist and law-enforcer to devise chemical tests for the different quality grades of oil, which in turn enter Italian and EU laws on olive oil, helping to make extra virgin olive oil the most tightly controlled food in the world—at least on paper.

Conte refilled my glass with the local white wine we'd been drinking, and together we enjoyed its crispness and cold floral notes. He explained that it was formerly called Tocai, a word which recalls the famous Tokaji or Tokaj wine produced in northeastern Hungary and southeastern Slovakia, but is made with different grapes that are locally known by Italian producers as Tocai. After vigorous protests from Hungarian and Slovakian wine-growers, however, the EU granted them the exclusive use of this denomination, and the Italians had to rename their wine.

"So it's a wine made from the Tocai grape varietal, but can't be called a Tocai," Conte said. "Now they've started calling it Friulano." He laughed, and made an odd face. "Another example of how different the wine and oil businesses are."

"One thing's for sure," he said, lifting his wineglass and gazing through the luminous liquid. "You don't see *this* stuff traveling around in tanker ships. You don't see tanker-loads of Bordeaux either, or single-malt scotch. But even though extra virgin olive oil is as fine and as perishable as any of these, tankers with 3,000-ton loads of extra virgin olive oil are crisscrossing the Mediterranean."

"Extra virgin . . ." he repeated, in his deepest, most theatrical voice, dripping with irony. "That's how they label it, anyway."

While working in the Fraud Repression Unit, Conte said, he learned quite a bit about olive oil tankers, and about the profound differences between the olive oil and wine businesses. He was a chemist at the unit's laboratory when the methanol scandal broke, and he saw the subsequent government crackdown that purged the Italian wine industry of many low-grade producers, vastly improving the overall quality of Italian wine. During the methanol scandal he and the other investigators in the Fraud Repression Unit were given a free hand to unmask unscrupulous producers who were adulterating their wines. In olive oil, by contrast, the deck frequently seemed stacked against them. Lab employees and other officials responsible for detecting adulterated oil were (and still are) criminally liable if their actions against suspected olive oil offenders proved unfounded and caused economic loss. "If you decide to block three thousand tons of oil and it turns out you were wrong, you pay out of your own pocket," he said angrily. "Who's going to take this responsibility?"

Conte said that since 1991, policy-makers at the International Olive Council and the European Union have attempted to improve olive oil quality by tightening the parameters for free acidity, peroxides, and other chemical values required for each olive oil grade. In the end, how-ever, they haven't been able to go far enough, because of resistance by producers and traders, many of whom fear that more stringent quality levels will bar their oils from the market. Conte says that the current free acidity level of 0.8 percent for the extra virgin grade is still much too high to ensure excellent oil, which typically has 0.5 percent or less, and he calls the current peroxide level of 20 milliequivalents per kilo "indecent."

We drank our wine in silence. Then, like several of the olive oil pro-ducers I'd spoken with, Lanfranco Conte wished aloud for a health scan-dal in olive oil equivalent to the methanol scare in Italian wine, which would lead to serious new laws, tough enforcement, and a generalized cleanup of the oil business, as he'd seen in wine. "Trouble is, olive oil has already had its scandal." He mentioned the so-called "toxic oil syn-drome," an incident in Spain in 1981 during which over 20,000 people were poisoned by fake olive oil made from rapeseed oil denatured with aniline, a highly toxic organic compound used to manufacture plastics. An estimated eight hundred people died, and thousands more were left with permanent neurological and autoimmune damage. Conte glanced at me to see if I understood. Fake olive oil had caused thirty times more deaths than methanol, yet the oil business remained as slippery as ever.

INDUSTRIAL OIL

Wild olives out of red earth
    (Blood of past praise and death)
    first tasted in a crooked orchard
    that clung on crumbling terraces—
    the peculiar taste of wild olives
    all the green of the world
    in their green smooth skins.
        —William Oxley, "The Peculiar
        Taste of Wild Olives"

Virgin Olive Oils: The oil obtained from the fruit of the olive exclusively
with mechanical processes and other physical processes, in conditions that
do not cause alternations in the oil, and which have not undergone any treatment apart from washing, decantation, centrifugation and filtration, exclud-

ing oils obtained with solvents or with chemical or biochemical reagents or
with processes of reesterification or any mixture with oils of other nature.

—European Union Law 1513/2001

*I*t wasn't the vials of liquid as black as tar which were labeled oil, or the smells of smoke, solvents, and rancidity, or even the ancient furnaces caked with charred, toxic-looking organic material. It was the starving cats that got me, standing among the furnaces and watching the workers eat lunch. The workers saw me looking at the cats, noticed my shock at their tattered, lumpy coats and spade-sharp hips and spent, streaming eyes, almost past caring. And the men raised their chins in defiance.

Food should not be made here.

I was touring the Rubino pomace plant with Michele Rubino, the friendly and plain-spoken director of quality control, a member of the family that has run this *sansificio* in the southern outskirts of Bari for four generations. "This used to be open countryside," he said as we walked through the courtyard, where the tall smokestack and jets of steam looked odd against the apartment buildings behind. "But now we're in the city. There have been complaints about the smell." In one corner of the yard were huge piles of pomace, the solid residue of olive skins, stems, pits, and leaves left over from olive oil extraction, which still contains about 8 percent of the oil made by the olives. The Rubino plant removes this residual oil.

We walked through the facility as Michele Rubino explained the process. Front-end loaders dump the pomace into a large hopper, from which it moves into a steel tube heated by the furnaces, that rotates slowly until most of the moisture in the pomace has evaporated. The dried pomace is transferred into tall silos and drenched with hexane, an industrial solvent. After the residual oil dissolves into the hexane, leaving the pomace, a blast of steam as loud as a cannon-shot drives the mixture of solvent and oil into a separate tank, where it's heated to evaporate off the hexane. What's left is a dense, black liquid known as crude pomace oil, vials of which Michele Rubino had shown me in his office. Before this oil can be sold as food, it's piped into a refinery in an adjoining building for desolventization, deacidification, deodorization, degumming, and other chemical processes. The resulting clear, odorless, tasteless fat is blended with a small quantity of extra virgin olive oil to give it flavor, and is sold as "olive pomace oil."

This substance is a poor cousin to extra virgin olive oil, with a dubious past. From time to time, Italian and EU health inspectors have detected toxins, mineral oil, and carcinogenic material in pomace oil; there have been Europe-wide health alerts for contaminated pomace oil, leading to product recalls and confiscations. In Italy, pomace extraction plants like the Rubino *sansificio* don't even need to be certified as food production facilities. Yet the pomace oil industry is widely subsidized by the EU, as well as by the national governments of Spain, Italy, and other oil-producing countries. Pomace oil is used extensively in the food service industry and in many restaurants, as well as an ingredient in foods such as pizza, pasta sauces, and snack foods, where it is typically marketed as healthy-sounding "olive oil." Pomace oil is commonly used to adulterate olive oil. It is widely sold in supermarkets, often in packaging that misleads customers into thinking they're buying olive oil.

All this is to be expected, however, in a business where opaque and misleading labeling is the order of the day. Where the term "olive oil" doesn't just mean the juice pressed from olives, but denotes a heavily refined concoction of low-grade oils which, like pomace oil, have been deodorized, deacidified, degummed, and the rest. Where "extra virgin olive oil," which actually *is* (or should be) olive juice, sounds vaguely unnatural, as though it had been processed. Where high-sounding terms like "pure" and "light" mean oils that have been stripped of nearly all of their sensory qualities and health benefits. A business whose laws and regulations have been written for (and frequently by) olive oil industrialists, rarely with the interests of olive farmers or honest extra virgin producers in mind. Much less of consumers.

———

THE PANEL taste test is an integral part of EU and Italian law regarding olive oil, yet Italian authorities rarely perform it, and private citizens who attempt to apply the law do so at their own risk. Witness the case of Andreas März, a Swiss agronomist who for the last three decades has produced extra virgin oil at a farm called Balduccio in the hills outside Pistoia, not far from Florence. März has the bulky, permanently dirt-stained hands of a farmer, yet his exuberant handlebar mustache, weather-worn leather vest, and red neckerchief suggest a character from the Old West—a steamboat gambler, perhaps, or a Texas Ranger. "I'm a farmer, but not the usual, silent kind of farmer," he says in Tuscan-accented Italian, breaking into German now and then for emphasis. Earnings from extra virgin olive oil are so meager that he's always had to do other jobs. He has unloaded trucks and hired out to other farmers as a laborer; when the great frost of 1985 ravaged Tuscan groves and killed 90 percent of his trees, leaving him with a mortgage and three young children to feed, he even stooped to journalism. Four years later he founded his own German-language magazine, *Merum*, dedicated to Italian wine and olive oil, and began to write a series of articles which denounced the poor quality of olive oil bottled—though rarely made—in Italy. He described the investigations of the Guardia di Finanza in Puglia and elsewhere in southern Italy, and told how major international brands had been caught selling adulterated oil. And he repeatedly pointed out that many big Italian producers were breaking international law, labeling oils as extra virgin whose taste and aroma were far inferior to the legal requirements for the extra virgin grade.

In 2004, he began his own investigation. He bought thirty-one bottles of extra virgin oil in supermarkets throughout Germany, and sent them to Florence for testing by three highly trained taste panels. The results were unanimous. Only one of the thirty-one oils was actually extra virgin grade. Nine were virgin, a grade below extra virgin. The rest, including oils by Bertolli, Carapelli, Rubino, and other major Italian names, were adjudged to be *lampante*, and therefore legally unfit for human consumption.

A few months later, März published the results of the tests in *Merum*. Carapelli promptly filed civil and criminal suits against the Florence chamber of commerce, whose panels had done some of the tasting, as well as against the head of the chamber's chemical analysis laboratory, Laura Mazzanti, and one of the panel leaders, the distinguished agronomist Marco Mugelli, on charges of abuse of office and interference with industry and commerce. An Italian court eventually threw out the case, but when the exasperated chamber decided to sue Carapelli for damages, they received a telephone call from a high official in the ministry of agriculture who instructed them to drop their suit. They did, and opted to avoid similar controversies in the future by discontinuing their panel test activities on behalf of private parties. "As an act of intimidation, it worked perfectly," Marco Mugelli says.

In December 2004, März published an interview with Mugelli in *Merum*. März began by summarizing the results of the 2004 tests. "Like the majority of supermarket extra virgins," März wrote, "samples from the Carapelli oil factory, in Florence, were also judged to be inferior. The taste panels of the Florence Chamber of Commerce have determined that the Carapelli extra virgins are incorrectly labeled. Independently from the tasting done by experts of the Chamber of Commerce, the inferior quality of the Carapelli oils was confirmed by another official panel (ARPAT in Florence). And now the counterattack: instead of classifying its oils correctly, the Carapelli group, based in Florence, takes aim at the individual taster. . . . If the press is critical of the anarchy that reigns in the olive oil market, then it must be silenced, and the most effective way to do this is to intimidate the experts."

März then asked Mugelli about the lawsuit which Carapelli had brought against him, and asked him to explain the existing laws governing olive oil quality, in particular EU Directive 796, passed in 2002, which sets out the most up-to-date quality requirements for each grade of oil.

"The law calls for the total absence of defects in an extra virgin olive oil," Mugelli said. "The law mentions no exceptions or special lenience."

"So in theory," Andreas März replied, "after 2002 the world of extra virgin oil should have undergone a revolution. If the law actually worked, extra virgin oil should be a real rarity?"

"It ought to have, yes. But in reality, nothing has changed."

"This means that the new law has outlawed most extra virgins currently on the market?"

"Precisely!" Mugelli agreed.

"So long as smelly, rancid oils and first-rate oils with the perfume of fresh olives bear the same name," März wrote, "quality producers in Italy and throughout the Mediterranean have no possibility of covering their costs. So long as olive producers are unable to earn a fair profit for their olives and their oil, groves around the Mediterranean will continue to die out. The leaders of the oil industry know what a clear differentiation among oil quality grades would mean for them. Putting consumers in the position to be able to choose between quality and quantity could threaten their sales. Carapelli apparently wants to avoid this threat by filing suit against one of the most inflexible and independent experts: Marco Mugelli."

In March 2006, soon after the interview appeared in print, Carapelli sued Andreas März for libel. They sought crushing damages, which, if granted by the judge, would cost März his home, his farm, and his livelihood.

When I visited März later that month, he and several Albanian hired hands were pruning his groves, and the air was pungent with smoke from the burning green cuttings. An old Tuscan adage says that when a tree is properly pruned, a swallow can pass through its branches in flight; extensive pruning, like green-pruning in grapes, helps concentrate the tree's energies on making olives rather than wood, and allows air and light to reach the fruit so it can mature properly. His trees, which number 4,000, grew scattered across the steep slopes, and were four to five meters tall—mere shrubs compared to the massive grandfather trees of southern Italy. About a meter up their short gray trunks, a few gnarled limbs curved outward and upward, creating chalices to catch the sunlight. The branches were densely covered with small, oval leaves, gray-green above and silvery beneath, which glimmered when a breeze turned them. März explained that these trees were regrowths after the 1985 frost.

Making extra virgin oil is expensive in hillside Tuscany, where land, labor, and materials are expensive. The harvest, which can account for over half of the total cost of making extra virgin olive oil, must be done largely by hand, not only because of the steep terrain but because hand-picking is the best way to avoid bruising the fruit—bruising triggers enzymatic processes associated with decomposition that spoil the flavor and aroma of the oil.

März was cordial but reserved until lunchtime, when he began to unwind. We walked out of the trees and into his low stone farmhouse, where, on our way to the kitchen, he selected a few of the dozens of olive oil bottles which sat in clusters just inside the door, in the hall, and at the foot of the stairs, samples that he had just reviewed in the latest issue of *Merum*. The kitchen was the largest room in the house, with walls of caramel-colored stone and ceiling beams as thick as a galleon's mainmasts. It was filled with a ravishing atmosphere of spices and herbs frying in oil, produced by März's wife Eva, who was maneuvering burnished copper pans over the blue flames of an enormous, professional-quality gas range. "I love to cook, and we both love to eat, so we allowed ourselves this extravagance," she said, gesturing at the broad kitchen with one of her pans. "Sometimes we spend the entire day in here, cooking and tasting all kinds of foods."

"And drinking," Andreas März added, handing me a flute of prosecco. "It's part of my job, after all." As we talked, the couple's two sons, now in their early twenties, drifted in, poured themselves wine, suggested in Tuscan or Swiss dialect a refinement to one of Eva's dishes, or took a pan and started cooking something else. This appeared to be a routine lunch at the März homestead.

März set the olive oil bottles he'd collected in a row on the kitchen table, a slab of age-polished oak ten feet on a side. Some were tall and slender-necked, others squat and square-shouldered like hip flasks, still others were colorful one-liter tins. He placed two white plastic cups beside each container, and poured samples for us to taste.

Like most oil-makers I've met, März loves to introduce people to real extra virgin oil, and watch their faces as they begin to realize what they've been missing. "I have a lot of visitors from Germany, Austria, Switzerland, and elsewhere in northern Europe, and many have never seen fresh olives before. I give them a handful and say to rub the olives, stick their noses in, and sniff—to really get physical with the fruit. And I say, 'This is what real extra virgin oil smells and tastes like, because *this* is the fruit it's made from.'"

He said that many northern Europeans were initially repelled, like Saint Hildegard of Bingen eight centuries earlier, by the bitterness and throat-burn of many first-class oils. Some Germans have reported olive oils to health authorities as adulterated because of these qualities—which are actually good evidence of authenticity. "People with no experience in the Mediterranean normally prefer mild, sweetish, slightly oxidized olive oils with very little character, just as, when people try wine for the first time, they usually prefer a mild *vin de pays* or a cheap Chianti to a big-bodied Barolo with heavy tannins. Which is perfectly fine—great oils and great wines are acquired tastes, and you need time to appreciate their subtleties, the variations from one locality or harvest to another. But the labels have to be accurate, so you get what you pay for. Just as you can't put 'Barolo' on a bottle of cheap table wine, you shouldn't be able to put 'extra virgin' on a bottle of piss-poor, *lampante* oil. But that's just what's happening."

He said he makes it a point to meet as many producers as he can, and visit their mills. "The best way to know for sure if an oil is good is to see where it comes from, walk among the trees that made the olives, shake the hands that did the picking," März said. "As far as I'm concerned, the only honest oil-makers are those who grow their own olives. By now it's a war between growers like us and the oil traders, who just buy, mix, and sell other people's oil—and profit from the inherently illegal condition of the olive oil industry."

We tasted oils from various parts of Italy, then experimented by pouring them over the dishes that arrived one by one from Eva's range. For all their variety, these oils had a few things in common. As März had said, each had the fresh, intensely green taste and aroma of recently harvested olives. And each was completely free of that flabby, cooked, meaty, faintly rancid taste of many supermarket oils. Ordinary extra virgin olive oils aren't necessarily bad, but premium extra virgin olive oil is a superior product—a fact explicitly stated in EU regulations. In fact, "ordinary extra virgin olive oil" is a contradiction in terms, and "premium extra virgin olive oil" a tautology: the "extra" in "extra virgin" means it's superior. As März said, "According to the letter of the law, a true extra virgin is a great oil, like a *grand cru* wine. It's an oil that makes you get down on your knees and say, 'Fuck!'"

At the end of the meal, after thick slices of Swiss walnut cake ("No *tiramisù* can touch this," März said), with the grappa still simmering on our tongues, I asked again about his audacious taste test, and Carapelli's lawsuit against him. "I'm happy that they're suing me," he replied. "Now I'll finally have the chance to bring the corruption in this industry to the attention of the world."

He was trying to put a bold face on his predicament—trying to play the cardsharp, the Texas Ranger. But in his voice, and in Eva's expression as she paused over the range to listen, I sensed the weariness and anxiety of farmers who longed to end this long detour through courts, and return to the calm conviviality of their meals, and to the silence of their trees.

FROM CLASSICAL TIMES until the beginning of the nineteenth century, Europeans (like people the world over) obtained their fats and oils from locally grown products. Small mills, presses, and workshops dotted the countryside, which in the north mainly processed animal fats, and in the south made olive oil.

In the early 1800s, first in England and soon after on the Continent, the factories of the Industrial Revolution developed vast new appetites for lipids. Steam-powered machines with precision, high-speed parts required more and better lubricants; textile mills consumed ever-growing quantities of fabric softeners; and a booming detergents industry called for a rapidly increasing supply of fatty acids. Traditional

sources of animal fats and vegetable oils soon proved insufficient. English traders began importing a series of exotic foreign oils from their
tropical colonies, most notably palm oil from Guinea and coconut oil
from India. The French likewise imported peanut oil from their African colonies and linseed oil from the Levant to supply the thriving soap
industry in Marseille. At first these oils were inedible, but over the next
several decades food chemists invented vegetable oil refining and hydrogenation, which yielded cheap, thick, spreadable fats with long shelf lives:
industrial cuisine for a new industrial society.

In 1866, Napoleon III announced a competition to create inexpen-
sive, healthy, easily conserved foods for the army and the working classes.
French chemist Hippolyte Mège-Mouriès won first prize with oleomargarine, an ersatz butter which he whipped up from rendered beef, water,
and casein, a protein extracted from milk. In 1871, Mège-Mouriès sold
the patent to Jurgens and Van den Bergh, two Dutch butter companies which soon specialized in margarine manufacturing. The companies found ways to replace beef and casein with cheaper vegetable oils,
especially Guinean palm oil and American cottonseed oil, and before
long opened factories in Belgium, Germany, and England. By 1895, European margarine production had already reached 300,000 tons, and by
1923, hydrogenated oils and solid fractions of liquid oils made up almost
90 percent of the fats consumed by Europeans. Jurgens subsequently
merged with several other oil and fat concerns, including the prominent
British soap manufacturer Lever Brothers, to form Unilever, a far-flung
multinational which extracted endless streams of oils from its extensive
tropical plantations, piped them through huge refineries, and funneled
them into people's mouths through worldwide trading channels.

As the distance between producer and consumer grew, extended by an
ever-longer chain of anonymous middlemen, food fraud became easier to
commit. In England, where the traditions of peasant foraging and cooking
were already being weakened by the enclosure movement, the Industrial
Revolution brought an age of rampant food adulteration: bread tainted
with alum and copper sulfate, beer "corrected" with narcotic picrotox-

ins, children's sweets colored with lead and mercury, and "demon grocers" who purveyed a range of revolting and sometimes deadly dry goods. In 1848, chemist John Mitchell observed that England was "about the only nation that has no laws, or no effective laws, for the protection of the public against the adulteration of food." Much of this was due to the British government's emphasis on free trade, and a faith that Adam Smith's "invisible hand of the market" would sort things out. The government's view, according to food historian Bee Wilson, was simple: "What happened between a man and his baker was no business of the state; free trade was best." As it happens, laissez-faire had shielded British swindlers long before the Industrial Revolution. Writing in 1726, Jonathan Swift had already consumed his fair share of adulterated bread and beer, and clearly thought little of free market economics. In *Gulliver's Travels*, his Lilliputians

> look upon Fraud as a greater Crime than Theft, and therefore seldom fail to punish it with Death: For they allege, that Care and Vigilance, with a very common Understanding, may preserve a Man's Good from Thieves; but Honesty hath no Fence against superior Cunning: And since it is necessary that there should be a perpetual Intercourse of buying and selling, and dealing upon Credit; where Fraud is permitted or connived at, or hath no Law to punish it, the honest Dealer is always undone, and the Knave gets the Advantage.

Fighting fraud in a world of long-distance trade was possible, as the ancient Romans proved at Monte Testaccio, and as the French government did in the mid-nineteenth century with a battery of stiff new laws against food counterfeiting. Yet without such concerted effort, most markets seem to take care of themselves, not their consumers. A slender but significant difference exists between *caveat emptor,* "let the buyer beware," and *floreat mercator,* "let the seller get rich."

Aside from outright fraud, however, the industrialization of the world food supply in the nineteenth century also marked the birth of what might be called legal fraud. Beginning with margarine and shortening and continuing in many thousands of other mass-produced foodstuffs, new processing techniques made it possible to assemble food in factories from an increasingly homogenized and anonymous range of materials. Oil refining and hydrogenation meant that "butter" could be created from rendered beef fat or palm oil, "lard" made from cottonseed oil, and "olive oil" concocted from peanut or poppyseed oil—or from whatever other commodity had the lowest price at that moment.

IN APRIL 2006, I visited the Bertolli refinery and bottling plant at Inveruno, in the industrial hinterland of Milan, where the Alps form a snowy curtain along the northern horizon. An ancient olive tree stood at the entrance to the plant, its leaves thin and browning, a few mummified olives clinging, unpicked, to its branches. Like that sad second-century Roman senator posted to the Danube, this tree was clearly out of its element in the cold northlands, where olives have never thrived. It and a handful of other olive trees had been dug up in their native Puglia and replanted here eight years earlier, to decorate the huge new facility, which produces 8 percent of the world's extra virgin olive oil. Despite this impressive market share, however, these may be the only olive trees that the Bertolli company, bought out by Unilever in 1994, has ever owned. Even back in the 1870s, the Bertolli family that founded the firm were bankers, not farmers or millers, and since then the company has always dealt in someone else's oil. Now tanker trucks arrive at the facility all year long, carrying oil which Bertolli buyers source throughout the Mediterranean. Only about 20 percent of it is Italian; the bulk comes from Spain, the Maghreb, and the Middle East. Marco De Ceglie, the personable oil executive who showed me around the facility, insisted that Bertolli doesn't rely on its Italian image to sell oil. "The country of origin means absolutely nothing to us," he said. "We've always maintained that the important thing isn't the '100% Italian' [label], but the Italian know-how in producing and blending oil—that's the real value-added." What's more, he rejected the criticism of supermarket oils by self-styled oil experts, who presume to educate consumers about what constitutes good olive oil, as paternalistic, even dictatorial. "Someone better think twice before they try to come into my home and 'educate' me, tell me what I should and shouldn't like," De Ceglie said. "We have to feed the whole population, not just please the rich and forget about all the rest. We're not like Marie Antoinette—'If the peasants don't have bread, let them eat cake.' And after all, those guys lost their heads!"

De Ceglie's talk of egalitarianism and fair play doesn't always square with Bertolli's marketing tactics, however. The company's television advertisements in Italy have, in fact, used Tuscan accents and settings to suggest the Tuscanness of its oil, and the Bertolli website for Canada, emblazoned with "Lucca" and *Passione Italiana*," still features a naïve pastel drawing of a four-generation family feasting on mozzarella, salami, and Chianti in a straw-covered bottle, against a backdrop of olive groves and cypress-clad hills that looks suspiciously like Tuscany. In Italy, other Bertolli ads have, in fact, presumed to dictate to consumers what constitutes a good olive oil—and have in the process misinformed them about the definition of extra virginity.

In the US, until 2001, Bertolli bottles were marked "Imported from Italy" and "Made in Italy," and the company used slogans such as "Born in the Tuscany Mountains" and "Like the Da Vinci [painting of the Madonna and Saint Anne], Bertolli olive oil is an authentic Italian Masterpiece." In 1998, however, Marvin L. Frank of the New York law firm Murray, Frank & Sailer brought a class-action suit against the company, charging that Bertolli oil was made from Spanish oil shipped to Italy for bottling, and that the company had used deceptive advertising because consumers were willing to pay more for Italian oil. (Frank says he settled the case in 2001, when Bertolli agreed to tone down its claims in its advertisements and labels.) A commercial that ran several years ago on Italian television shows two attractive oil-tasters, a man and a woman, sipping Bertolli oil in regulation tulip glasses. "It's what we wanted, no?" the man says. "Gentle on the palate." The woman agrees: "It's not peppery in the throat, it isn't heavy—it's what we were looking for!" In reality, "gentleness" or mildness is a frequent attribute of low-quality oil, and pepperiness is one of the three official positive attributes, together with bitterness and fruitiness, identified in the legal definition of extra virginity. Other big producers continue to rely on similar marketing sleight-of-hand: in a recent television advertisement by Carapelli, an actor dressed in lush Renaissance silks and brocades to resemble Lorenzo de' Medici praised the taste of Carapelli oils in a thick Florentine brogue. This bait-and-switch fuels revenues: customer surveys suggest that most Italians buy oil they believe is made from Italian olives, and prefer it to oil from other countries. The same preference undoubtedly exists in many other countries.

At Inveruno, the various oils Bertolli buys were stored in towering silos, which with their observation catwalks and gantries of pipes resembled ballistic missiles, and held €10 million in oil—liquid assets that had drawn unwanted attention in the past. Several years earlier, De Ceglie told me, the plant was robbed by sophisticated oil thieves, who jammed the surveillance cameras to prevent detection and then siphoned off several million euros in oil into tanker trucks. After this theft, Unilever installed an alarm system which senses motion and changes in pressure and temperature throughout the facility, and automatically dispatches text messages to alert the personnel. "Oil is cash," said De Ceglie with a shrug. "You take it and you sell it instantly."

But each day, Bertolli faces a more insidious kind of crime. Every shipment of oil that arrives at the Inveruno facility is tested at least eight times for adulteration, starting with a probe dipped into the tanker trucks as they arrive at the factory to detect hidden compartments, and ending in the company's oil laboratory, among the most sophisticated in the world, where a battery of chemical tests is performed. De Ceglie showed me the lab with obvious pride, pointing out its impressive range of mass spectrometers and other high-tech devices, some of which cost over $500,000. Naturally, now and then even Bertolli makes mistakes, as in 1991, when they and other major olive oil companies bought oil from Domenico Ribatti that had been adulterated with hazelnut oil, and resold it to consumers as olive oil. But Simone Dominici, Bertolli brand manager, told me that Bertolli rejects as suspect about 70 percent of the oil it receives. This oil soon finds another buyer, however. "It doesn't get tossed in the river," Dominici said. "Someone else bottles it. As extra virgin, naturally." With their state-of-the-art laboratory, De Ceglie said, "We've made an impregnable fortress for oil. But the rest of the market is, let's say, fairly permeable."

The trickiest kind of fraud to detect is deodorization—inferior olive oil that has been processed at low heat to remove unpleasant odors and tastes. De Ceglie indicated that sophisticated and hard-to-identify *deodorati* are made by mysterious companies which sometimes possess the same level of chemical know-how and advanced equipment as Bertolli itself, whose identity he clearly suspected, but wouldn't reveal for fear of lawsuits. "Well, we're talking about criminal charges here, so I have absolutely no names for you. But let's say they could be trading companies, brokers, refineries, and so forth that can do these things." He said that Bertolli is constantly developing new test methods to detect fraud, while its shadowy foes dream up ever more inventive new frauds. "It's a continual game of cops and robbers. With us on the side of the cops."

"They also know our limit of detectability, and they adjust the oil," added one of the lab technicians, who had been listening to our conversation. "Because they don't just give us pure deodorized oil, they mix it in such a way that we're always—as far as they're concerned . . . at the end of the day . . ." She exchanged looks with De Ceglie, and her voice trailed away.

Much of the oil that Bertolli rejects as potentially adulterated will be bought by their competitors, the most cutthroat of whom these days are discount supermarkets, which sometimes sell "extra virgin" oil at under €2 per liter. A recent chemical and sensory analysis of discount extra virgins by the food quality laboratory at the University of Bologna, headed by noted olive oil chemist Giovanni Lercker, determined that 70 percent of the oils sold below €3 per liter were actually not of extra virgin grade, and probably contained deodorized oil. Bertolli views these discount oils as the biggest threat to their sales. "By breaking down the natural defects of these oils, deodorization is habituating consumers to this flat taste," Simone Dominici told me. "When a consumer tries a robust oil, very rich and fruity, they say, 'Oh no, this is a bad oil!' He's become used to the flat taste of the *deodorato*. And what's happened there is the worst thing that could possibly happen—the incredible value of the extra virgin olive oil category has been destroyed." Dominici said that the practice of deodorization was "penalizing both us and the consumer."

Here is an ancient lament. The Garda oil-makers of the seventeenth century accused dishonest Venetian merchants of corrupting German palates with substandard oil, and makers of high-quality oil like Andreas März and Grazia De Carlo blame Bertolli, Carapelli, and other big brands for doing the same thing, selling "gentle" oils that erode the consumer's taste for authentic extra virgins. A swift and widespread dumbing-down of olive oil quality has occurred, which in the end is everybody's loss.

Still, Bertolli employees know good oil when they taste it. De Ceglie took me into their panel testing room, where a world map on the wall was marked with hundreds of locations where Bertolli buys oil. They have analyzed and recorded the tastes and aromas that each of these oils should have at a given time of year, which helps them to select good oils and to unmask frauds. "You need both the taste test and chemistry—they're two sides of the same coin," De Ceglie said. "Once I know that in a specific season a *coratina* oil must have a certain taste profile, when I taste it and it's much sweeter, something's wrong."

We sat in the tasting booths and an assistant brought us three of the many thousands of oil samples which the Bertolli taste panel would try during the course of the year. We tried a splendid *racioppella* from the area near Benevento, with hints of artichoke and chicory, a *coratina* with a serious bitter bite and a strong aftertaste of almonds, and a milder Greek *koroneiki* with notes of fresh-cut grass. De Ceglie and his colleagues tasted the oils expertly, slurping and rolling their eyes with obvious pleasure.

We tasted nothing from a Bertolli bottle, however. Unlike these unblended oil samples, each so characteristic of a specific locality and harvest, Bertolli oils are mixed to fit rigid taste profiles. "We know what our customers expect, every time they buy a bottle of our oil. And that's what we give them. The great art of Italian oil-making consists in producing a consistent product from a huge range of different oils that change constantly throughout the year." Bertolli must also produce enormous quantities in order to satisfy its high-volume customers, such as Walmart. He said that the smallest quantity of oil the company would buy was a tanker truck, or thirty tons; he remembered, during his years traveling the oil regions of the world as a buyer for Bertolli, his hard negotiations with the big Spanish cooperatives, which produced so much oil and had such enormous storage facilities that they could drive a hard bargain. The situation was reversed in Puglia, where oil-makers and agricultural cooperatives had invested so little in storage silos that, as the *olio nuovo* began to arrive during the harvest, they frequently didn't know what to do with the previous year's oil. "It was a delight to go and buy there," he remembers. "The producers didn't know where to put the oil, and I basically named my own price. It was absurd."

High volume, intense price pressure, and an identical product every time—Bertolli extra virgin olive oil is a textbook commodity. Not long after my visit to Bertolli, Unilever sold the company to the Spanish oil and fat conglomerate Grupo SOS, which had recently purchased Carapelli and several other historic Italian brands as well. A substantial part of the oil sold under Grupo SOS's Italian brands now comes from Spain, though marketing campaigns still stress their Italian origins. "These companies have basically become just bottling plants for Spanish oil," one former Carapelli executive told me. But Grupo SOS, which in July 2011 changed its name to Deoleo, has its own troubles, due to plummeting oil prices, the economic downturn in Spain, and the company's lawsuit against its former heads, Jesús and Jaime Salazar Bello, which alleges fraud, money-laundering, misappropriation of €240 million in company money, and other misdeeds. (The case is currently being heard before the Audencia Nacional de España, a Spanish national court in Madrid.) The company, burdened with debt and a plunging stock price, has sold Dante and other brands to raise working capital, but this may not be enough. More recently, in February 2011, investigators of the Nucleo Agroalimentare e Forestale del Corpo Forestale, a food quality corps of the Italian Forest Service, said they discovered falsified transport documents in the Deoleo office in Tavarnelle val di Pesa regarding a shipment of 450,000 kilos of oil valued at about €4 million. Prosecutors hypothesize that these documents were altered to conceal the real nature of the oil, which, instead of being extra virgin, they say may have been low-grade olive oil containing deodorized oil, worth three times less. "We asked for this hypothesis to be verified using the alchyl esters test, an important new chemical method for detecting the use of deodorized olive oil," said the investigative head of the corps, Colonel Amedeo De Franceschi. "To tell the truth, it seems possible that our request itself accelerated the approval of this analytical method at the EU level, unfortunately with parameters too permissive to prevent many frauds—far more permissive than the parameters published in professional journals by the scientific community two years ago." (The Florence district attorney is evaluating the accusations; investigations are still under way, and so far no charges have been brought against Deoleo.)

ON MAY 12, 2009, having considered Carapelli's request for damages against Andreas März because of his article in *Merum*, and heard a statement by März's lawyer in his defense, the presiding judge in the case, the Honorable Luciano Costantini of the district court in Pistoia, near Florence, read his verdict.

Carapelli's accusations against März, Costantini observed, regarded five statements that he had made in his article. He reviewed each statement in turn.

1) Like the majority of supermarket extra virgins, samples from the Carapelli oil factory, in Florence, were also judged to be inferior. The taste panels of the Florence Chamber of Commerce

have determined that the Carapelli extra virgins are incorrectly labeled. Independently from the tasting done by the experts of the Chamber of Commerce, the inferior quality of the Carapelli oils was confirmed by another official panel (ARPAT in Florence).

"Regarding the first affirmation," Constantini said, "the accused has described the events in a manner that corresponds entirely with what actually occurred."

2) Instead of classifying its oils correctly, the Carapelli group, based in Florence, takes aim at the individual expert.

"Regarding the second affirmation, it is demonstrated by the documentation provided to the court, and by statements by the witnesses themselves, that Carapelli S.p.A. brought suit against Marco Mugelli, director and leader of the panel, and Laura Mazzanti, head of the chemical analysis laboratory of the Florence Chamber of Commerce, and other functionaries of this last organization, at the public prosecutor's office in Florence on September 23, 2004."

3) If the press is critical of the anarchy that reigns in the olive oil oil business, then it must be silenced, and the most effective way to do this is to intimidate the experts.

"Regarding the third affirmation, the opinion expressed by März regarding the judicial action undertaken by Carapelli S.p.A. appears entirely legitimate, also in light of the results of the preliminary investigations that have been carried out, and the requests for damages made in the libel suit [brought by Carapelli]. One must also note that [Carapelli's] opposition to a settlement of the proceedings by decree indicates an explicit desire, not merely for restitution of damages suffered, but for the punishment of those who might eventually be found responsible, leading the accused to believe that the suit was brought with punitive intent."

4) So long as smelly, rancid oils and first-rate oils with the perfume of fresh olives bear the same name, quality producers in Italy and throughout the Mediterranean have no possibility of covering their costs.

"[Regarding] the fourth affirmation, . . . the lesser quality of the oils was determined by the analyses done in Florence at the chamber of commerce and ARPAT, from which result the various negative characteristics of aroma and taste expressed with the terms 'smelly' and 'rancid.'"

5) The leaders of the oil industry know what a clear differentiation among oil quality grades would mean for them. Putting consumers in the position to be able to choose between quality and quantity could threaten their sales. Carapelli apparently wants to avoid this threat by filing suit against one of the most inflexible and independent experts: Marco Mugelli.

"Regarding the fifth affirmation, the observations made in point three above, regarding the motivation behind the judicial action of Carapelli S.p.A., apply here as well."

"Andreas März carried out his journalistic investigation scrupulously and diligently," Justice Costantini said, before concluding, "The court pronounces März Andreas Anton innocent of the crime of which he is accused, because the crime itself did not occur."

Moments after the sentence, Andreas März was ecstatic. "We've shown them! The judge confirmed my statements word for word! This is just the beginning!"

A week later, though, he had returned to earth. "The verdict got no coverage in the Italian press—*nobody* picked it up. No lab or panel will do tests in the future, after the ruckus I kicked up here. And even if they were willing to test, no private citizen will dare to bring them any oil." His voice was a monotone, and had grown softer as he spoke. I could barely hear his last three words: "Nothing has changed."

6

FOOD REVOLUTIONS

The mortal moon hath her eclipse endured,
And the sad augurs mock their own presage;
Incertainties now crown themselves assured,
And peace proclaims olives of endless age.
— William Shakespeare, Sonnet 107

"Too much love kills, even more than hatred. That's what we've done to olive oil. Our reaction to it is totally visceral: oil belongs to the most sacred things, which are paradoxically the first things that we vilify. 'Grease the palm,' 'Oil the works'—oil has become a synonym for corruption."

I'm sitting with Paolo Pasquali, in a broad, low-ceilinged room with an antique breakfront and an enormous, age-sleeked table that came from a church sacristy, and a holy water stoup against the wall with a tap over it that spouts olive oil. He calls this place an *oleoteca*. "Wine has the *enoteca*, and the wine cellar, but until now, oil has had nothing analogous. It wouldn't be the mill, of course, which is a noisy, aggressive, stressful place, where people rush to process as many kilos of olives per hour as possible. So I created the oleoteca. It's a place of merry holiness, where you can enjoy oil in its multiple tonalities—mythological, scientific, and culinary."

Pasquali taught philosophy at the University of Florence, and quotes Aristotle, Aquinas, and Lévi-Strauss with an intensity that reveals how their words have shaped his mental warp and woof. He also trained as a musician, and made a fortune as an entrepreneur in publishing, then sold his business for another fortune just before the Internet swallowed it. He's handsome, with the jutting chin and hooked nose of a battle-hardened *condottiero*. Now he's trained his Renaissance-man energies on the art and science of making great olive oil, in a place where the arts and sciences have melded in creative ways for centuries. He owns Villa Campestri, a thirteenth-century estate in the Mugello, the hill country north of Florence, where he makes oil from small groves in various parts of the property. The Mugello has been called the cradle of the Renaissance: Giotto was born around the corner, Fra Angelico up the road, and philosopher Marsilio Ficino taught and wrote among the olive groves of nearby Cafaggiolo, the ancestral home of the Medici. Pasquali believes the time is ripe for a modern renaissance of olive oil, based on a new philosophical and aesthetic understanding of great oil in the twenty-first century.

To begin with, he says, the language we use to talk about oil is all wrong. Olive oil labels, with their opaque references to production methods and oil chemistry, give the consumer no sense of what the oil will be like to eat, and no desire to find out. Pasquali thinks no better of official taste testers, who brandish spiderweb charts of sensory characteristics and spout terms borrowed from lipid chemistry, "as if they were nurses trying to talk like doctors." Pasquali finds that even the basic words people use to describe olive oil are charged with unwanted meanings, and need to be retooled. "Pungent" and "bitter" have far more positive connotations in the Mediterranean than in North America, for example, where they sound harsh to many people. In China, "eat bitterness" is an ancient curse.

"We must reclaim the nobility of language which oil has lost. The language of music, for example, which is the natural way to speak about beauty. We talk about an oil's 'floral notes' or its 'harmonious' structure, instinctively borrowing from the musical lexicon."

Before his talk grows cloying, Pasquali hops to his feet, because like all Renaissance men he's also a man of action. He walks to a console on the wall built in gleaming copper and stainless steel, which despite its modern materials fits with the thirteenth-century decor. He takes three tulip glasses, holds them one by one under the three spigots of the console, and out come three green and gold ribbons of oil, three different extra virgin experiences. He invented this device to shelter fine olive oil from its three worst enemies: oxygen, heat, and light. It's part of a new business model Pasquali has devised, OliveToLive, which he says will allow restaurants and stores to serve the highest-quality olive oil, and to make a profit doing it.

"Oil is the opposite of wine. Wine ages, oil goes bad. The instant an oil is bottled, the decay accelerates. Bulk oil is the only way to go—super-premium bulk oil."

This console, he explains, contains three light-proof vessels that preserve the oils in an oxygen-free environment, at 16 degrees Celsius, the optimum temperature for oil storage, until the moment it's served. Oil that's kept in the OliveToLive system, which has been installed in a handful of high-end restaurants and oil bars in Italy and the US, maintains its freshness and sensory qualities longer than bottled oil.

Pasquali fills three more glasses, then brings all six back to the table, where he sets three in a line before me, and keeps the others for himself. He tells me to start with the gentler oil, made at the McEvoy Ranch near Petaluma, California, and then work up to the more pungent and bitter oils from Andalucía and from Pasquali's own trees. He cups a glass in the palm of his left hand and cranks it around with his right, to warm it. I do likewise. He shoves in his sizable nose, and breathes.

While we snuffle and muse over the oils, Pasquali describes his personal education in the substance, which, as with most things he does, has been hands-on. He's made oil at Villa Campestri for the last five years, and participates actively in the milling, the harvest, and the year-round care of the trees. "When I first started, I'd go out with local farmers, the oldest ones I could find, and spend the whole day with them among the trees, pruning or hoeing or picking. I found they were able to talk about oil for eight straight hours, and saw that olive oil must have a power even greater than soccer! They had the oil bug, and I caught it."

Since then Pasquali has made Villa Campestri a center of R&D and communication about fine oil. He's hosted study groups and retreats for sensory scientists and other scholars from the University of Florence and the Culinary Institute of America, and has more research planned for the future. Guests at Villa Campestri enjoy a complete olive oil experience: guided tastings, mill and orchard tours, seminars on sensory science, massages with olive oil, and magnificent oil-based meals in the hotel restaurant. His daughter Gemma, who holds a PhD in agronomy, leads the seminars, often accompanied by her young children, including Pasquali's newest grandchild, two-year-old Cosimo, after whom this year's oil at Villa Campestri is named. "The children love tasting oil," Pasquali says. "They seem to sense its innate goodness and healthfulness, perhaps because of the percentage of the linolenic acid in olive oil, which is just like mother's milk, and is fundamental for its absorption in the intestine."

By now we're tasting the third oil, made at Villa Campestri. It's a fierce oil: floridly fruity, brazenly bitter, lip-puckeringly pungent. I slurp some, then cough and hack like a character in *The Magic Mountain*. Pasquali smiles unblinkingly, with glistening lips.

Then he's off on another of his carefully reasoned tangents: how to make money from oil. As he says, he loves the myth, poetry, and science of olive oil, but he remains an entrepreneur. "People don't ask for free wine at a restaurant. Why should they expect free olive oil? Until premium olive oil becomes a profit center in restaurants, we producers will never make a fair living." In his restaurant, he says, he charges €9 for a flight of three oils, and business is brisk. The Culinary Institute of America recently opened one of his *oleoteche* at its campus in Napa, California, and likewise charges for an oil experience. Pasquali says he aims to open another four oil bars soon, in Spain, Greece, Japan, and Singapore, and to use them as springboards to educate fifty top chefs around the world in the fine art of fine oil. "They'll become opinion leaders, spokespeople for how real oil works."

A door opens behind him, and his grandson Cosimo toddles in, his round cheeks pink from the cold. *"Ciao nonno!"* he chirps, leaning heavily on his grandfather's leg. He sees our oil and reaches up for the nearest glass on the table, the potent Villa Campestri oil which bears his name. As Pasquali cups his hands under it to prevent it from falling, Cosimo brings the oil to his lips and gulps it.

He shakes his head as if he's been slapped across the face, and coughs loudly, his eyes filling with tears. I think he's going to cry—that he's crying already. Then, still coughing, he chokes out a word: *"Buono!"* And he holds out the glass to his grandfather for more.

Pasquali's expression shifts between pride, tenderness, and what can only be described as hope. For a moment, I think *he* may cry.

"Can you imagine a better opinion leader?" he says at last.

THE MODERN HISTORY of olive oil began shortly after World War II, when Ancel Keys, the Minnesota epidemiologist, visited hospitals in Naples, Madrid, and on the island of Crete. Keys found an incidence of coronary heart disease that was drastically lower than in America, though people in these places had recently suffered the extended dietary privations of wartime, while Americans had had access to a varied and plentiful food supply. Keys, who had developed the K ration for the US Army ("K" stands for "Keys") and had recently concluded pioneering research on the physiology of human starvation, suspected that the root cause was the differing fat consumption of the two populations. Not so much the quantity of fat—paradoxically, he found that the Greeks and Italians actually had a moderate to high fat intake—but the type of fat they ate.

Spurred by his observations, Keys began an ambitious epidemiologic survey of traditional diets and lifestyles in Greece, Italy, Yugoslavia, the Netherlands, Finland, Japan, and the United States, which was eventually called the Seven Countries Study. He concluded that the trouble was with saturated fat, and the correspondingly high levels of cholesterol in the blood, which clogged arteries and led to heart attacks and strokes. In countries like the US and Finland, where most fat came from saturated sources such as meat and dairy products, coronary heart disease was high, while in the Mediterranean, where fats came primarily from monounsaturated olive oil, people were comparatively free of heart disease. (In Japan, where the diet was low in fat of any kind, heart disease was likewise very low.) In a series of publications in the 1960s and 1970s culminating in a definitive volume on the subject, *Seven Countries*, published in 1980, Keys recommended that Americans (and everyone else who cared about heart health and longevity) reduce their fat intake to 30 percent or less of their total calories. He urged what he termed a "Mediterraneanstyle regime," rich in vegetables, fruit, fish, bread, and pasta, with moderate amounts of dairy products and wine, and large quantities of olive oil. Keys had christened the Mediterranean diet, and put oil at its core.

Key's work had unexpected and ironic consequences. The United States government, in large part prompted by his emphasis on low-fat diets, declared unconditional war on fat. In 1977, the Select Committee on Nutrition and Human Needs headed by Senator George McGovern drew up a set of strongly anti-fat dietary goals, which were echoed by the USDA and the National Institutes of Health in anti-fat recommendations of their own. A series of clinical tests followed, purporting to prove the causal links between fat intake and heart disease, as well as connecting fat with cancer and obesity. Initially, hard saturated fats were targeted, but in the press and the popular mind, the demonization of fat rapidly spread to anything containing fatty acids, even healthy monounsaturates like olive oil. Dietologists dreamed up low-fat diets and food companies churned out low-fat foods to fill them, gradually making "low-fat" a synonym for slimness and health, though these foods frequently contained unhealthy amounts of sugar and salt, and all too often encouraged people to eat more total calories than before. Eventually the message spread far beyond the United States, working its way into the eating habits of the developed world. Today, many people in various parts of the globe believe that fat, saturated or not, is the root of all dietary evil.

Yet in the four decades since America condemned fats, the scientific consensus behind this condemnation has collapsed. After hundreds of millions of dollars spent in clinical studies, and after countless billions more spent in government nutritional education programs and food marketing, there is no proof that eating fat causes pathologies like heart disease, cancer, and obesity. Though hydrogenated fats are unambiguously unhealthy, there is no firm evidence linking unsaturated fats with heart disease, and even with saturated fats the science is far from incontrovertible. There is no proof that fat causes cancer. And although fats do contain five more calories per gram than carbohydrates, the wholesale substitution of fats with carbohydrates widely mandated in America may actually have accelerated the spread of obesity; the number of obese Americans has climbed from 14 percent of the population in 1980, when America went on a low-fat diet, to 34 percent today. What's more, fat plays many essential roles in the human body, and some researchers believe that reducing lipid intake may impair a range of functions including metabolism, cell membrane permeability, and neural transmission (the brain is 70 percent fat).

The current state of science regarding dietary fat was summed up by Walter Willett, chair of the Department of Nutrition at the Harvard School of Public Health, in his critique of the USDA's "Dietary Guidelines for Americans, 2010," which still recommends that Americans limit their fat intake to 35 percent of total calories. "There is really no basis for setting an upper limit on total fat," Willett wrote. Nevertheless, after decades of well-intentioned misinformation, fats of all kinds are still widely considered taboo. Olive oil, the healthiest fat of all and the crux of the Mediterranean diet, remains in nutritional and psychological limbo for many people.

While Ancel Keys was observing hospital patients in Crete and Italy and attempting to frame the debate about olive oil and fat, oil-makers and lawmakers in Europe and around the Mediterranean were gradually forging the modern language of oil. In 1959, the United Nations founded the International Olive Oil Council (since renamed the International Olive Council, or IOC), an intergovernmental agency composed of eighteen olive-growing and oil-producing countries from around the Mediterranean, whose purpose was to supply financial and technical assistance to growers and millers, fund research in oil quality and chemistry, and promote olive oil consumption throughout the world. Additional help for the industry came from the central European government, which began to take shape shortly after World War II in order to promote cooperation among member nations, thus making "war unthinkable and materially impossible," as Robert Schuman, the French foreign minister, said. Agricultural policy was a central part of this new unity: to ensure adequate and reliable food supplies in war-torn Europe, leaders created a Common Agricultural Policy (CAP) with generous subsides, incentives, and price guarantees to farmers. Olive farmers and oil-makers benefited from CAP aid, first in Italy, a founding member of the European Economic Community, and later in Greece, Spain, and other member states as they joined the EEC (which became the EU in 1993). European subsidies on olive oil continue to this day.

In addition to safeguarding the quantity of olive oil produced, Europe and the IOC also began, in the late 1950s, to address a growing qualitative divide among olive oils. While oil refineries remained widespread and profitable, and most producers continued to make oil with old-fashioned grindstones, mats, and presses as their ancestors had for cen-turies, new technology for olive crushing, malaxing, and centrifuging of the sort pioneered in Puglia by the De Carlo family had begun to produce increasingly high-quality oil, made quickly and efficiently from fresh olives. The gulf in taste and nutrition between refined oil, old-fashioned pressed oil and this new premier oil widened steadily, yet no sharp legal distinction existed between the bland, the bad, and the beau-tiful. Finally, on November 13, 1960, the European Parliament passed a groundbreaking law on olive oil quality, which created several new oil grades. The highest of these had an odd-sounding name, with overtones of science and religious mystery: extra virgin. The law stipulated that extra virgin oil be made solely by mechanical methods, without chemi-cal treatment, and set a number of chemical requirements, including a maximum of 1 percent free acidity. The law also announced that such oil "must not demonstrate disgusting odors such as rancidity, putridity, smoke, mould, olive fly and similar," though how these tastes were to be determined, or by whom, was not specified. Extra virginity was born, but the means for determining it were still lacking.

The task of creating a scientific taste test for olive oil was taken up by the IOC. Starting with a seminal tasting method developed in the early 1980s by the National Organization of Olive Oil Tasters, an olive oil school based in Imperia, Italy, a small team of chemists and sensory scientists from Italy and Spain immersed themselves in olive oil for two decades of painstaking experimentation, during which they identified the various flaws in taste and aroma which can arise in oil, and codi-fied a rigorous and reproducible tasting protocol to determine the qual-ity grade of an olive oil. The resulting IOC taste methodology, together with a set of chemical requirements, became the basis of a new EU olive oil law, passed in 1991 and, with some modifications, still in force today: to be called extra virgin, an oil must have zero taste flaws and some perceptible fruitiness (pepperiness and bitterness are also identified as positive attributes). With this law, olive oil became the first food in the world—and to this day one of a mere handful—whose quality was legally determined at least in part by its taste. The chemical limits for the extra virgin grade, though stricter than the original 1960 standards—the level of free acidity, for example, was lowered to 0.8 percent—were still loose, but the legal taste test appeared to promise a new seriousness in fostering olive oil excellence.

The mid-1990s were a high point for the IOC. Production boomed in many parts of the Mediterranean, and as new extraction technology spread, oil quality rose rapidly. The IOC recognized and coordinated a growing number of taste panels throughout the Mediterranean, regularly subjecting them to strict ring tests to verify their abilities and disqualifying panels that failed the tests. The IOC's executive director, Fausto Luchetti, a charismatic entrepreneur and member of a family of distinguished Italian diplomats, led promotional campaigns in a number of countries outside the EU, which successfully spread the message about olive oil's culinary and nutritional benefits. "The work of the IOC under Fausto Luchetti helped put olive oil on the map in Australia," says Paul Miller, president of the Australian Olive Association. "They created a critical mass of public awareness, and paved the way for the popularity that olive oil now enjoys in this country."

For all the successes of oil in the 1990s, these years were also a high-water mark for olive oil crime. Generous EU subsidies on olive oil encouraged widespread fraud in many olive-producing nations, particularly in Italy, the historic heart of the oil trade, where in many areas the entire production chain became, in effect, one huge criminal network, with farmers overstating the quantity of olives they picked, millers inflating the amount of oil they produced, and companies exaggerating the number of bottles they sold. Even olive oil unions got caught up in the scam, pocketing large sums and building lush headquarters in Rome, while neglecting the olive growers and oil-makers they nominally represented. In the mid- to late 1990s, olive oil became one of the most frequently adulterated agricultural products in the EU, leading OLAF, the European anti-fraud office, to set up a special olive oil task force. Domenico Seccia, the investigative magistrate in Bari who prosecuted Domenico

Ribatti and Leonardo Marseglia, wrote a book, *Olive Oil Fraud in the European Union*, which described the illegal consortia of oil producers, oil traders, banks, and food companies that had formed to reap the dual rewards of oil adulteration and European subsidies, and detailed investigative techniques for detecting and disbanding these networks. In olive oil fraud, an EU investigator told me, "profits were comparable to cocaine trafficking, with none of the risks." Widespread adulteration and huge supplies of refined olive oil fueled a price war, which forced even the largest oil companies like Unilever and Nestlé to seek ever cheaper sources of oil, with the risk of purchasing and reselling, knowingly or not, adulterated products themselves. While the quality of estate olive oils soared, supermarket extra virgins plummeted.

This quality divide between true extra virgins and industrial oil eventually split the IOC. According to its charter, the council was responsible for promoting all grades of olive oil. Yet as the quality gap between real extra virgins and lesser oils widened, producers of high-quality oil demanded more recognition for the extra virgin grade. At the same time, large olive oil companies with substantial sales in refined blends and supermarket extra virgins showed less and less enthusiasm for the IOC's taste test protocol, especially after it was written into EU law and could be used to exclude low-grade oils from the extra virgin category. Through lobbyists and direct participation in EU committees, these same large companies played an important role in formulating EU policy on olive oil, and exerted considerable influence on the IOC itself, since 80 percent of the IOC operating budget was supplied by the EU.

The crisis came in 2002. Fausto Luchetti was accused by the EU of mismanaging IOC funds, and resigned from the council. (The case is still being heard in a Madrid court.) Luchetti denies all charges against him, which he says were part of a scheme by certain high-level EU functionaries to divert funds from olive oil promotion by the IOC and channel them into the promotion of seed oils from northern Europe. His friend Flavio Zaramella, who followed the events closely, blames olive oil industrialists instead: "The big industry players wanted him out,"

Zaramella says. In any event, after Luchetti's departure the EU slashed IOC funding, severely curtailing the council's ability to carry on olive oil research and promotion. The funding cut also hamstrung the IOC's network of taste panels, since the council no longer had the money to perform ring tests on its recognized panels to verify their accuracy. The IOC remains a repository of invaluable experience and expertise, and its scientific brain trust still boasts some of the preeminent oil chemists in the world, like Lafranco Conte. But today this once-progressive organization, which invented a revolutionary new definition of olive oil quality and spread the gospel of good oil in many parts of the world, all too often helps to hold extra virgin quality to the lowest common denominator, protecting the interests of Big Oil rather than helping producers of genuine extra virgins—much less consumers.

ON SEPTEMBER 20, 2010, an eclectic group of chemists, chefs, sensory scientists, musicians, culinary visionaries, and quality control engineers from seven countries gathered in Verona, Italy, at a three-day conference called Beyond Extra Virgin, to discuss the future of olive oil. It was a historic moment for extra virgin oil. The Mediterranean diet, built on a shining foundation of olive oil, had just become part of UNESCO's Cultural Heritage of Mankind, and the extra virgin grade, created in 1960, was about to celebrate its fiftieth birthday. Yet the enthusiasm of the participants was tempered by moments of somberness, even of disorientation, as they realized how little they themselves actually knew about great olive oil, and how hard it would be to communicate the truth about oil to the world.

Speakers explored the mysteries of extra virginity in many ways. Harold McGee, the noted American writer on food chemistry, showed eye-popping slides of futuristic olive oil dishes made by trendsetting chefs like Ferran Adrià, the mad genius from Catalonia, who has formed a research group to devise unique new extra virgin edibles: oil-filled spheres of alginate that look like fish roe, which Adrià calls "olive oil caviar," and olive oil foam made from tapioca maltodextrin, a fine powder which absorbs the oil and liquefies in the mouth, like room-temperature ice cream. Luis Rallo Romero, professor of pomology at the University of Córdoba, described rare Spanish olive cultivars conserved in his plasma bank which most people in the audience had never heard of, which were rapidly disappearing from agriculture, together with their unique-tasting oils. Paolo Pasquali of the Villa Campestri compared the impact of oil on our senses of taste and smell to that of music on the ears, observing that oil produced the same progression of attack, decay, sustain, and release known to sound engineers, and virtuoso composer Luca di Volo and his ensemble interpreted olive oil's fruity, peppery, and bitter notes on violins and saxophones. In perhaps the most thought-provoking presentation of the three-day conference, sensory scientist Erminio Monteleone from the University of Florence described recent blind taste tests he'd conducted in Helsinki and Florence, during which consumers tried three oils and expressed clear preferences, yet often reversed these preferences when the same oils were served with food. "Olive oil combines chemically and kinesthetically with food, changing both itself and the food," Monteleone said, "so we can properly assess an oil only when we taste it in a dish."

This point was brought home with a number of tastings. World-class chefs prepared a variety of dishes at the cooking station at the front of the hall: Paul Bartolotta of the Bartolotta Ristorante di Mare in Las Vegas cooked his signature *triglia alla ponentina*, a red mullet encrusted in salt; star Greek chef Christoforos Peskias made a simple yet subtle chickpea soup; and María José San Román from Spain playfully whipped up a banana mousse and a salad of salmon and mango. When they finished cooking, waiters passed through the aisles carrying trays to the spectators, which held nuggets of the food that the chefs had just prepared, along with three gleaming plastic beakers of premier oil: gentle *biancolillas*, tart *cornicabras*, big boisterous *koroneikis*, and other top estate oils made in several countries. The audience tasted the oils on their own, after which the chefs explained how to blend them into the foods, pointing out how oil brought out hidden flavors in the dishes, and how each oil, with its own distinct pungency, fruitiness, aromatics, and mouthfeel, changed the fundamental character of the food in different ways, highlighting the succulent flakiness of the mullet and the floral notes hidden in the chickpea soup, and causing the mousse's sweetness to linger luxuriously on the tongue.

Occasionally a big-bodied oil would set off little eruptions of coughing, the loudest of which often came from Claudio Peri, the organizer of the conference. Peri is a retired professor of process control and food safety at the University of Milan, and looks it: tall, slightly stooped, with a slender white mustache that he fiddles with when he speaks, and a gentle, hopeful smile, someone for whom rules and procedures are deeply reassuring, even satisfying. At first blush he seems a bit too staid, and, well, professorial, to have dreamed up this three-day carnival of cutting-edge creative thinking about oil. But talk with him awhile and you'll see telltale flashes of an oil obsession: the mill in the Umbrian hills that his father ran when he was a boy, the dreamy sensuousness he says he feels when olive oil touches his lips, his love of oil's sacred and mythic dimensions. You begin to sense behind his mild demeanor a sharp thinker and a risk-taker, even something of a rebel, all catalyzed by oil.

"I'd spent my whole professional life teaching theories of food quality and food technology in a university. When I retired, I decided to see if these theories could actually produce something concrete, actually do good in the world outside. It was a kind of challenge I set for myself."

At the university, Peri had done research in a number of food industries, including wine, dairy products, vegetable proteins, and seed oils. But for him olive oil was the obvious choice as the food with which to bring his theories to life, not only because of his fond childhood memories but for oil's three unique characteristics, which had long puzzled him. First, despite what he saw as the inherent nobility of the product, oil fraud was rampant and ethics in the industry exceedingly low. Second, olive oil had no widely agreed on parameters of excellence, since the term "extra virgin" had become emptied of meaning. And third, despite the culinary and cultural value of fine oils, making them was rapidly becoming an economic impossibility. The three concepts of ethics, excellence, and economics became the watchwords of his new mission, and the name of Association 3E, the nonprofit organization which he founded in 2004. Through 3E and its members, which currently include eighteen world-class oil producers in Italy, Spain, Greece, and the US, Peri aims to set a new quality standard for great olive oil, which he calls the "super-premium" grade.

To join 3E, a producer's oil must pass the association's chemical and sensory tests, which are far more stringent than those prescribed by IOC and USDA guidelines. A 3E auditor documents the harvest of each member company, checks milling procedures, measures the quantity of oil produced, and monitors the stocks in real time in the storage silos until the last drop is sold. But despite these detailed procedures, Peri says, "membership in 3E is less about the quality of oil than about the quality of the people who make, sell, and use it. This isn't just a certifying agency. It aims to be more like a movement." In addition to creating great oils, 3E also attempts to help its producers earn better profits, by clearly explaining the superior qualities of their oils to consumers and distributing them through elite sales channels like Paolo Pasquali's Villa Campestri, the oil bar and restaurant at the Culinary Institute of America, and a handful of other fine restaurants in Europe and America.

In fact, Peri sees the strategic alliance he has formed with the Culinary Institute to be a vital step toward taking great oil into the mainstream. "Olive oil has had enough of the static language of taste panels and the hieratic hocus-pocus of the various olive oil sommeliers. It's the sensory dialogue between chefs and their customers that will open the road to excellence, which soon will be followed by people in their homes."

IF KRITSA, CRETE, is the heartland of olive oil consumption, then Jaén, deep in the Spanish south, is the mecca of oil-making. This province of the Andalucía region produces about 500,000 tons of olive oil per year—as much oil as all of Italy. Jaén is covered by an ocean of olive trees that flows across the lowlands of the Guadalquivir river valley, rides up over the rolling hills, and climbs as high as 1,000 meters on the steep mountainsides, wave on wave of trees planted in satisfyingly straight rows. There is no better place to experience the systematic, almost martial rigor with which Spain grows its olives and extracts their oil, an approach so different from the picturesque and haphazard farming of most of Italy and Greece. Over the last half-century, Spanish growers have uprooted hundreds of thousands of ancient olive trees and replaced them with efficient, high-output modern groves. Many of these new trees were planted in the 1940s, 1950s, and 1960s under *El Generalísimo* Francisco Franco, the military dictator, who promoted large-scale olive cultivation in Andalucía and other parts of Spain as part of his program to free the country of dependence on foreign food imports. More groves went in during the 1970s, when the Spanish government drew up a series of ambitious nationwide plans to renew the country's oil-making infrastructure, and still more were planted in the years preceding Spain's entry into the EEC in 1986, when Spanish farmers and oil-makers became eligible for generous agricultural subsidies.

Yet as in the second and third centuries AD, when this area was the olive basket of the Roman Empire—Monte Testaccio was built mostly with Andalucían amphorae filled with oil made hereabouts—historically Jaén oil-makers have concentrated on quantity, not quality. Ninety percent of the trees here are of the *picual* cultivar, chosen for its extremely high oil content (20–22 percent by weight); most growers wait until the content peaks, when the olives are overripe and beginning to fall off the trees, then bring down what fruit still clings to the branches with four-wheeled mechanical shakers that maneuver like huge crabs among the trees, and vacuum the olives off the ground with vehicles that resemble street sweepers. About half of the oil made in Jaén each year is *lampante*, and less than a quarter is extra virgin; of the four hundred mills and cooperatives in the province, only a handful produce fine olive oil. Refineries and pomace extraction plants dot the landscape, their chim-

neys spouting dense, sour-smelling smoke, and the practice of deodorization is reportedly widespread—it was here that Flavio Zaramella
saw deodorizing columns in mills, which are used to remove unpleasant
smells and tastes, and turn inferior oils into pseudo extra virgins. Both
the *picual* cultivar and the province of Jaén have become synonymous
with low-grade bulk oil; about 80 percent of the oil made here is shipped
to Italy, as in Roman times, and sold under Italian brand names.

On a high hill in the heart of Jaén, rising like an island from this
olive-green sea, sits the Castillo de Canena, a lowering, turreted fortress
built in the Renaissance on the remains of earlier medieval, Moorish,
and Roman strongholds. It's a homey place, with huge hearths and deep
comfortable couches and an Italianate loggia along the top of its eastern wall, but its warlike origins are unmistakable: the ten-foot-thick
stone walls are hung with spears, shields, and antique firearms, along
with several dozen trophy heads of big-game animals shot in forests and
savannas the world over. In fact, the Castillo de Canena remains a cita-
del to this day, and on the morning I arrived in Canena, its master and
mistress, Rosa and Francisco Vañó, members of the noble family that
has grown olives and made oil in these parts since 1780, were holding
a council of war, one of many they have called in their eight-year campaign for oil quality in the heart of Jaén. Rosa and Francisco, siblings
in their late forties, sat at the breakfast table with laptops and smart-
phones crackling, trying to locate an oil shipment that had gone missing
somewhere in Asia. The wireless and phone signals were a bit sluggish
due to the heavy masonry of the walls, but after an intense half-hour of
brainstorming and negotiation, they'd tracked down the oil and sped it
toward its final destination.

The Vañó family has made olive oil for over two centuries, but until
2002, it was the low-grade bulk oil typical of Jaén. In that year, Rosa
and Francisco left successful business careers in other industries—she
as marketing director of Coca-Cola International, he as a senior executive at Banco Santander, the prominent Spanish commercial bank—to
begin running the family business together. Since then, with a combina-

tion of entrepreneurial flair and slow, meticulous farming, this sister-and-brother team has turned Castillo de Canena into one of the world's premier producers of extra virgin oil. "We run this company like a little Coca-Cola," said Rosa Vañó, a handsome, energetic, crisply tailored woman with large, slanting brown eyes, as she crushed the pulp from a tomato over a piece of toasted bread and poured on some of her oil. "In each of the thirty-eight countries where we sell, we draw up a business plan, a marketing plan, a complete profile of our competitors, and an analysis of market trends." She said she enjoys the challenge of selling olive oil to people in cultures where it's little known, or even mistrusted. After her experience at Coca-Cola, where she made presentations in English to the corporate board of directors which included Warren Buffett, no negotiation is too ticklish. "I could go to hell and fight for my soul with the devil!" she laughed. She handed me the slender bottle, made in red glass with art nouveau decorations, which apart from its size looked more like perfume than oil. "Try our *picual*."

Actually, I had intended to try the other oil on the table, the *arbequina*, because of my instinctive aversion to *picual* oil. Most *picual* made here in Jaén has a distinctive musky stench; this oil is the primary ingredient of many supermarket oils, which have this same defect, known by Italian tasters as *pipí di gatto* ("cat pee"). Nevertheless, not wishing to offend, I poured Rosa Vañó's *picual* over my toast and took a bite. Fleeting flavors bloomed and faded, with an evanescent complexity more like old cognac than olive oil. Here was a stereotype-breaker: a gourmet *picual*, with a lovely, crisp mouthfeel and perfectly balanced fruit, spice, and bitterness, and no hint of the familiar feline pong.

Rosa Vañó said that when she started working at Castillo de Canena, she found it hard to convince potential customers that their oils were different from the Andalucían run-of-the-mill. "People would say, 'Oil from Jaén? No thanks, I don't need any more bulk cooking oil.' Or they'd say, 'A high quality *picual*? You must be kidding.'" To change people's minds, she paid countless *puerta fría* ("cold door") visits to restaurants and food stores. "At Coke I used to drive around in a blue Jaguar com-

Harvesting ancient olive trees can be physically demanding, involving acrobatics that the older generation of farmers is less and less able to perform, and long hours that their children and grandchildren have little taste for. *Donatello Brogioni/ Contrasto/Redux*

Ancient olive trees grow throughout the southern Mediterranean, some reputedly over 2,000 years old. *Courtesy of N'ora Futura*

In super-high-density olive groves in California, Spain, Portugal, and elsewhere, 700 or more trees are packed into an acre of land, and are harvested by over-the-row harvesters like those used in the wine industry. *Courtesy of Corto Olive*

In open-air Masses held in olive groves, a common event in southern Italy, the power of the rite is enhanced by the religious resonance of the trees themselves, familiar biblical symbols of peace and fortitude. *Gianni Berengo Giardin/Contrasto*

An estimated 700 different olive cultivars grow worldwide (this plate alone holds fifteen), each containing a distinctive—and sometimes radically unique—oil. *Paul Vossen*

Traditional mills continue to operate throughout the southern Mediterranean, like this donkey-driven mill in Tin Mal, Morocco, a village in the High Atlas Mountains 60 miles from Marrakesh. *Jerzy Strzelecki*

These granite millstones in Calabria, Italy, similar to those used by Roman millers, are still widely employed, though they are steadily being replaced by stainless steel hammer and disk grinders. *Paul Vossen*

Modern grinding machines, like this stainless-steel disk mill made by Alfa Laval, are replacing old-fashioned grindstones, because their speed, precision, and ease of cleaning often produces better oils. *Alexandra Kicenik Devarenne*

Olive oil plays a central role in Christian rites and symbolism, and is considered a vehicle of conversion, health, and cleansing. Here Bishop Gerald M. Barbarito celebrates the Eucharist with the blessing of oils at the Cathedral of Saint Ignatius Loyola in Palm Beach Gardens, Florida.
Taylor Jones/Palm Beach Post/ZUMA Press/Newscom

Villagers on Crete frequently bring a bottle of their early harvest oil to the village church to be blessed by the priest, and used as medicine and in church rituals. *Nikos Psilakis*

In *yağlı güreş* ("oil wrestling"), a popular Turkish sport that continues the Greco-Roman tradition of olive oil in athletics, contestants (known as *pehlivan* or "heroes") slather themselves in olive oil and then try to come to grips. *Reuters/Fatih Saribas*

As with wine, the appreciation of a fine oil and the detection of a flawed oil start with the nose, in tulip-shaped tasting glasses that concentrate volatile aromas. *Leah Bradley*

Chemical analysis of an olive oil helps to reveal its freshness and nutritional value, as well as certain frauds—though lab tests are far easier to satisfy than a trained taste panel. *UC Davis Olive Center*

Droning like twin jet engines, these centrifuges at the California Olive Ranch in Artois, California, spin crushed olives at thousands of rpms, separating the oil from the water, pits, skins, and pulp also contained in the olives. *Paul Vossen*

Olive-pomace plants, like this facility in Puglia owned by Fratelli Rubino, use industrial solvents to remove the last oil from the solid waste produced by olive oil mills. *Paul Vossen*

pany car. I had a personal secretary and thirty people working for me, and a marketing budget of 5 billion pesetas [about 30 million in today's euros]. It was different when I started selling our oil. I'd go in through the servants' entrance with samples under my arm. 'You don't owe me anything,' I'd tell people. 'Just *try* this.' One month we only sold €50 worth of oil. We were sitting around this table, asking each other, 'Do you think all this effort is worth it?'"

A breakthrough came when she left a sample for Jean-Pierre Vandelle, a prominent chef in Madrid. Vandelle called her a short time later. "There has been a mistake," he said. "You have given me an oil labeled *'picual'* that is not *picual*." When she insisted that the label was accurate, he told her, "Come and see me." Since then, Rosa Vañó says, Vandelle has become an ambassador for their oil, along with a number of other leading chefs and food critics, as well as a famous bullfighter, an opera singer, and a graphic artist, all of whom have signed a vintage of Castillo de Canena oil. Rosa travels incessantly on four continents, and has developed a strategy for overcoming jet lag using eyeshades, noise-cancelling headphones, carefully timed naps, and fractional doses of Ambien, the sleeping pill. "There are many new markets in the world that have huge potential," she said. "Even here in Spain, the consumption of good extra virgin olive oil is very low. Ninety percent of Spaniards eat butter on their bread for breakfast. They should be eating our oil instead!"

I took another piece of toast and drizzled the *arbequina* oil over it, and had yet another awakening. Oils made from the *arbequina* cultivar are usually low in polyphenols, oleic acid, and personality, but this oil was robust and nuanced, with a hint of green apples and bitter almonds.

"Our *arbequina* has 250 in polyphenols and 68 percent oleic acid this year, which is unheard-of for the cultivar," Francisco Vañó said. "We get these levels by stressing the trees, reducing their irrigation—polyphenols are the olive tree's response to a stress situation. At the same time, we've increased the irrigation to the *picual*, removing some of its natural bitterness and pepperiness, which can be quite aggressive." (This year their *picual* weighs in at a whopping 500+ mg/kg in polyphenols and

80 percent in oleic acid, and a remarkably low free acidity—less than 0.1 percent.) While Rosa travels the world selling Castillo de Canena oil, Francisco stays home in Canena and makes it, on the family's 1,500 hectares of olive groves and 280,000 trees. "When I worked in the bank I worked hard, but as soon as I left the building at night I was a normal person. Here, I'm an olive oil maker twenty-four hours a day. I've become a little like an animal—I often sniff new things as a way of learning about them. The sense of smell gives you a huge amount of information, so many inputs. Until I was forty-two years old, I paid no attention to my nose." Francisco says that the profession of making oil has an epic quality, because so many factors lie outside his control. "You pray for wind, rain, sun—you're always praying for something, looking at the sky. This contact with nature makes you more human, more inside the universe. Olive-oil-making is really Homeric."

It's also stressful: Francisco's nails were chewed to the quick, and he occasionally paused, drew a deep breath, and let it leak out slowly through pursed lips, as if to settle his nerves. Rosa, who had recently arrived from San Francisco and would be leaving for Moscow the next day, looked weary, her eyes bloodshot with dark circles beneath.

After breakfast, we drove out of town into the endless groves which surrounded Canena, so even and uninterrupted that it was impossible to tell where one property ended and the next began. It had been raining off and on for several days, and growers had stopped harvesting to let the olives dry out. It was late January, by which time the makers of fine oil around the Mediterranean have long since finished collecting their fruit, but these trees were still heavy with plump black *picual* olives, and many more had fallen in dark patches around the foot of the trees.

When the Vañós started making extra virgin oil in 2002, they hired a consultant from Córdoba, who instructed them to use only their oldest trees, harvest the olives at maximum ripeness, and strive to produce a homogeneous oil, one that tasted the same from year to year. After their first harvest, Rosa and Francisco brought samples of their oil to a food show and proudly offered it to industry experts. One well-known taster took a sip and asked how many months it had been in the bottle, though they'd made it only two days earlier. "We were humiliated," Francisco remembered. "That's when we started to understand that 'homogeneous,' that bloody word, was completely the wrong way to think about extra virgin olive oil. The olive tree is a living creature, and produces different harvests every year. Variety isn't a weakness in good oil, and can actually be a strength." The Vañós began to study olive growing and oil-making with agronomists and oil experts at IFAPA, a nearby agronomics institute widely recognized for its expertise in extra virgin olive oil. By the next harvest, they were ready for another examination. "I smelled and tasted our oil, and it seemed good," Francisco said. "But I didn't trust my own judgment. So I took a sample and drove as fast as I could to IFAPA. I handed it to Brígida Jiménez Herrera, their top taster. She poured the oil into a tasting glass, warmed it in her hands, uncovered it, smelled it, sipped it. She looked up at me. '*Francisco, es estupendo!*' she said. And I burst into tears."

By now we were driving through the Vañó groves. Rosa and Francisco described their harvest routine, which begins in early October, when they collect samples of ten to fifteen still-green olives from representative trees, produce test batches of oil using a tiny custom oil-making machine, and analyze each batch for flavor profile and chemical properties. When the test results are right, they quickly harvest all the olives for their "First Day of Harvest" oils in an eighteen-hour blitz, then pick the fruit for their Family Reserve oils in the days that follow. We saw the experimental grove which they'd planted three years ago, containing forty-five different cultivars from around the world that they would begin harvesting the following year. "We're going to find out, scientifically and for the first time, which olives produce the finest oil in our soil, altitude, and climate," Francisco said. "When we do, we'll plant a lot of the three or four best cultivars. And in a few more years we'll start making premium blends with them—not blends with olives that happen to be growing on our land, as most producers do, but the best blends possible." They're also planning to start an oil-making operation in California, where they'll focus on native cultivars, like the mission olive. "California wouldn't be a new market for Spaniards like us, but a return to an old one," Francisco laughed. "After all, when the Vañó family started growing olives in 1780, California was part of the Spanish crown." They showed me their irrigation system, which employs a novel technology developed in Australia, and their new solar farm. They spoke of the close attention they pay to their carbon footprint and to water conservation. "We're looking twenty to thirty years into the future," Francisco said, "starting projects that we're hoping our children and grandchildren can continue."

Driving back to the castle, we passed mile after mile of muddy roads and fallen, rotting olives. The rain began again, making the landscape even more desolate. It had been a difficult harvest, Rosa explained, and these rains only made it worse—as did the current economic crisis in Spain, which is particularly acute in Andalucía, where unemployment is close to 30 percent. "It's hard to see a way of life that has been a livelihood for fifty years come to an end," she said, scanning the sodden groves. "Profit margins are disappearing in low-end oil made like this. Bulk oil is dead." The Vañós know the bulk oil market well. Though their company concentrates on making superior extra virgin oil, they continue the family business they took over in 2002, which also produces low-grade bulk oil in a separate mill. In volume, this oil represents 95 percent of their production, though high-quality extra virgin oil already accounts for a quarter of their profits.

I ask about a recent open letter to the Spanish environment minister, Rosa Aguilar, written by a number of trade organizations representing the nation's bottling companies and oil producers. In it, the signatories complained about a chemical and sensory test of fifty extra virgin oils that the Andalucía regional government had performed in Spanish supermarkets not long before, which revealed that half of the oils labeled "extra virgin" were in fact virgin or *lampante*, leading to product seizures and widespread negative press. The signatories condemned the taste panel as a subjective and unreliable method, and demanded that the minister immediately halt its use in determining olive oil quality. The signatories represented big Spanish oil bottlers and producers like Grupo SOS and the giant growers' cooperative Hojiblanca, but the letter had also been signed by INFAOLIVA, an association of olive oil producers to which Castillo de Canena itself belongs.

"They're trying to drive down the quality of extra virgin oil to the lowest common denominator, to turn olive oil into a commodity," Francisco said. "Farmers in Jaén continue to make their oil the cheapest way possible. They still don't believe they'll be paid for quality, or understand that making true extra virgin-grade oil is the future of the industry."

I asked why these organizations, faced with plummeting profits in the bulk oil business, didn't start making quality oil like Castillo de Canena does. "They have the resources," Francisco replied. "They could hire fifteen Francisco Vañós, or fifteen people better than me. But they don't, and their few attempts in premium oil have been failures. They don't feel the passion, which is the only way to make great oil. It's not just the money—we aren't making nails here. We have to put in so much passion and faith, so much love. In the end, I think they are afraid of us." He fell silent, as if he'd just had this idea, and found it shocking.

It was raining hard when we reached the castle. Rosa Vañó said goodbye and trotted to her car; she was driving to Madrid, to catch her Moscow flight early the following morning. Francisco offered to show me around the castle. We saw the cellar with its Moorish and Roman masonry, where two dilapidated horse-drawn carriages stood covered in dust, slowly collapsing into the earth. We walked through the ballroom, the dining hall hung with sixteenth-century Flemish tapestries, and the loggia with its view over rainy Canena. We peered into rooms tucked away high in the castle towers, which seemed not to have been opened for weeks, perhaps months. Now and then Francisco paused to study a network of cracks forming in a masonry arch, or a patch of plaster that had fallen from a ceiling far above, reminders of how much upkeep this ancient, 2,500-square-meter building must require. Everywhere the herds of dead game animals on the walls stared their glassy stares, interspersed with oil paintings and photographs of past generations of the Vañó family, looking down at us proudly, inquisitively.

"I'm not a hunter," Francisco said with a touch of impatience. "These are my brother-in-law's trophies. Rosa won't allow them in their house." As if to explain his aversion to violence, he pointed out the wedding portrait of his grandfather, for whom he was named, and said that soon after the photo was taken, his grandfather was shot by one of Franco's firing squads, in the first months of the Spanish Civil War. The family portraits continued, men in morning suits and women in ballgowns, as well as photos of Francisco's and Rosa's children, now in their teens.

Meeting their gaze, Francisco said, "Rosa and I feel that our ancestors have given us the mandate. They're telling us, 'You have to do things better than we have done.' We love this job, but we both agree that we don't want to work this hard, day and night, for the rest of our lives. Someday we want to be able to hand on the company to the next generation. And somehow we feel that if we can't manage that, we'll have a lot of explaining to do."

Then, as if continuing his earlier thought about fear in the oil business, he added, "I suppose we are afraid, too. In the last few years, the economic crisis in Spain and the crisis in Spanish oil have driven down the quality of mass-market oil, but they've also forced quality producers to differentiate, to innovate. We can't afford to stop working, stop making our oil better and better, or we'll be swallowed up."

BILL BRIWA, chief instructor at the Culinary Institute of America at Greystone, the Napa Valley campus of the largest cooking school in the world, stood at a blazing range, pointing a gun into a pot of olive oil. Briwa was measuring the heat of the oil with an infrared thermometer as it rose to 220 degrees Celsius, the smoke point for most olive oils at which they begin to break down and to produce an acrid bluish smoke. Every ten degrees he spooned some of the oil into a saucer, marked it with the temperature using a yellow Post-it, and set it on an adjacent

counter. He processed four different olive oils this way, three extra virgins of varying qualities and a refined oil, as methodically as master
chefs know how to be. By the end of the experiment there were forty
saucers in four neat rows on the counter. He was ready to taste them,
and to learn something new about cooking with olive oil.

"I've read all kinds of contradictory opinions about frying with olive
oil," Briwa said. "Some people say it's good to use because it has a high
smoke point and holds up well chemically to heat, others say it's better
to use peanut or palm oil instead. Oftentimes the only way to tell fact
from fiction is to try it at the range."

He handed me a spoon, and we tasted the four oils in series, ascend-
ing the temperature scale, pausing now and then to clear our palates
with sparkling water. After trying the first few samples, Briwa said,
"This tastes like popcorn!" All the others did too—flat, browned, faintly
nutty—even those that had been cooked at moderate heats, including
the very best extra virgin he'd used, a high-priced Spanish oil. In fact,
the Spanish oil was the worst, since cooking had driven off all of its subtle flavors and aromatics, leaving an overbearing bitterness that made it
almost inedible. The oil that had changed the least, predictably, was the
refined oil, since the flavorful elements of the extra virgin oils, which
suffered in the heat, had already been removed from it at the refinery.
"I can't speak for the chemistry or nutrition, and I'd need to test a lot
of other oils to say anything definitive," Briwa concluded, "but for now,
cooking at high heat seems a waste of good olive oil."

Briwa, whom I met at the Beyond Extra Virgin conference in Verona,
is like most cooks a big fan of fats, which play leading roles in the kitchen.
They dissolve and amplify flavors, soften foods by entering into and
weakening their cell structures, create soft, creamy textures, and cook
at temperatures well above the boiling point of water, which crisps and
browns the food surface. But thanks to its complex flavors and aromatics, Briwa says, "great olive oil is the queen of fats, a multiplier of flavors
that creates a long-lasting taste of joy." He likes playing with unusual
pairings, such as olive oil cooked in and poured over sweets. "There's

a huge difference between eating a rich chocolate ganache, and eating that same dessert with a fine oil poured over it. The oil gives depth and complexity to the sweetness, and adds a fresh, green sensation of health. Now it has a 'grown-up' flavor profile, becoming something to really savor, not just 800 calories to ingest mindlessly. Things should taste good but also *think* good."

Briwa admits he has a lot to learn about olive oil. "I still find myself cooking dishes and then going to look for the right oil to put on them, instead of considering the oil as an integral part of the dish, and choosing it before I start cooking." Many top chefs feel the same, and are left speechless by their first encounter with excellent oil. Paul Bartolotta, who also attended Beyond Extra Virgin in Verona, vividly recalls his initiation into extra virginity, during an impromptu meal in a cave in Lucca beside an active olive press. "They're cooking grilled *baccalà* and bean soup and *fett'unta* right there while they're making the oil," Bartolotta remembers, "and they're pouring the fresh oil all over the place, and the oil is dripping everywhere and the whole room smells of it, until I want to rub it in my hair and all over my body—I'm so in love with this moment! And I'm thinking, 'Where do I get this oil? How do I share this experience with my clients?'"

If you can't visit Bartolotta's cave in Lucca, a good place to learn about oil is a restaurant where the chef has a range of quality extra virgins, and knows how to pair them with foods. Big oils, like big wines, can seem harsh and intimidating to the fledgling taster. "As a chef I can take a client by the hand and reassure them that where they're going is a good place," Briwa says. "I start with some olive oil and they cough, but then I give them some olive oil sorbet, and they like that. Then I get them to add a little olive oil on top of the sorbet, then a little more. These are lessons that people will take home with them, and pass along."

In April 2010, to foster this kind of guided learning and experimentation, the Culinary Institute installed an *oleoteca* or oil bar, which Briwa took me downstairs to see. Visitors sat along a broad stainless steel counter, tasting oils dispensed from a slightly upgraded version of Paolo

Pasquali's invention. (As at Villa Campestri, the oils are all 3E-certified, and are rotated regularly to provide a maximum diversity of styles.) The manager of the bar, Patricia Donnelly, was talking to an elderly couple in shorts and Hawaiian shirts, explaining the characteristics of the oils and how to use them on the sampler of foods she had brought.

At the bar we were joined by Greg Drescher, strategic director of the Culinary Institute, a sharp dresser with a melodious, crowd-pleasing voice, who clearly thought of olive oil in long-range strategic ways. "Part of our mission at the Culinary Institute is to provide the best culinary education in the world, and great olive oil is a fundamental part of that education," he said. He explained that American cuisine is undergoing a rapid transformation—"the old saying 'American as apple pie' has less and less meaning"—and that a major challenge for olive oil in the United States would be to find roles in Latin and Asian cuisines, which are beginning to set the new culinary agenda.

I listened, and watched the people in Hawaiian shirts ooh and aah at the oil bar. The Institute is visited by 300,000 people a year, Californians and tourists alike, along with 4,000 chefs in training. Often their experience at this counter must transform their understanding of olive oil. Yet I couldn't help thinking of the De Carlos in Puglia, and the thousands of growers like them around the Mediterranean, who are barely able to cover their costs in a market awash in low-priced imitation oils, and who will probably never sell their oil here. And I thought of people in the Midwest, of America and every other consumer nation, for whom the Culinary Institute is as inaccessible as that magic cave in Lucca where Paul Bartolotta had his oil epiphany—people who simply can't get good oil, or even get oil that's actually made from olives.

I mentioned these people to Drescher, the suffering farmers and the oil-deprived consumers, the unanointed masses. And I asked, trying not to be snide, how this glitzy oil bar in Napa would improve their lot.

Drescher looked at me evenly. Working with the Harvard School of Public Health, he played a key role in codifying and communicating the Mediterranean diet in America in the early 1990s. He has spent years travelling the Mediterranean. He has seen the endless groves of Andalucía, and the ancient trees of Crete beside the pale green sea. He has been in Puglia at harvest time, and shared meals with the harvesters.

He shrugged, and said simply, "What we're doing here, will help them there. Excellence is contagious."

7

. . . .

NEW WORLDS OF OIL

Picking the olives,
Marriages are made.
If you don't go to the harvest
You'll never fall in love.
What power must they have, Mother,
In matters of the heart,
The olive trees?

—Andalucían folk song

Kangaroos sometimes bound through the olive groves of New Norcia, a Benedictine monastery in Western Australia not far north of Perth, but they don't harm the trees. Parrots are the real problem, the great noisy flocks of black cockatoos and pink and gray galahs that swoop down on the groves around harvest time and gobble the green olives. "It's really frustrating," says Gordon Smyth, the head of grounds at the monastery. "Dom Paulino used to say that shooting five birds a day would affect their numbers, but personally I think you'd need five shotguns firing continuously to make any difference."

Smyth recently took over responsibility for olive cultivation and oil-making from Dom Paulino Gutierrez, a Spanish monk who managed the groves for decades until shortly before his death in 2010, at the age of ninety-nine. The brothers of the New Norcia community, which is located in the dry, fertile Victoria Plains, fifty miles inland from the Indian Ocean, have grown olives and made oil for over a century, led by a series of Spaniards that stretches back to the founders of the mission, bishops Rosendo Salvado and José Serra, who arrived in Perth harbor on a sailing frigate in 1846 and set to work converting the Noongar Aboriginal people to Christianity. In the first year of their work, Salvado and Serra lived the nomadic life of their Aboriginal hosts; sometimes, when their familiar monastic victuals ran out, the reverend fathers got by on bush tucker—grubs, tubers, lizards, and the occasional opossum. With the help of an Aboriginal guide, they eventually located a promising site along the Moore River, where the monastery stands today. They began clearing the native eucalypts, river gums, and wandoo trees and planting familiar Mediterranean crops like figs, wine grapes, bitter oranges, and a large olive grove. Soon they had created a self-sufficient Christian community, which they named after Norcia in faraway Umbria, the birthplace of St. Benedict and of St. Sanctulus, the sixth-century priest who taught pagan Lombard millers how to use holy (or boiling) water to extract olive oil.

Bishop Salvado kept three bottles of oil in his church, which are now visible in the New Norcia museum, each blessed for different uses: oil of catechumens for anointing converts before they were baptized, chrism oil for the baptismal rite itself, and oil of the sick to heal wounds and comfort the dying during extreme unction. The oil of the sick was particularly famous for its therapeutic powers. In his diary, Salvado describes how he and Bishop Serra cured an Aboriginal boy they'd found lying half dead in the bush with a spear through his stomach—"a wound so bad that the only thing we could do for him was to prepare him for death." The bishops cleansed both the entrance and the exit holes with oil, and eased him into bed; to their amazement, after nine days the boy had recovered completely, and trotted back into the wilderness. (Not that olive oil was the only cure at the monks' disposal—when suffering from severe abdominal pains, Salvado himself recovered on a diet of parrot soup and bread dipped in Communion wine.)

As in Benedictine monasteries everywhere, olive oil also served the monks in more mundane ways, as soap, for hair care, and above all as nourishment, to be eaten with their bread. The oil made at New Norcia has been first-quality from the monastery's earliest years, receiving a high commendation at the 1886 Indian and Colonial Exhibition in London, and soon after being praised in the *Western Australia Settler's Guide and Farmer's Handbook*, published in 1897, whose author called the monk's table olives "a treat," and wrote that their oil was "real Simon pure . . . no cottonseed here." The monks of New Norcia imported olive trees and seeds from Andalucía and Sicily, and during frequent trips to the Mediterranean they studied the agronomic methods and oil-making techniques being used in Spanish, Italian, and French monasteries, which they later employed to improve their oil back in Australia.

Down through the end of the twentieth century, Spaniards continued to run the monastery and care for its olives. Dom Paulino, the last of them, arrived in 1928 as an eighteen-year-old. "He was a remarkable man, incredibly resourceful, with a beautiful heart and mind," Gordon Smyth remembers. "And you should have seen him scream around on his quad bike—he'd really go tick!" Dom Paulino taught Smyth the traditional harvesting and milling methods of the monastery, which often employed generations-old equipment. He introduced Smyth to the grove's benchmark trees, venerable giants which, through the condition of their fruit, signalled when to start the harvest. The monks knew these trees by name: Clarence, whom Smyth describes as "a stiff-upper-lip, public school kind of tree, with a 'don't mess with me' attitude," and Rosa, who is "like an Italian lady, lovely, graceful, and robust."

Nobody knows which cultivars the Spanish monks of New Norcia brought over from their homeland. Many trees died during the ocean journey, and as Gordon Smyth says, those which survived the salt air of the voyage "were as tough as old boots by the time they got here." Over the last 150 years, in the antipodean sunshine and the breezes off the Indian Ocean, these trees have grown apart from their Mediterranean ancestors and are now considered a separate cultivar, the West Australian mission olive. Similarly, since taking over from Dom Paulino, Gordon Smyth employs a new, native Australian approach to making oil at the monastery, based not only on the age-old sensibilities of Spanish Benedictines but on his own experience in the groves of South Australia, where he grew up. To start with, Smyth thought the trees had grown unmanageably tall and dense, and gave them a vigorous pruning. "I opened them up like cocktail glasses, to let the light and air in. People used to go all swoony walking among the trees. They really shuddered when I pruned them back. But I told them, 'You just try going up in a cherry-picker at seven or eight meters off the deck in the winter wind, mate! I'm here to make great oil.'" He stopped using the old mill on the monastery grounds, and began processing the fruit at a modern facility in the nearby town of York. And he started relying on his instincts. "I use the senses God has given me to tell how the trees are doing. I close my eyes and run my hand down the foliage. Is the leaf slightly inverted, starving for water? Is it sticky, or full of dust?"

When harvest starts in May, at the beginning of the Australian autumn, Smyth pinches and prods the olives that arrive in crates from the groves, rejecting any fruit that is mushy or damaged by birds. He squeezes juice from an olive now and then, to examine its color and viscosity, and tastes raw olives to judge their levels of bitterness and pepperiness. Finally he lays them out on a sorting table and, with a painter's eye, tries to create the assemblage of colors that will make the best New Norcia oil. "I want the right palette in the fruit between green, on the turn, and fully ripe. If it's not just right I tell someone, 'Go out and get greens, pick ten crates!' We work to that recipe."

Smyth's New World perfectionism is paying off; last year the monastery's oil won four awards at national olive oil competitions in different parts of Australia. "To continuously improve the product is what the Bible is about," he says. "I'm applying that fundamental idea in my oil-making and other agricultural work. I represent the monastery and its long history here. Hopefully someone will come and carry on when I'm gone, and make it even better."

I asked Smyth if he had traveled in the Mediterranean, heartland of the olive tree, where Dom Paulino and earlier generations of monks at New Norcia had learned to make oil. Did he have any plans to visit Spain or Italy, to study olive growing or oil production?

He sounded as if he'd considered this question before. "Listen, the stars look great at night around here," he said. "How good does the caviar have to be? I have no desire to have an overseas experience."

OLIVE OIL came to Australia, just as it spread everywhere else in the world where olives can grow, with a series of voyagers from the Mediterranean: missionaries, explorers, and conquistadors in the fifteenth to seventeenth centuries, followed in the eighteenth and later centuries by wave upon wave of immigrants and merchants. Everywhere these wide-eyed, ambitious, and lonesome people went, they brought oil from their homelands and planted olives, sometimes grafting them onto hardy local relatives of the olive that grew there. Olive trees now climb the slopes of Table Mountain in South Africa, dot the hot plains of northern Argentina, and ring the Hauraki Gulf in New Zealand, familiar Mediterranean shapes rising against horizons once alien to them.

Olives grow throughout Australia, from the steamy subtropical forests of Queensland in the northeast to the cool subarctic plains of Tasmania to the south, and on out past the arid Red Center to the Karri country of Western Australia. Though the monks of New Norcia have been making oil since the 1850s, large-scale modern olive cultivation in Australia began in the 1980s, the years of the so-called "oil fever," when the federal government offered substantial land grants, subsidies, and tax breaks to growers. Soon the demand for olive oil, originally low except among the large populations of Greek and Italian immigrants in the big cities, began to grow, thanks to IOC promotional campaigns, cooking shows on television which popularized Mediterranean food, and an increasing interest in healthy natural products. Growing demand, in turn, stimulated production. Today Australian companies produce 18,000 tons of oil, making Australia one of the largest producer nations outside the Mediterranean, and Australians eat far more oil than they make. Australian oil companies are among the most technologically advanced in the world, and have developed new orchard practices and oil-making techniques; the country's largest producer, Boundary Bend, manages 2.5 million trees, exports its flagship oil to fifteen countries, and builds Colossus, a huge, state-of-the-art mechanical harvester. Top Australian companies are making superb oil at competitive prices. Some have Mediterranean names like Mark Kailis and Felice Trovatello, but their outlooks are distinctively New World. And they're beginning to question the Old World order.

As the Australian oil industry has grown in skill and size, local producers have pushed for existing laws against unfair competition to be applied to some supermarket extra virgins imported from the Mediterranean, which they point out don't measure up to the legal definition of the extra virgin grade. With a measure of government support, some oil fraudsters have been prosecuted, while CHOICE, the magazine of an independent consumer association, has conducted a series of surveys of supermarket oils, most recently in 2010, all of which have revealed that close to half of supermarket extra virgins in the country are mislabeled. Some critics go further, and question the basic definition of extra virginity as enshrined in IOC guidelines. "The chemical requirements set by the IOC are a complete joke," says Richard Gawel, a chemist and oil blender who formed the first IOC-certified taste panel in Australia and frequently judges international oil competitions. "Take the free acidity level of 0.8 percent, for example. Olives can fall from the trees and lie on the ground for five months before milling and still come in below 0.8 percent! Peroxide levels—a measure of the oxidation state of the oil—are set at twenty, but trade buyers of extra virgin olive oil wouldn't touch an oil with a peroxide higher than twelve with a barge pole. Levels like these serve one purpose: to sell a lot of old or poor-quality oil and put money in people's pockets, at the expense of the consumer."

Modern Olives, a lipid laboratory in the state of Victoria that has become one of the most respected olive oil labs in the world, has started applying new tests, known in chemical shorthand as DAGS and PPP, to detect old and illegally deodorized oils. The IOC claims these methods are flawed and refuses to include them in their official testing protocols, but Gawel says he has never seen a peer-reviewed reference to problems with DAGS and PPP. "I think it's all crap. There's nothing wrong with these tests, it's just a case of the IOC wanting to maintain their stranglehold on olive oil testing. They have proposed an alternative test to these, but in fact that test has had less scientific scrutiny than the ones that they have been criticizing. The EU subsidizes producers to stockpile a lot of oil when prices are low, and it sits in the tank for a long time. Sophisticated tests like those proposed can detect this practice. I'd be surprised if the suppliers of these back-blended oils weren't concerned at the adoption of these robust and sophisticated tests, which can detect the practice of back-blending of old oils." In 2011, the Australian official standards organization drew up stiff new standards for olive oil quality, which include DAGS and PPP, another step in the country's steady move away from the Mediterranean.

Where does the definition of "extra virgin" come from? Who gets to decide? Throughout the new worlds of oil, these questions are being asked by producers who are starting to challenge the Mediterranean hegemony over oil. True, they only represent 2 percent of world olive oil production, but that share is growing, especially in the high-quality end of the market. What's more, precisely because of their relative inexperience and small size, these newcomers are free from certain age-old prejudices and economic obligations that encumber the oil business around the Mediterranean, and they may be able to see the question of olive oil quality more clearly. They are everywhere, and form a rising chorus, each country and region with its own original and evolving history of oil, its own collection of the individualists and eccentrics who always seem to gravitate to olives. But potentially the most important new world of oil is California. Today the state produces under 3,000 tons of oil per year, a sixth of Australia's output, and a seventieth of the Puglia region of Italy alone. Yet California is the fifth-largest agricultural economy on earth, and part of a nation of 300 million people, many of whom are just beginning to discover the joys of great olive oil. In 2009, America overtook Greece as the third largest olive oil consumer in the world, and the potential for further growth is enormous, considering that the average American eats only 0.9 liters of oil a year—half of Australian consumption, and 4 percent of that of the Greeks. If Americans learned to love oil even half as much as the Italians, the US market would far exceed Greece, Italy, and Spain—the world's three leading consumer nations—combined. "Australia has helped set the new quality agenda, but there are only 23 million of us," Paul Miller of the Australian Olive Association says. "America, with 300 million strong, has a vital role to play in taking this agenda global, and making it stick."

IN *LIFE on the Mississippi*, published in 1883, Mark Twain recounts a breakfast conversation he overheard aboard a steamboat between two "drummers," or traveling salesmen, whom he describes as "brisk men, energetic of movement and speech; the dollar their god, how to get it their religion."

One of the salesmen holds out a slab of butter on the end of his knife and says, "Look at it—smell of it—taste it. Put any test on it you want to. Take your own time—no hurry—make it thorough. There now—what do you say? butter, ain't it? Not by a thundering sight—it's oleomargarine! . . . You can't tell it from butter; by George, an *expert* can't."

His company has found a way to turn the excess fat from slaughterhouses into an imitation butter that costs far less to make than the real article: "We can sell it so dirt-cheap that the whole country has *got* to take it—can't get around it, you see. Butter don't stand any show—there ain't any chance for competition."

His companion, not to be outdone, pulls out two bottles of olive oil. "There now, smell them, taste them, examine the bottles, inspect the labels," he says. "One of 'm's from Europe, the other's never been out of this country. One's European olive-oil, the other's American cottonseed olive-oil. Tell 'm apart? 'Course you can't. Nobody can. . . . We turn out the whole thing—clean from the word go—in our factory in New Orleans: labels, bottles, oil, everything."

He explains that his company is taking cottonseed oil, extracted from the waste products of cotton gins, altering it chemically, and selling it as olive oil to the guileless consumers on his beat: "We turn out an olive-oil that is just simply perfect—undetectable! We are doing a ripping trade, too—as I could easily show you by my order-book for this trip. Maybe you'll butter every-body's bread pretty soon, but we'll cotton-seed his salad for him from the Gulf to Canada, that's a dead-certain thing."

"Cotton-seed was comparatively valueless in my time," Twain remarks, "but it is worth twelve or thirteen dollars a ton now, and none of it is thrown away. The oil made from it is colorless, tasteless, and almost, if not entirely, odorless. It is claimed that it can, by proper manipulation, be made to resemble and perform the office of any and all oils, and be produced at a cheaper rate than the cheapest of the originals. Sagacious people shipped it to Italy, doctored it, labelled it, and brought it back as olive oil." This shuttling back and forth across the Atlantic, Twain says, provided import stamps from US customs that lent an air of authenticity to the fake oil, enabling dealers to earn "no end of cash" from it. Subsequently, however, these "sagacious people" further perfected their system, and found a way to procure customs stamps without going to the trouble or expense of exporting and reimporting their oil.

By 1883, from the Gulf of Mexico to the Canadian border, much of the olive oil that Americans were eating on their salad was fake, the product of systematic fraud.

THE FIRST olive oil importers to the New World were the conquistadors, for whom, as for their contemporaries in Spain, olive oil was a crucial food, fuel for lamps and engines, and active ingredient in medicine and religious rites. Spanish explorers packed quantities of olive oil, together with wine, salt pork, sardines, raisins, sandals, and weapons, in each ship they sailed to the Americas. As in Roman times, when the legions planted olives wherever they were stationed, olive trees grew in the furrows of the conquistadors' swords, becoming a vivid symbol of conquest. Olive oil dazzled the indigenous populations with its myriad beneficial properties (the Aztecs, devotees of the sun, admired the brilliance of Spanish olive oil lanterns), and became, together with Toledo steel and Arabian stallions, an emblem of technical and cultural superiority. Olive groves were planted in royal *encomiendas* and *reducciónes* in Mexico and Peru, and soon after in Argentina and Chile. Some of these first arboreal immigrants to the New World still stand, like *el olivo viejo* ("the old olive tree") at Arauco in northeastern Argentina, one of several trees planted shortly after the conquest. However, after the initially rapid spread of olive cultivation and oil-making, the Spanish government curbed olive production in the colonies, in order to prevent American-made oil from competing with Spanish oil—to keep the New World hungry for Old World oil.

Since olive oil, the main ingredient in chrism, was also a vehicle, literally as well as allegorically, for the spread of Christian doctrine and divine grace, holy oil became a symbol of the conversion of the indigenous populations to the Christian faith. Religious orders planted olives in their settlements throughout South America; as the missionaries moved northward, so did the trees. In 1769, Fray Junípero Serra and a group of fellow Franciscans introduced olives to North America when they founded a mission with an olive grove on San Diego Bay. Over the next half-century the Franciscans founded twenty-one more missions along the California coast, each with its own grove of olive trees of a cultivar that subsequently became known as "mission," still among the most widely-grown in California. Olives were also planted in America by the eager hands of a Founding Father. Thomas Jefferson first saw olive trees on a trip by muleback across the Alps in 1788, and was entranced, marvelling at how they "gave being to whole villages" and calling them "the richest gift of heaven," as well as "the most interesting plant in existence." Jefferson promptly began an olive plantation in South Carolina. He imported several gallons of "virgin oil of Aix" each year for the rest of his life, and saw to it that an olive branch, heavy with fruit, was placed in the talons of the eagle on the Great Seal of the United States.

In the latter part of the nineteenth century, new ambassadors of olive oil arrived in the Americas. Waves of immigrants fled impoverished southern Italy for the New World, only to find that their new homeland lacked one of their most beloved foods. Some entered the olive oil trade to make good this deficit, and ended up turning a nice profit as oil importers. Giuseppe Profaci was born in Villabate, Sicily in 1897, emigrated to America in 1921, and eventually founded Mamma Mia Importing Company in Brooklyn, New York. By the 1950s, the company was the leading olive oil importer in America and Joseph Profaci, as he now called himself, was known as the "Olive Oil King." But Profaci actually seems to have made most of his fortune in less savory ways: drug trafficking, loan-sharking, extortion, prostitution, and where necessary, murder. Joseph Profaci was a leader of La Cosa Nostra, and was described by Attorney General Robert F. Kennedy as "one of the most powerful underworld figures in the United States." (Mario Puzo, author of *The Godfather*, used Profaci as a model for his protagonist gangster Vito Corleone, and gave Corleone his own olive oil business, Genco Pura.) Profaci was one of many Italian American mafiosi who used the olive oil import-export trade as a front for criminal activities.

One of his sons, John J. Profaci, founded Colavita USA, the American subsidiary of the Italy-based olive oil company run by Leonardo Colavita, which makes one of the leading olive oil brands in America. John Profaci is still chairman emeritus of the company, which he runs together with his four sons. (Profaci points out that his father died over a decade before Colavita USA was formed, and says there were never any links between the company and his father.)

Back in nineteenth-century Italy, trading companies sprang up to finance the bold gambles of millions of Italians who emigrated to the Americas. One such company was the Francesco Bertolli Bank and Exchange, founded by Francesco Bertolli in Lucca in 1875. Soon after his first clients arrived in the United States, they began to send him postcards with greetings to him and his family, and plaintive requests for a crate or two of olive oil, the flavor of their homeland. Bertolli complied, and by the 1890s was making more money in olive oil than in finance. His oil business spread from New York, Philadelphia, and Chicago westward across the US and south into Latin America, assuaging the culinary homesickness of countless Mediterranean immigrants. Francesco Bertolli's son Giulio opened the Brazilian market by traveling on muleback from village to village in the Minas Gerais region, carrying a supply of sorghum brooms and olive oil. At first he sold the brooms and gave a tin of oil free with each purchase; within six months he had abandoned brooms entirely, and was selling ever-growing quantities of olive oil.

FOR TWAIN, bogus olive oil and fake butter symbolized the growing artificiality of American life, and he considered the people who made and sold them to be the epitome of the slick riverboat grifters that often crop up in his fiction. In fact, cottonseed oil manufacturers had found a crafty way to spin straw into gold: in 1894, *Popular Science Monthly* observed that cottonseed had been garbage in 1860, fertilizer in 1870, cattle feed in 1880, and "table food and many things else" in 1890. Actually, *Popular Science* was behind the times: already in 1879, knowingly or unknowingly, humans as well as cattle were eating large amounts of cottonseed oil. In that year alone, 73,782 barrels of the stuff left the port of New Orleans for Europe, and the transatlantic flow increased in the coming decades. Much of it went into oleomargarine, invented eleven years earlier by French chemist Hippolyte Mège-Mouriès, which quickly spread, and was spread, throughout America. By the time Mark Twain overheard the two beaters gloating on the Mississippi steamboat, fifteen margarine plants were operating in America, which between them had an estimated $7 million in sales—almost $10 billion in today's dollars.

Not all of the cottonseed oil exports from New Orleans went into margarine, however. Over half of the 1879 shipment was destined for Italy, where it was widely used to adulterate olive oil. The British consul in Livorno reported that oil merchants frequently topped up olive oil flasks with cottonseed oil, and the *Atlanta Constitution* sardonically noted that Italian oil makers increased their output by setting a cask of cottonseed oil at the foot of every tree.

Butter and olive oil substitutes converged, as more and more margarine producers replaced the animal fat in their wares with less expensive cottonseed oil, and later with other cheap vegetable oils—corn, sunflower, peanut, colza, rape. These products became edible thanks to recent chemical and technological breakthroughs in vegetable oil refining, which allowed food manufacturers to decolorize, deodorize, and otherwise denature what had previously been unpalatable if not downright revolting substances, fit only for making soap, greasing axles, burning in lamps, and feeding hogs. Hydrogenation soon followed, which turned liquid oils into semisolid pastes at room temperature and paved the way for still wider use of vegetable oils in margarine and many other foods.

No wonder Mark Twain's two beaters were gloating in 1883, at the prospect of reaping ever fatter margins on cheap, easy-to-make butter and olive oil substitutes. Yet for industrial and political reasons, the two businesses faced very different futures. The powerful farm lobby, recognizing that margarine represented a serious threat to the dairy farmer's livelihood, took up butter's cause. They objected to margarine's being labeled with alluring terms like "refined butter" and "pure butter," and complained that dishonest shopkeepers were cutting their butter with cheap margarine. The fierce legal battle which ensued, lasting over a century, saw the butter lobby seeking to limit the ability of margarine-makers to compete with butter, while the margarine lobby fought each of these measures under the banners of free speech, free enterprise, defense of the poor—and by arguing that margarine was healthier than butter. States began to legislate against margarine; in 1881, Missouri outlawed the manufacture, sale, or possession of margarine with intent to sell, while other states forbade coloring margarine yellow to resemble butter, or even required that it be dyed pink.

Congressional hearings on margarine began in the early 1880s and continued through 1950. In 1886, Congress enacted a Margarine Act, slapping stiff taxes and restrictions on margarines; when he signed the act into law, President Grover Cleveland remarked that one of its main benefits was "the defense accorded the consumer against the fraudulent substitution and sale of an imitation of the genuine article of food of very general use. I venture to say that hardly a pound of oleomargarine ever entered a poor man's home under its real name and in its real character." Around the turn of the century, the Supreme Court heard several cases concerning margarine. "We need insistent recognition of the fact of the interdependence of the human animal upon his cattle," Herbert Hoover intoned. "The white race can not survive without its dairy products and no child can be developed on short or bad milk supply." The world wars and butter rationing boosted the margarine industry, but strong limits remained on the way the product could be marketed and sold: through the 1950s, federal taxes remained in effect on the product, and in many states margarine could only be sold as a white block, with a pellet of yellow coloring that the consumer had to knead in. In Wisconsin it was still illegal to sell yellow margarine until 1968, and in Quebec, the substance was only legalized in 2008, after Unilever brought suit against the provincial government.

No American president or Supreme Court justice ever spoke in defense of authentic olive oil, however. The industry had no powerful special interest to defend it, just a few small-scale producers in California and a crowd of highly competitive east coast importers who all too often were cashing in on fake oil themselves. Hence the adulteration of olive oil with cottonseed and other vegetable oils went largely unchallenged. Already in 1863, the *New England Journal of Medicine* reported as "a well-known fact that the olive oil sold in America and elsewhere is very seldom pure, but mostly adulterated with other cheap vegetable oils," such as beechnut, poppy, sesame, and peanut oils. Two decades later, reporting the conversation he'd overheard between the two traveling salesmen, Mark Twain described the pervasive use of cottonseed oil to cut olive oil. In 1903, an investigation by the US Department of Agriculture revealed that adulteration continued apace, even in domestic oils: "The inspection of home-made oils has been so loose that cottonseed is put in here at home without paying freight twice across the Atlantic," the department's inspectors reported. Olive oil adulteration helped prompt the passage of the 1906 Pure Food and Drug Act, a groundbreaking federal law that aimed to remove adulterated foods, poisonous drugs, and harmful patent medicines from commerce, and that gave the Food and Drug Administration new prominence and authority. Yet the trade in bogus olive oil continued undisturbed: in 1922, two years into Prohibition, US Health Commissioner Royal S. Copeland observed that "there is more profit in adulterating olive oil than there is in bootlegging. The practice of adulterating this oil has grown until it has become a menace to the honest importers in the trade." Continued testing by the Department of Agriculture and the Department of Health, and later by the FDA, revealed extensive adulteration in the 1930s, 1940s, 1950s, 1960s, 1970s, 1980s, and 1990s, not

only by oil importers but also by certain California producers themselves. In the late 1990s, having failed to halt oil adulteration, the FDA
stopped testing for it.

Despite enduring problems with fraud, the olive oil market in America is large and fast-growing, and shows encouraging signs of renewal.
Olive bars are opening at high-end locations like the Culinary Institute
of America in Napa and Eataly NYC, the hyperdeli on Fifth Avenue,
as well as at a growing number of delicatessens and food stores which
source and sell high-quality oils. Olive oil franchises like Oil & Vinegar and We Olive have opened in eighteen states, and excellent online
resources have emerged, like the Olive Oil Times (www.oliveoiltimes
.com) and the Olive Oil Source (www.oliveoilsource.com). Large oil
companies, which traditionally have produced oils with a limited number of taste profiles, are beginning to pay attention to different cultivars and terroirs. Colavita USA soon plans to introduce a new line of
regional oils made from olives grown on estates in California, Australia,
Spain, and Greece, each oil distinctively packaged to highlight its unique
flavors and aromas. "I'm not retiring!" John J. Profaci, the company's
seventy-four-year-old founder and chairman, says of the initiative. "I'm
excited. It's like I'm starting all over again."

The regulatory environment is also evolving. In October 2010, the
USDA finally updated the previous trade standard for olive oil, which
dated from 1948, thereby replacing quaint, Truman-era terms like
"choice," "fancy," and "superior" with terminology and chemical requirements that follow IOC guidelines. The California Olive Oil Council and
the North American Olive Oil Association, two trade groups, are taking active part in the debate about quality. Perhaps most significantly,
the three-year-old Olive Center at the University of California, Davis,
is becoming a vital forum for chemical, sensorial, agronomic, and nutritional knowledge about olives and oil. America, it seems, is developing
an appetite for good oil.

What's more, though the US currently imports 98 percent of its olive
oil, within its borders lies a production area of enormous potential. If

olive trees could choose where to sink roots and grow fruit, many would move to California. The state is the fifth largest agricultural economy on earth for very good reason: everything grows here, in reckless profusion, four hundred crops including more than half the national production of vegetables, fruits, and nuts. Olives, highly adapted to hot, dry climates, thrive here. In fact, they've been cultivated in California since Spanish missionaries began to grow their "mission" olives here in the seventeenth century. But in the last fifteen years, Californians have started to get serious about making first-quality oil, using varying degrees of Silicon Valley innovation and old-fashioned farming grit. "The California olive oil industry's relationship to the Mediterranean is a little like a child to a parent," says Alexandra Kicenik Devarenne, an independent olive oil consultant and educator based in Petaluma. "At first we adopted Mediterranean practices—and prejudices—without questioning them, but now we're maturing and becoming more like teenagers, with that uneasy mix of rebellion and reliance." Like pioneers in other fields, many California oil women and men have strong, independent personalities. Despite their common trade they often mistrust, and sometimes detest, one another. But each, in very different ways, shares a uniquely American ambition: to be the best at what they do.

DINO CORTOPASSI always dreamed of being a farmer, though his father, who immigrated from Italy in the 1920s and worked through the Depression on minimal wages, tried hard to talk him out of it. As a child Cortopassi made toy tractors out of cleats and toy disks out of old valve springs, and used them to farm his sandbox. His heroes were farmers, like his great-grandfather Serafino, a sharecropper in the hills near Lucca who saw a grain thresher at an agricultural fair around 1855, took out a loan to buy two of them, and eventually made enough money to buy land and raise his family out of poverty. As Cortopassi grew he developed a farmer's build—six foot three, barrel-chested and long-armed—and seemed cut out for the trade. But in his senior year in high school he caught rheumatic fever, which damaged his heart, and doctors ruled out farming or manual labor for two to three years. "I felt like I'd been dealt some bad cards," he remembers. "But sometimes the worst breaks turn out to be the best ones."

Cortopassi grew up in Stockton, in California's Central Valley, in an Italian environment where people bought cars, bread, and insurance from Italians, and most spoke the Genoese dialect which his mother's family used. (His father, who was from Lucca, learned *genovese* to fit in.) Cortopassi was sitting at home nursing his heart, longing for the farming he couldn't do and watching friends go off to college, when a family friend suggested he try the two-year agriculture program at UC Davis, sixty miles away. Cortopassi jumped at the chance—sort of. "Actually, I majored in poker. But poker gave me the skills I needed to set myself up in agriculture later on: numbers and probabilities, discipline, money management, and how to judge people. Above all it taught me how important it was to get an edge, and when you got one, to ride it hard. If I ever write the book of my life, that'll be the title: *Getting an Edge.*"

Cortopassi has wavy, iron-gray hair and black, expressive eyebrows, the head of a nineteenth-century Italian statesman set, incongruously, on the body of a lumberjack. He is frequently in the company of Tank, his equally barrel-chested Labrador, and his conversation is loud and fast, peppered with splendid obscenities and genuine life wisdom. In 2005 Cortopassi received the prestigious Horatio Alger award for his rags-to-riches success story, and he and his wife, Joan, spend a substantial part of their time and money helping inner-city kids in nearby Stockton and Lodi. The rest of his energies are directed at fine-tuning the family business for maximum efficiency. "He's constantly experimenting with different methods, always asking 'Why? Why? Why?'" says Brady Whitlow, his son-in-law, who runs the family olive oil operation. "He pushes us pretty hard."

Cortopassi found his first edge in agriculture shortly after graduating from UC Davis, when he took a job with a grain trading company,

Pillsbury, and began driving his white VW throughout the Central Valley to buy grain from farmers. His heart gradually healed, and as he traveled the farm countryside he became convinced he could compete in farming. He didn't have the money to buy land, so he began renting, and by double-cropping winter wheat together with kidney beans he started turning a profit. "People said I was crazy, that beans planted so late would get rained out, which was the risk I ran each year. Sometimes they did, and that was like a bad beat in Texas hold 'em. But more often, I made money while everyone else was just getting by." Soon he was purchasing less productive land, which he levelled and improved.

His next big edge came in tomatoes, in the early 1960s, when, like his great-grandfather Serafino, he caught wind of a new machine, this time for harvesting tomatoes, just as a labor crisis broke out because of a shortage of hand-pickers. While other tomato farmers were pulling out their crops, Cortopassi invested heavily in the new technology, and eventually became one of the biggest tomato canners in the state. He continued diversifying in a range of successful row crops and tree fruits, as well as grapes and kidney beans; at one time he was the largest producer of kidney beans in the world.

Finally, in 2004, Cortopassi tackled olives. He was flying over California near the town of Gridley, the location of California Olive Ranch, the largest olive producer in the state which used the recently invented super-high-density (SHD) system. In traditional olive groves, where the fruit is picked by hand or with simple rakes or shaking devices, the trees are planted at about 100 to the acre; SHD groves, by contrast, pack in 700 trees or more per acre, set in straight hedgerows like grapes or corn. SHD olives are collected by twenty-foot-tall mechanical harvesters that ride over the rows, engulfing tree after tree, gobbling up the fruit and spitting it through a chute into a trailer paralleling it one hedgerow over.

"When I saw those groves I said, 'Goddamn son of a bitch, Cortopassi, this is it! This is 'the edge' in olives! But I gotta know more! I gotta know the costs!'" He and a team of coworkers chartered a Flexijet and took a rapid tour of areas in Spain where the SHD system had been pioneered. "I wanted to talk to the farmers themselves," Cortopassi says. "Farmers talking to farmers, they'll level with you." Having convinced himself that the SHD system had competitive advantages over conventional methods of olive production, Cortopassi threw himself into the business with characteristic decisiveness, eventually planting 1,200 acres of olive trees and building a high-tech mill with a throughput of 250 tons of olives a day.

Today the Corto Olive company, managed by Brady Whitlow, makes about 600,000 gallons of first-rate extra virgin olive oil a year. The trees, nine feet tall and planted in die-straight lines like dwarf cypresses, have lost their poetry, but the entire operation sparkles with efficiency and runs day and night. Seeing a gigantic harvester move down a row in the dark, floodlit and clanking like a mechanized cavalry unit, makes you think about the olive harvest very differently. Some competitors object that the handful of cultivars suited to SHD are specialized clones which can't produce the wide range of oil styles made with traditional olive-growing methods. Others say that *arbequina*, the most popular SHD cultivar, is low in oleic acid, polyphenols, and flavor. "It's the Pink Chablis of olive oil," one small producer told me.

When I repeated this to Brady Whitlow, he shrugged. "Look, it's early days for this system, and we're still learning. Many other agricultural innovations you see in California took a few years to get themselves sorted out, then took off. Besides, we're trying to compete in taste with the supermarket oils, the Bertollis and Carapellis of this world, and we're already doing that very well." He handed me a cup of fresh, jade-green Corto oil, which made his point better than any words could.

All that's missing is profitability. When I asked Dino Cortopassi about his margins, he made a sour face. "Thanks to European labeling fraud there's no level playing field in this industry, and it's tough to compete with the prices of inferior oils camouflaged as extra virgin. But our product, real olive oil, makes other things taste better, and the center of the plate is always the center of the consumer's consciousness. Eventually we'll win the olive oil game, on the basis of superior taste at reasonable prices."

IF DINO CORTOPASSI is the epitome of all-American efficiency in the oil business, the prize for the most global vision of oil goes to Mike Bradley, an independent oil producer and trader based in Oakland. Bradley, together with his wife, Veronica, and their two grown children, runs Veronica Foods, a company founded in 1924 by Italian immigrant Salvatore Esposito, Veronica Bradley's grandfather. The company headquarters is a 160,000-square-foot industrial warehouse near the Oakland dockyards, where the cranes of the port bristle on the horizon. In Bradley's second-story office you can hear Latino music and whirring forklifts from the shop floor below, where workers prepare pallets of different oils for shipment to specialty olive oil stores, delicatessens, and restaurants across America. On the day of my visit, his desk was crowded with oil samples from producers trying to sell him their product: an elegant red bottle from Castillo de Canena, rustic tins from Italy, Greece, Portugal, Turkey, and Syria, and a screw-top PET bottle filled with oil made in a partially abandoned grove in the nearby Sierra foothills, harvested and pressed by the local high school football team. "There are some great trees in that area, up around Copperopolis, missions and *manzanillas* and *arbosanas* planted by the Italian immigrants of the late nineteenth and early twentieth centuries who came to work in the gold fields and the mines," Bradley said. "We're thinking of setting up a little mill out there. These small farmers are paying fees for picking and crushing of over $800 a ton, which is three to four times the going rate in Europe, and makes their oil expensive beyond all reason—in some cases almost 300 percent above the world market price for extra virgin olive oil."

Bradley is sixty-two, with a square jaw and a buzz cut and little round glasses that highlight the brilliance of his blue, true believer eyes. He poured me a dose of what he called a "radioactive *koroneiki*," one of his favorites this season, from the Asopos Valley in southern Greece; we both tasted, he doing his unique *strippaggio*, a two-stroke slurp that sounds like heavy hydraulics at work. We both coughed, hard. Bradley removed his glasses to wipe his watering eyes, and grinned. "Gotta love those whips and chains!"

Bradley knows the economics of the international oil trade like no one else I've ever met. On a desktop calculator (which he seemed not to need) he punched out line by line the impact that agricultural subsidies to European oil-makers have on the price of their oil, which represent an unfair economic advantage over American oil. He detailed the import restrictions imposed by the central European government, which hurt growers in California, Australia, Chile, and every other producing nation outside the EU. "That's a really strong headwind to do business against," he concluded. "The most efficient producers in the world out-side Europe are barely surviving in this dysfunctional market, and even Europeans receiving EU subsidies can barely make a profit, if they're making decent olive oil."

But in addition to calculation, Bradley's affinity for oil has poetic and historic depth. He tells with obvious glee the story of Thales of Miletus, the legendary philosopher and mathematician of ancient Greece, who made a fortune in olive oil by correctly predicting a big harvest and rent-ing a number of mills to process it. He recites with admiration the lines from *Oedipus at Colonus* where Sophocles praises the olive tree, calling it "the gray-green nurturer of children." Bradley himself has written odes to the olive, like the poem which coalesced in his mind after years of traveling the back roads of the Mediterranean at harvest time, watching entire villages of women and children pick green, red, and black olives and bounce back to the mill with them in battered flatbed trucks:

CRUSHING GREEN FRUIT

Even the hungry Starling will not take
What we suffer to gather;
Crushing is more heroic than curing

The green true fruit,
The clingstone fruit.

Tight skinned, unyielding;
Firmer than a morning ache.
Too muscular for weeping.
They ride the rocky wagon
Dressed in burlap,
Millbound.

Fragrant is the Miller's song,
Precious is the emerald juice,
Sweet is the bitter fruit,
A gift from the Goddess
To the City of Light.

But all is not fragrance and light in American oil. In the early 1990s, Bradley lost a longstanding customer to an olive oil wholesaler who underbid him by a wide margin, and whose identity the customer wouldn't reveal. "We were producing premium extra virgin olive oil in our own mill in Tunisia, as well as buying fruit on the tree in different parts of the world and having it custom crushed to our specifications," Bradley remembers. "So we knew very well what it cost to produce high-grade extra virgin olive oil. And our profit margin was already razor-thin on that key account. Extra virgin olive oil simply could not be produced anywhere in the world at the prices offered by our mystery competitor." He explained this to his customer, but lost the account anyway. Other customers began to defect to low-priced competition. Bradley heard reports from experienced oil salesmen of oil marked as Italian extra virgin being sold at impossibly low prices in major restaurant supply chains. "More and more we began to feel like we were under attack from hidden but powerful competitors, who had an incredible pricing advantage over us and the rest of the market."

Eventually Bradley learned, the hard way, the identity of one of these competitors, and the nature of the product that they were passing off as extra virgin olive oil. In order to help a client with a sudden shortfall of organic olive oil, he called a major oil trader in Los Angeles, one of the few people in California who could deliver the required quantity on short notice. When eighty drums of oil arrived in a tractor-trailer from down south, Bradley took what he thought were ample precautions to ensure its authenticity, tasting and chemically analyzing numerous samples, all of which were fine. Over a year later, however, his customer notified him that certain lots of the oil had turned out to be adulterated. Bradley checked a retained sample from his bottling run and, sure enough, found that refined oil had been mixed with extra virgin in that lot. When the oil had arrived from Los Angeles, Bradley had only tested the first and last few drums of oil from the load; he speculates that drums in the middle of the shipment contained the adulterated oil. "We'd resold the oil itself long before. All that was left was the retained sample, and the gut-wrenching realization that we'd been had."

Bradley became obsessed with oil fraud. He began testing olive oils and blends on the market, spending tens of thousands of dollars in laboratory fees and identifying a number of dishonest producers. With the help of a hired investigator who frequently passed himself off as an oil buyer, he pieced together the linkages between these producers and their clients, food companies large and small, which in turn were selling huge quantities of counterfeit or mislabeled olive oil to the ingredients and baking industries, to restaurants, hospitals, nursing homes, schools, and the US government.

Yet no one was interested in his findings. He spoke with officials at the FDA in Oakland and at the California Department of Agriculture in Sacramento, but neither office took action. No lawyer would take the case, because the main fraudsters reputedly held their earnings in offshore bank accounts, which would be difficult to access even if they were successfully sued. Most discouraging of all, Bradley found that many clients of dishonest oil dealers, when informed that they were buying adulterated oil, said they didn't care. "Yeah, we know, but it's cheap, and that's what our customers want," the oil buyer for a nationwide super-market chain told him. "I'm not here to change the world." Some buyers became aggressive with Bradley, advising him to mind his own business. "The whole anti-fraud thing started to consume me," Bradley remembers. "My wife said she was worried about my sanity."

While remaining convinced that something had to be done about the fraud, Bradley redirected his energies into quality. He had already made fact-finding missions to the Mediterranean. In 1995, during a trip to Tunisia, he'd formed a partnership with Habib Douss, a Tunisian American chemist; together they bought an olive grove at Monastir on the central Tunisian coast, near the ancient Roman city of El Djem, and built a technologically advanced mill complete with nitrogen-flushed storage silos. Now Bradley intensified his travels in the Mediterranean, making extended trips, which he refers to as "pilgrimages," through the major production regions of Spain, Italy, Greece, and North Africa at harvest time, sometimes for months on end. He toured groves and watched harvesting, milling, and storage, and tasted as many oils as he could lay his hands on. "I wanted to find out where the good stuff was coming from," he says. "I was after the where, what, when and how of fine olive oil—where the olives are grown, what cultivars and chemistry they have, when and how they're processed."

After several years of travel and experience, Bradley figured he'd finally cracked the quality code. But oil held another big surprise in store. "By then I'd built a great network of suppliers, whose work I'd seen, tested, and trusted. I finally knew what the term 'extra virgin' meant—or ought to mean—and understood the essentials of making first-class oil: healthy fruit, processed immediately after harvest in a clean facility, properly stored, and bottled at the last minute, just before sale. I knew what efficient production looked like." He began to identify what he considered the great, archetypal oils from around the Mediter-ranean, and to form alliances with mills that could deliver these oils in large quantities.

No sooner had he created this tidy world of olive oil, however, than it was demolished by the arrival of a large wooden box from Mildura, Australia, sent by a recently formed company he'd never heard of, called Boundary Bend, which wanted him to buy their oil. Bradley's previous experiences with Australian oils had been uninspiring, so he put off opening the box for several days. Finally he did, and discovered an array of tiny vials containing a dozen different oils, each neatly labeled with its cultivar, chemical composition, and taste characteristics. "It was late May or early June," Bradley remembers, "and most of the European and Californian oils were beginning to soften, to lose their fresh-crushed aroma and fruity profile. I tried one of these Australian oils, which had been made only a week or so earlier. I tried another, and another. They were amazing, all of them: bright, fresh, crisp, and grassy green, with strong pepper finishes. I'd spent eight or ten years working out where to buy the best oils in the Mediterranean, and here was this noisy thing in the room that was better than any oil I had. I was literally trembling—at first I didn't want to accept what I was seeing and tasting."

Until that moment, Bradley had overlooked what might be called the antipodean advantage: being six months out of phase with the northern hemisphere, olives properly harvested and crushed Down Under during May and June, the antipodean fall, make oils that are at their best just when northern oils are beginning to lose their legs. Soon he was off to Australia, New Zealand, Chile, Argentina, and South Africa, to complete his oil education. "Once I got the two-hemispheres thing going, I fully understood that freshness is the key to great oil. From the moment the olives are crushed, the aging starts, and the oil begins to lose its magic. The taste and essence of what's in the bottle is all I'm interested in, not what's written on the label. Provenance is often used as a marketing device." Finally, Bradley was ready to share his global vision of olive oil quality with the world.

Today Bradley imports over one million gallons of premium, single-cultivar extra virgin oil each year, from twenty countries around the world, a portfolio of about seventy oils that changes with each harvest, which he sells wholesale in ten-liter boxes (like Paolo Pasquali, he insists on bulk storage as the best way to minimize oxidation and preserve oil quality). Bradley is now the exclusive supplier to a rapidly growing number of specialty food stores and oil bars across America, and teaches regular seminars in extra virgin olive oil for store managers. Each year for the last three years, his business has doubled. Many of his customers do little or no advertising, relying instead on word of mouth—and on the selling power of great oil. "We virtually insist that shoppers sample the oils before buying them, and we teach them to ask the right questions," Bradley says. "When they put it on their tongue, the light goes on, they get it immediately. We're witnessing a paradigm shift in the olive oil business. It's like experiencing the rebirth of olive oil. Finally, consumers are beginning to realize that oil is made from fresh produce, and that expiration dates measured in years rather than months are a cruel joke."

In January 2011, Bradley and his family opened Amphora Nueva, their own oil store, in Berkeley, where the walls are lined with antique and replica Roman amphorae like the ones from Monte Testaccio, as well as panoramic photos of the groves where Bradley sources his olives, and banks of gleaming stainless steel *fusti* containing fifty great single-varietal oils from around the world, each labeled with the cultivar name, taste profile, and chemical analysis. I stood with him at the grand opening, as crowds of curious oil newcomers read the unfamiliar words aloud off the *fusti*, sipped oil, coughed, laughed, and questioned Bradley and his staff. "There's a renaissance happening here, that not even rampant fraud can stop," he said.

ED STOLMAN, inventor of the Dove bar, likes to say he's had fourteen careers, and has made money in all but one of them. Stolman is an entrepreneur in the classic American mold, gregarious, well-connected, and infectiously big-picture, and can hardly help making money. He has worked in hospital management, invested in real estate, run a volunteer ambulance service, renovated the city centers of historic towns in Tennessee, where he grew up, and made ice cream, and has prospered every time. So when the IRS noticed a fifteen-year string of losses that he'd reported at the Olive Press, the oil mill and shop he owns with several partners in the countryside not far from Sonoma, they became suspicious. "They called me in, and were pretty tough with me at first," Stolman remembers with a sunny smile. "Then I told them my story. By the end of the meeting, the agents had tears in their eyes." This year, his sixteenth in the business, he has finally turned a profit in olive oil, though he might still be in the red if it weren't for some help from Oprah Winfrey.

I met Stolman at the Olive Press, which is housed in a faux-Tuscan palazzo owned by Jacuzzi Wineries, near the wine-tasting room. The Mediterranean, particularly Tuscany and Provence, is a recurrent theme of conversation in these parts, and a favorite destination for long, leisurely journeys. (Stolman himself lives in another Tuscan-inspired villa, in the hills above nearby Glen Ellen, surrounded by his 1,000 olive trees.) So in 1995, Stolman and a group of other northern California residents, most of whom had accumulated comfortable fortunes and were looking for something to do, decided to make olive oil, a Mediterranean icon. They traveled together to southern France on a scouting trip to learn about milling, and visited Pistoia, not far from Florence, to order several thousand trees, which arrived in San Francisco harbor a month later wrapped in huge rolls of damp burlap. That day they held a big party in gazebos on Stolman's property—dwellings hereabouts are referred to as "properties," not "houses," and most deserve the term—complete with opera music, prosecco, and Italian flags. Then the partners took their shares of the trees back to their properties, and planted them.

Somewhere along the way, Stolman and several others of the group, which also included Nan McEvoy, a newspaper heiress, caught the oil bug, and began to make oil that was first good, and then superb. Olive Press oils have won more national and international awards than any other oil in America. But the company still wasn't profitable. "I don't think there's a producer in the state who is making money in olive oil, at least the honest way," Stolman says. He is trying to marshal governmental action to tighen up laws and push enforcement, through his various contacts in the state capital and in Washington. So far he's had little success.

Still, in a series of fortuitous events that mostly seem to happen to outgoing and well-connected entrepreneurs like Ed Stolman, the TV financial guru Suze Orman began shopping at the Olive Press. Before long she mentioned their oil to her friend Oprah Winfrey, and it promptly made the O List, the catalog of gift recommendations that Oprah has compiled each Christmas and publicized in her show and magazine. The resulting spike in sales finally nudged the Olive Press into the black.

Stolman walked me around the showroom. The Olive Press is a place you instinctively want to spend hours in: warm-lit and wood-paneled, filled with a profusion of attractive and interesting objects and the murmur of happy browsing. The oil bar contains a dozen ready-to-taste oils arranged from mildest to most full-bodied, as well as oils infused with lemon, basil, parmesan, and hot pepper. The bottles are sleek and the labels memorable, and there are oils in slender little aluminum cans as well that are custom-made in Austria. On shelves and tables around the room are other things made from and for oil—soaps, tapenades, cruets, *fusti*, and olive oil ice cream—all carefully positioned by the marketing director, Christine Harrison, formerly of Victoria's Secret, to evoke a sense of bounty, yet order.

I tasted the oils, one by one, starting with a soft-spoken mission and ending with a screamingly peppery *coratina*. I'd been expecting a letdown after the Olive Press's high-profile marketing, but these oils were sublime, every one so fresh and spicy and distinctive it made my teeth hurt. Who had made this oil?

In the back wall of the room was a door with a plexiglass window in it, through which the mill was visible, a shiny one-ton Pieralisi. The harvest was in full swing, and the machinery ran twenty-four hours a day. Five people were hard at work loading olives, checking the malaxer, measuring temperatures, adjusting valves, and performing the hundreds of other tasks that milling is made of, which together determine whether an oil will be great or mediocre. In their midst was a slender woman with a red bob and a pale, pretty face a bit like a china doll's. As I watched, she called one of the workers over. No sound came through the plexiglass, but she was clearly correcting a small error he had made. Something in the set of her mouth, the lips a little pinched, and the way the worker leaned forward attentively toward her while she spoke, like a slight bow, made her seem faintly intimidating.

"That's Deborah," Ed Stolman said. "When it comes to making oil, I've learned just to do what she says."

We walked through the door, passing from the fragrant serenity of the showroom to the roar and fluster of "the crush," as Californians call the milling season. (This term, which captures the act as well as the intensity of milling, is far more appropriate than the verb "to press," which is passé nowadays, since virtually all good oil is made with centrifuges, not presses.) Deborah Rogers, the master miller of the Olive Press, doesn't like to leave the mill during the almost four months it runs at full capacity, not even at night, and though she sometimes drags herself away, by the end of the season she's badly sleep-deprived. "Deborah is very passionate about her home, family, and making healthy food," says her husband, Doug, "but during milling season she becomes somewhat of a ghost. Even when she's standing right in front of you, she is usually a million mental miles away." Rogers says she trusts her staff, but is always concerned that something will go wrong and spoil a batch of oil, or a split-second adjustment will crop up that requires her advice. "This is like living four months in a pressure cooker," she half-shouted over the noise. Her expression, though, was happy.

Rogers studied horticulture but her real passion was food, ever since she learned to cook as a girl with her Polish grandmother, preparing kielbasa and kapusta and rolling out dough for homemade pierogi while standing side by side in the kitchen. "Our house smelled amazing, fragrant with cooked onions, cabbage, and dried mushrooms sent by my grandmother's family back in Poland," Rogers says. "She would tell me stories about immigrating to the US and the various jobs she worked to support herself. She was quiet and stoic and very stern. I learned so much from her—my early passion for gardening and growing my own food, wasting nothing, and the joy of cooking from scratch using only the freshest ingredients." Even as a schoolgirl, Rogers was so fascinated by food that she'd pretend to be sick so she could stay home and watch *The Galloping Gourmet.*

She discovered olive oil in a little store in St. Helena, near Napa. "It was the tiniest, cutest, Old World family store I'd ever seen. The owners would fill the half-gallon jug and stick on a label, often a little crooked. I got a great feeling just going to that store to get oil. I decided to do something horticultural and culinary at the same time: make olive oil."

In 1993, she sold her house and used most of the money to buy five acres of land in Glen Ellen, to plant olive trees. Then, not wanting to delay her entry into oil-making for the five to seven years that the trees would need to fruit, she contacted two bulk oil dealers and bought a 55-gallon drum from each, plunked them down on the living room floor of her tiny new apartment, and started bottling her own signature blends. "It was a mess. I didn't have a drum pump, so I siphoned the oil out by mouth, sitting on a milk stool between the drums. Then I hand-bottled them, but the first time I bought the wrong-sized corks, so I had to drip wax over them to seal the bottles." The system worked, though, because at the next farmer's market her oil stand, set among a dozen or so people who actually made oil from their own olives, drew the biggest crowds, and she sold out her entire stock of wax-corked signature blends priced at $18 a half-liter. Business grew rapidly, and soon she was able to quit her day job and devote herself to oil. (She never did plant olive trees on her land in Glen Ellen.) "But I still didn't know what good oil tasted like," she admits.

That began to change in 1995, when she traveled to southern France with Ed Stolman and a group of other northern California residents, the future partners of the Olive Press. Significantly, she remembers less about the oil she tasted than about the mills she saw. "I walked into one mill and was amazed by how clean the machinery was, a big modern Pieralisi. The air smelled clean, too, with no trace of rancidity. That was an awakening."

Back in California, Rogers continued making her blends, though occasionally she was reminded that buying other people's oil had its risks. In oil from one of her suppliers, from whom she'd just bought twenty drums, she noticed red flecks and large black blobs, and had the oil tested. The laboratory found paint chips, feather barbules, and rat feces, though the identity of the black blobs was never determined.

Soon the Olive Press partners imported their trees from Pistoia, bought a modern hammer mill, and started making oil, first with olives they purchased from local growers and then, after their trees fruited, with their own. As she'd learned cooking from her grandmother, Rogers mastered milling standing long hours at the side of several mentors, the few self-taught masters of the craft in California at the time. She says the key to great milling is the ability to see, hear, and react to many things at once. Some people, she finds, have the knack, and others don't. "Restaurant guys get it. They know how to perform, and actually thrive, under pressure. In fact, the satisfaction of milling is a bit like short-order cooking. When things in the kitchen are humming and you're getting all the plates up there in the window, and the diners are all happy—it's a high, and quite addictive."

Rogers walked me over to the malaxer so she could check the progress of the latest batch. The reddish-brown paste glistened with tiny droplets of oil, which were beginning to pool in larger green puddles in the folds of the paste. The warmth and the smell steamed up invisibly from the paste, aromas and aromatics dancing like angels in my nose. I could almost feel the green on my face.

"That's *leccino*," she said, gazing at the paste. "See the clumpiness, how beautifully it's setting up? And the gloss of the oil? *Leccino* is a miller's dream."

Rogers said she'd worked so long and hard at the Olive Press, nose to the millstone, that she hadn't traveled much. Yet olive oil had brought her together with many talented and intriguing people from distant lands, who had come here to the mill or whom she'd met at oil tastings and competitions. "Oil is like a universal language wherever you go."

In fact, she told me, she was going into semi-retirement after this harvest, so she could travel the world and visit these far-flung friends. Given her unmistakable love of milling, this surprised me. I asked where she was going, and she listed her destinations, naming the oil friends first and then where they lived. There were many Australians and New Zealanders, and quite a few Chileans and Argentinians, too. She mentioned no one from the Mediterranean.

"Of course, I'll still be running the Olive Press mill each harvest," she added. "I'm just going down south when things get quiet around here."

Then I saw. She was heading south to follow the olive harvest. She was chasing the crush.

PROBABLY THE ONLY small producer in California to defy Ed Stolman's dictum and make a regular, honest profit from olive oil is Mike Madison, and he's done it with no help from Oprah. Educated at Phillips Andover and at Harvard, where he earned a PhD in botany, he took a job as a plant collector for the Harvard Botanical Museum, roaming the rainforests of South America, sometimes for a year at a time. Eventually, when what had been a big adventure began to feel too much like hard labor, he returned to his hometown, Davis, and bought twenty acres of prime farmland on Putah Creek, near a farm where he had lived as a child.

Madison, a wiry sixty-three-year-old with a short brown beard and a baseball cap, claims that his modus operandi in farming is "trial and error followed by error and error," and that his motto is "aim low." Yet as I walked with him around his farm on Putah Creek, his real plan appeared more and more to be "aim right."

Madison has made money in oil each year since 1991, when he planted his first trees, by keeping his costs almost incredibly low. Instead of hiring a contractor to put up a new building for his olive mill, he bought an abandoned barn for one dollar, deconstructed it with a chainsaw and a crowbar, and reassembled it on his farm. Instead of buying a fancy mill from a big-name manufacturer, he hired three men in a shed in Perugia, who also liked to work with their hands, to build him a custom mill. "This mill has thirteen motors," he said, laying his hand on it like a stockman with a champion stallion. "If the sound changes in any of them, I know something's going wrong." And while most growers hire a crew to harvest their olives, he hand-picks them himself during the day, and runs his mill at night. "This is strictly a one-man operation," he says. "It takes me ten or eleven weeks of ten-hour days to harvest 1,500 trees."

When it comes to selling his oil, Madison is equally frugal. He has no website, he doesn't ship his oil, he doesn't advertise, he doesn't even have a telephone. He sells most of his oil at the farmers' market in nearby Davis, at modest prices, and gives the rest to the local food bank. His total investment for the trees, a drip irrigation system, a half-ton-per-hour mill, a building, and plenty of stainless steel tanks for storing his oil, was $98,000. "Most people putting together that package would spend eight or ten times that amount. And if you've spent three-quarters of a million dollars to set up a small operation, you will never make a profit in olive oil."

Olives and oil fit Madison's larger aspiration to farm, and to live, at a pre-Industrial Revolution pace and scale. "I set the price of my oil low enough that people hopefully won't be inhibited from using it liberally. I sell most things within ten miles of here. This style of commerce is a throwback to the eighteenth century, when most trade took place between people who knew each other, and knew what to expect from each other. Nowadays virtually everything you buy is made by strangers, who need to impress you with pretentious bottles and fancy labels and high-priced marketing, and all the awards they've won. But if you're selling to people you know, you don't need all that."

Madison chooses his crops with care, and only grows the ones that seem right to him. He doesn't grow sweet corn with the new sh-2 gene which boosts the sugar content of the kernels, because, as he says, he likes his corn to taste like corn, not Cap'n Crunch. Other crops he grows—quinces, almonds, and tart heirloom Wickson apples as small as a five-year-old's fist—all fit this pattern of complex, tart, even bitter, rather than sweet. Olives and their oil do too. "The bitterness of fresh olive oil is rich and interesting, and lingers on the palate. Like music in a minor key, it sets a mood of contemplation and regret."

Yet Madison also recognizes, and heartily enjoys, the slippery side of oil. As we stood among his trees, heavy with *taggiasca* olives just like those that were growing on the old tree near my home in Liguria, he told the story of an oil-maker he knows, good-hearted but bumbling, who ran a shabby mill north of Davis and somehow managed to win top prize at a major competition.

"Soon after, two Sicilian gentlemen showed up with a fat sales contract and offered him twice what the mill was worth. He pounced on the offer, because he didn't really like making oil anyway. The Sicilians took that prizewinning label of his and began slapping it on bottles of rancid, fusty oil of doubtful origin. They didn't even use the mill, which they abandoned; for a time it was used to dump old cars. Trouble is, buried deep in that sales contract was a clause that allowed them to annul the sale and return the mill to the seller within two years, which they promptly did. They left that guy with a broken-down mill and a mill-yard strewn with car carcasses!"

He chortled as he remembered the story, shaking his head. "When a product sells for a hundred dollars a gallon or more, the temptation to fraud must be nearly irresistible."

EVERYONE IN the oil business in California, and in America, knows a fraud story, because everyone knows a fraudster. The United States, whose oil consumption is third in the world and is growing at 10 percent annually, a market worth over $1.5 billion and climbing, has long had some of the loosest laws on earth concerning olive oil purity, and the new USDA standards passed in October 2010, which mirror the lax regulations of the IOC, remain voluntary, with no provision for enforcement. The United States of America is an oil criminal's dream.

A recent survey of supermarket extra virgins performed by the UC Davis Olive Center, in cooperation with the Australian Oils Research Laboratory, revealed that 69 percent of oils tested had taste flaws such as rancid, fusty, and musty, which meant they weren't extra virgin oils at all, and had been mislabeled. (The California oils surveyed weren't perfect, either.) Such cases of "legal fraud" are common in American supermarket oils, as they are in many parts of the world: similar findings were reached by Andreas März in Germany, by *CHOICE* magazine in Australia, by the regional government of Andalucía, and by documentaries on Swiss and German television about extra virgin quality in those countries. "We've pulled olive oils off the shelf," says Paul Vossen, a University of California oil specialist, who beginning in 1997 trained and then led America's first IOC-recognized tasting panel, "and I would say very seldom do we ever find one that passes as extra virgin." The same is often true at gourmet retailers and websites. "Price is by no means an indicator of quality," Vossen says. "The high-ticket items can be equally bad."

In the wholesale market, a lot of oil is adulterated outright with cheap vegetable oils. After years of lab testing and observation, Mike Bradley concludes that "the market is awash in counterfeit olive oil to the point that most legitimate sellers have given up trying to sell the real thing to wholesale suppliers or restaurants. It is rare to find authentic extra virgin olive oil in a restaurant in America, even in fine restaurants that ought to know better. It's nearly impossible in some localities, such as southern California, where large-scale counterfeiters pump out blends of low-grade olive oil and soybean oil dyed bright green, and sell it to their fences, the big-name 'legitimate' wholesalers." John J. Profaci, chairman of Colavita USA, says such buyers are motivated merely by low prices, not by quality, and are "as responsible as the adulterators" for the prevalence of fake olive oil on the American market. "Because if I'm offering my extra virgin olive oil at $5 a bottle and somebody comes in at $3, the buyer's got to say, 'You know what? Something's wrong here. There can't be such a big difference in price if the quality's the same.' But they close their eyes to it."

Much of the fake olive oil sold in America is imported. In 2006, in a rare intervention by authorities, federal marshals seized about 61,000 liters of what was supposedly extra virgin olive oil and 26,000 liters of olive pomace oil from a New Jersey warehouse. Some of the oil, which consisted almost entirely of soybean oil, was destined for a company called Krinos Foods. In a shifting of responsibility that recalls cases of oil fraud in Italy, Krinos blamed its supplier, DMK Global Marketing, which it says had guaranteed the quality of the oil; DMK, in turn, blamed the bottlers in Italy from whom it had purchased the oil, which according to an FDA document were Fabio Mataluni & Co. and Oleificio Fratelli Amato, both members of ASSITOL. The marshals destroyed the oil, but no criminal charges were brought against Krinos or any other companies. (This wasn't Krinos's first encounter with the authorities. In 1997, federal marshals seized a shipment of an olive pomace oil brand imported and distributed by Krinos, which actually consisted partially or wholly of sunflower seed oil, and in 1988 the company's founder, John Moschalaidis, pleaded guilty in a federal court in New Jersey to conspiring to import feta cheese contaminated with benzene hexachloride, a carcinogenic pesticide.)

Large quantities of fake oil are also being mixed up on American soil, where fraudsters take advantage of the lax regulatory environment. In California, the hub for fraud is greater Los Angeles, where a number of companies are blending soy, seed oil, or cottonseed oil with low-grade olive oil and selling it as extra virgin. "There's a river of bad oil flowing through here," says Mustafa Altuner, a Turkish-born olive oil and specialty foods importer based in Long Beach, who has struggled for years to sell real extra virgin in the Los Angeles market. "The volume is phenomenal. Even pomace oil gets cut with soybean oil." Michele Rubino, the olive and pomace oil producer in Puglia, thinks the problem is nationwide; he estimates that 50 percent of the oil sold in America is

fraudulent, with particularly acute problems in the food service industry. "In America, people can pretty much put whatever they want in the
container," he says. Leonardo Colavita agrees. "The American [authori-
ties] tell me, 'So long as a product isn't toxic, you can sell it however you
like—so long as it isn't toxic. Because if you put seed [oil] inside extra
[virgin olive oil], you don't poison anyone. So they say, 'It's the consumer's
choice whether to buy it or not.'" Leonardo Marseglia believes the FDA's
approach is ultimately more sensible than that of the Italian authorities.
"They do more intelligent checks than us. What do they do? They check
to make sure that [the oil] isn't poisoned, that it doesn't harm anybody's
health. But regarding the quality, the buyer has to defend himself. . . .
They say, 'If you bought yourself some extra virgin that turns out to be
lampante, that's your tough shit.'"

The FDA considers olive oil adulteration a low priority. "We're
inclined to spend our money on things where there's a clear public health
benefit," Martin Stutsman, an FDA specialist in adulterated food, told
me. Stutsman said that the FDA has no ongoing program to test olive oil
quality and was unaware of any such programs in the past. Instead, the
agency relies on major producers, as well as trade associations like the
North American Olive Oil Association (NAOOA), the US counterpart
to ASSITOL, to alert it to suspicious products. With the industry act-
ing as a watchdog, he says, "you don't waste your resources on surveys
that are likely to make somebody comfortable but that don't do much
toward protecting the public health."

Stutsman's faith appears misplaced. NAOOA members include
ASSITOL itself, as well as Krinos and Bertolli, which have had problems
with faux olive or pomace oil in the past. Therefore, the NAOOA may
not always be the most objective source of information about fraud—it
is, after all, a trade organization, not a regulatory agency. Nevertheless,
the NAOOA is the only body in America that performs widespread
oil testing, and it regularly notifies the FDA and other federal and
state authorities when test results point to fraud. According to a letter
recently sent by the NAOOA to the FDA, in April 2010 the NAOOA

analyzed samples of Genco Extra Virgin Olive Oil (evidently named after the olive oil company in *The Godfather*), which is marketed by Coachella Valley Edibles in Rancho Cucamonga, a suburb of Los Angeles. These tests revealed that the product was adulterated with cheaper oils. The NAOOA writes that it performed similar tests in 2005 and 2007, with similar results. "That means that for at least five years this company has demonstrated a pattern of defrauding consumers," the letter concludes, "and robbing them of the health benefits outlined in FDA's health claim for olive oil and olive oil–containing products." The NAOOA has written similar letters regarding other companies. It sent the FDA test results regarding extra virgin oil produced by Gourmet Factory, a company in Glendale, New York, showing that the product actually consisted mostly of pomace oil; the letter ends with a request that the FDA "take whatever action possible to protect consumers and legitimate businesses from these unscrupulous practices." The NAOOA has also written to the Orange County district attorney to report the activities of Italcal Trading (also known as Gemsa Enterprises), based in La Mirada, another suburb of Los Angeles. The letter cites six of the company's labels, including Di Stefano olive oil, La Dolce Vita extra virgin oil, and Angela extra virgin oil, which, it says, its tests reveal "to actually contain large amounts of seed oil," and urges the district attorney "to actively pursue an investigation of Italcal Trading."

Other sources report adulteration by Italcal Trading. Mustafa Altuner and other Los Angeles oil companies have had this company's olive oil products analyzed by reputable laboratories, with test results that point to adulteration with cheaper oils. Mike Bradley has done the same, especially because Italcal was the Los Angeles-based oil dealer from whom he bought the eighty drums of organic oil, part of which appeared from later testing to have been adulterated. A former employee of Italcal, who is currently in dispute with the company, reports having observed extensive adulteration by the company. He claims that Italcal systematically lied about the nature and origins of the oils it sold, and ignored traceability and other procedures required by the FDA.

He speaks of a worker in the Italcal warehouse, whom he nicknamed "the gondolier," who he says blended up adulterated oils using a five-foot metal paddle, adding a coloring agent procured by the head of the company, Emilio Viscomi. Viscomi kept the recipe for the agent a closely guarded secret. "You want it greener, less green?" the former employee said. "You want it emerald green? However you want it, that's how he makes it." The employee also describes Italcal's illustrious client list, which he says included some of the leading food distribution companies in America, who he claims must have known the true nature of the "olive oil" they were buying, given that it was being sold at far below the market price of olive oil.

I attempted to contact Emilio Viscomi, head of Italcal, numerous times by phone and email to request an interview, but he never replied. I even dropped by unannounced at the Italcal warehouse in La Mirada, where the receptionist told me Viscomi had just stepped out; I asked if I could speak with someone else at the company, or tour the warehouse, but she cordially refused. So I can't say how Viscomi would respond to the charges of his former employee, or the claims of the NAOOA and other oil traders who say he sells fake olive oil. I can say, though, that while sitting in the parking lot of the Italcal warehouse, a series of tractor-trailer trucks with the names of prominent American food companies painted on their sides pulled up to the truck bay, loaded goods, and drove away. These were the same names that the former employee of Italcal said had purchased the company's products, and the same that Mike Bradley painstakingly documented during his investigations— companies which, as both men point out, can hardly be ignorant of the real nature of the product they are buying.

So far, however, despite repeated reports from the NAOOA and independent oil businessmen, neither the FDA nor other authorities appear to have taken action against reputed oil fraudsters. What's more, the FDA *has* performed its own tests in the past, with results that have been far from reassuring. David Firestone, an FDA chemist from 1948 to 1999 who acted as the agency's olive oil specialist, instituted a survey program in 1983 to curb what he calls "the rampant adulteration of olive oil products" in America. Of twenty-five products collected at random, nearly half were adulterated; two years later, a follow-up survey of sixty-one olive oil products found 32 percent adulteration. Some of the adulterated products were by major producers, whose names Firestone would not reveal. "My experience over a period of some fifty years suggests that we can always expect adulteration and mislabeling of olive oil products in the absence of surveillance by official sources," he says. More recently, in 1997, the Canadian Food Inspection Agency, Canada's answer to the FDA, began testing retail olive oils for adulteration; since then, over 20 percent of the oils it has tested have proven to be fraudulent. Today in the US, where oil companies know there is no systematic testing, the incidence of fraud is surely higher.

The FDA's Martin Stutsman says his agency is hesitant to commit the resources to fighting olive oil adulteration because such activity, though wrong, doesn't represent a serious public health hazard. This too is debatable. True, olive oil mixed with a cheaper vegetable oil doesn't compare in danger or virulence to anthrax, botulism, or salmonella. Yet how many people with a peanut or soybean allergy have become sick after eating olive oil adulterated with peanut or soy oil? Italian investigators have found hydrocarbon residues, pesticides, and other contaminants in fake olive oils, and pomace oil, a common adulterant, sometimes contains mineral oil as well as PAHs, proven carcinogens that can also damage DNA and the immune system. Then there's the 1981 case of toxic oil syndrome in Spain, when rapeseed oil adulterated with an industrial additive, sold as olive oil, killed eight hundred people and seriously injured thousands more.

In 2008, Mike Bradley imported organic extra virgin olive oil in a flexi-bag, a 24,000-liter polymer bladder which, when filled, looks like a small green whale. When it arrived, Bradley's quality assurance team discovered that the oil had a peculiar chemical odor, and refused to unload it. The producer insisted that the odor hadn't been there when he'd loaded the oil, while the shipping company denied all knowledge and demanded that the container be returned empty. Bradley declined, and, despite growing late fees for the container, consulted prominent chemical laboratories and flexi-bag manufacturers to try to determine the source of the problem. He eventually found that the oil, as well as the paint on the inside of the container, was contaminated with naphthalene, a pesticide that is the active ingredient in mothballs; the oil had 390,000 times the allowable limit. The container had evidently been sprayed for insects before an earlier shipment, and the insecticide had passed from the container through the plastic membrane of the flexi-bag, contaminating the oil. Bradley called health officials at the state and federal level to report the incident and ask what to do with the oil, but they told him they had no jurisdiction over imported products, and instructed him to take the issue elsewhere. Despite numerous attempts, he was unable to locate an agency anywhere in America that was willing to deal with the problem. Finally, in frustration, Bradley alerted health authorities that he was about to release the load of contaminated olive oil, still inside its original container, back to the shipping company, and that he would not be responsible for the consequences. The next day, he says, federal, state, and county officials arrived at his warehouse en masse. One read Bradley his rights, while others placed the container and its contents under embargo. Over six months later, the container and its contents were transported under state supervision to a refinery, where all traces of naphthalene were removed. (Final liability and responsibility for the incident are still being decided in a suit between Bradley's insurance company and the shipping company, being heard in a court in Tel Aviv, Israel.)

Instead of facing such complications, some dealers in this situation might have let the smell of the tainted oil fade, mixed it with good oil and sold the resulting blend without a word to the authorities. Many others wouldn't have caught the problem in the first place, especially if the level of contamination hadn't been so high. "As far as I know, the practice of treating empty containers with naphthalene continues, and the flexi-bags that most importers of olive oil use don't prevent this kind of contamination," Bradley says. "Which is alarming, when you realize that millions of tons of produce and foodstuffs move in ocean containers that have been treated inside with pesticides, and that neither shippers, receivers, nor the government officials I spoke with were aware of the potential problem." Bradley sees this incident as symptomatic of a wide-spread mistrust of official supervision. "People have been brainwashed into believing that all government regulation and oversight hamper free enterprise, and are the bane of industry. They aren't willing to pay the up-front cost of effective vigilance."

In fact, the FDA is itself the victim of a generalized bias against government regulation. The same laissez-faire attitudes lamented by Jonathan Swift, which helped turn Britain after the Industrial Revolution into a haven for adulteration, have undermined the agency's ability to protect the US food supply. In November 2007, in an internal review of the agency, the FDA's own Subcommittee on Science and Technology decried the "appallingly low inspection rate" of US food:

> FDA cannot sufficiently monitor either the tremendous volume of products manufactured domestically or the exponential growth of imported products. During the past 35 years, the decrease in FDA funding for inspection of our food supply has forced FDA to impose a 78 percent reduction in food inspections, at a time when the food industry has been rapidly expanding and food importation has exponentially increased. FDA estimates that, at most, it inspects food manufacturers once every 10 years, and cosmetic manufacturers even less frequently. The Agency conducts no inspections of retail food establishments or of food-producing farms.

"FDA does not have the capacity to ensure the safety of food for the nation," the report concluded. "FDA's inability to keep up with scientific advances means that American lives are at risk."

There are signs that this risk is being addressed. In 2009, President Barack Obama formed a Food Safety Working Group to advise him on how to upgrade the US food safety system. In late 2010, after a series of food poisoning incidents involving eggs, spinach, and peanut butter, both the Senate and the House of Representatives passed new food safety bills that aimed to expand the FDA's powers to inspect and recall tainted foods. For olive oil authenticity, help may be on the way from the private sector as well. In August 2010, responding to the UC Davis study that reported widespread mislabeling in the extra virgin grade, the Orange County law firm of Callahan & Blaine filed a class action complaint against the manufacturers and distributors of many of the oils cited in the study, including Unilever, Carapelli, and Sysco. The complaint accused these companies of fraud, negligent misrepresentation, false advertising, breach of warranty, and unjust enrichment, and of "misleading and defrauding California consumers for years." (Callahan & Blaine later decided not to pursue the case.) Mustafa Altuner says that, at least in Los Angeles, the atmosphere in the oil business appears to be improving. "Right now the bad guys are sleeping with one eye open."

Yet so far nothing concrete has actually been done to strengthen the FDA, and no arrests have been made in the olive oil business. The bad guys may be resting a little less easy, but they're still blending up bad oil.

Epilogue

MYTHOLOGIES

A re we witnessing a renaissance in olive oil, or the death of an industry? Will extra virgin olive oil become the next premium food phenomenon—the next microbrewery beer, Starbucks coffee, or quality chocolate—or will it sink into the anonymous mass of fat that is the legacy of our post-industrial food supply? Why don't we respect great oil as we respect great wine? And why have oil and wine evolved in such fundamentally divergent ways over the last half-century?

For several years now I've been asking these questions of people I've met in orchards, restaurants, monasteries, warehouses, and courthouses, in places farther and farther from my home in Italy, where my questioning began. Some of their responses—guesses and musings rather than answers—make up this book. In many of my conversations, wine, oil's

age-old companion and rival, has been the unspoken point of compari-
son. Recently, back in western Liguria where I live, I saw how the enduring dialectic with wine may, if not explain the enigma of oil, at least
provide clues to oil's real nature. I learned this from my neighbor Gino
Olivieri, an eighty-five-year-old farmer who is the wisest man I know, as
I watched him make oil and wine amid the terraced fields and limestone
cliffs of our village.

Each year I help Olivieri with two ancient rites of the fall: gathering
in the wine grapes and the olives. From the beginning, I've been struck
by the differences in these two activities, and in Olivieri's underlying
attitudes toward wine and oil. We harvest the wine grapes in late September, and the whole Olivieri clan turns out, including distant cousins
who rarely see each other during the year. It's easy, jolly, companionable
work; the warm autumn sun shines green through the fat leaves, and
swarms of fruit flies and wasps and bluebottles buzz in celebration. We
snip the grapes from the vines in heavy bunches, a hundred or more at
once, bunch after bunch until our arms are tired. Now and then we eat
a few grapes, their sweetness and warmth filling our mouths and drib-
bling down our arms, which like our shears are sticky with grape juice.

The olive harvest, by contrast, is bitter. It begins one morning in early
December, when the cold air smells of wood smoke and a raw wind
sluices through the trees. Bundled against the cold, Olivieri and I and a
few of the hardier members of his family walk into his groves carrying
ladders and long canes. We clamber up into the wet-limbed trees, strip
the olives we can reach with our hands and knock down the others with
the canes, into nets spread at the foot of the trees. Unlike the warmth
and ease of the *vendemmia*, this is hard, tiring work, with a constant
risk of falling—I worry about Olivieri with his arthritic knees on those
wobbly ladders. Olive trees have no bunches of fruit dangling there for
the taking. They give up their fruit unwillingly, which we often must
pluck one by one from stubborn stems. Olives offer no sustenance as you
work: most fresh olives are fiercely bitter from the natural antioxidants
they contain.

But the biggest differences come after the harvest. Olivieri makes the wine himself. He has taken enology courses offered by the Italian government and the European Union, and knows the latest methods for filtration, malolactic fermentation, must treatment, and the other arcana of the wine-maker's art. He practices this art in the vaulted cellar beneath his old stone farmhouse, amid the soft drip and simmer of fermenting wine, a place of stillness where he can stop and sip and meditate on his work, as all the while time works on the wine, helping him make it better.

His approach to olives is different. He has never studied olive-growing or oil-making, and employs the same methods he learned from his father and his grandfather, like canes to bring down the fruit, which Roman agronomists already advised against because they knew it bruised the olives. Nor does he make his own oil. Instead he drives his olives to a local mill, where a scene occurs that has been repeated throughout Italy since ancient times: in the noise and the flurry of the crush, as people hurry to process the most olives in the least time, Olivieri walks his fruit through the entire extraction process, olives to paste to oil, to ensure that the miller is not playing tricks—part of the bitter tinge of deceit that oil-making often has.

Olivieri's wine is a respectable white table wine, honest but undistinguished, and he knows it: he calls it his *vinello*, his "little wine," and to celebrate New Year's or a christening he buys a bottle of something better. But he'd never buy someone else's olive oil. Not so much because he thinks his oil is the best in the world, but because to him, at some level, it's the *only* oil. And despite the hardships of the olive harvest, which are considerable for an old farmer whose joints and spine have labored three city lifetimes, Olivieri loves it more than the *vendemmia*. Recently, after our tenth harvest together, I asked him why. He shook his head, as if trying to remember something, and then said, "Because it's harder."

This difficulty brings an attachment to olives that doesn't come with wine. Grapes are wanton, giving away their juice in huge quantities with the gentle pressure of the fingertips. Fresh olives, from a tree that knows the thrift and patience of the desert, cling to their oil—to wring it out you must grind and crush the olives under immense pressure, almost like an act of sacrifice. Olivieri's attachment to the olive harvest, and respect for the fruit and the tree, continues in the oil. The most recent harvest was a good one, and his new oil is the brightest and most complex it's been since I started tasting it ten years ago. I said it was something to be proud of.

"I'm happy, but not proud," he said simply. "I didn't do this. The olives make the oil." This suggests another fundamental difference between wine and oil. Grapes contain not wine but grape juice, which must be transformed by the vintner's art. Oil is already there in the olive, if we can only coax it free. Wine in the final analysis is man-made, while oil is made by nature, through the medium of the strange tree—mysterious, because it comes from something greater than ourselves. Wine in a meal is the soloist, set apart in its gleaming glass, while oil permeates the food, losing itself but subtly changing everything. Wine's effects on us are vivid and swift, while oil works on the body in hidden ways, slow and lingering in the cells and in the mind, like myths. Wine is merry Dionysus; oil is Athena, solemn, wise, and unknowable.

Wine is how we would like life to be, but oil is how life is: fruity, pungent, with a hint of complex bitterness—extra virginity's elusive triad.

GLOSSARY

For a more in-depth glossary of olive oil terms, see *www.extravirginity* *.com*.

Antioxidant – A substance that inhibits oxidation, i.e., a chemical reaction with oxygen. Oxidation, though vital for biological systems, can also produce free radicals and cause cell damage; therefore, plants and animals typically employ antioxidants to reduce oxidative stress. Extra virgin olive oil contains a number of antioxidants, including tocopherol (vitamin E) and a range of **polyphenols**.

Bitter – One of the three characteristics, together with **fruity** and **peppery (or pungent)**, which are mentioned as desirable in the definition of extra virgin olive oil endorsed by the IOC, the EU, the USDA, and many other institutions. Bitterness is often associated with the presence of **antioxidants** and other health-promoting constituents of the oil. A recent survey of olive oil consumers in northern California performed by UC Davis sensory scientists revealed that the majority of consumers disliked oils with marked bitterness or pungency, in sharp contrast to olive oil experts.

Cold-pressed – An outdated production term, now used for marketing purposes and largely devoid of meaning. Until a half-century ago, when oil was made with hydraulic presses, after the first pressing had removed the best oil, the nearly spent paste was drenched with hot water (as Saint Sanctulus of Norcia taught) and pressed again, yielding a second-press oil of inferior quality. Nowadays, extra virgin olive oil is "first-pressed" and "cold-pressed" almost by definition. (EU regulations state that "cold-pressed" can be used only when the olive paste is kept at or below 27 degrees Celsius during the malaxing process—a level respected by nearly all serious producers—and when the oil is actually made with a press, nowadays a rare occurrence.)

Crush, crushing – See **Extraction** and **Milling**.

Cultivar – A distinct variety of olive (or other fruit or vegetable) and of olive tree, which has arisen through selective cultivation, often over many centuries. There are approximately 700 olive cultivars in the world, which frequently have strongly divergent agronomic properties, and produce oils with distinctive sensory, chemical, and nutritional properties. Some of the most commonly grown cultivars are: *arbequina, ascolana, barnea, chemlali, chétoui, cobrancosa, coratina, cornicabra, empeltre, frantoio, galega, hojiblanca, koroneiki, leccino, maurino, manzanillo, memecik, mission, pendolino, picholine, picual, picudo, sevillano, souri,* and *taggiasca.*

Deodorized oil, mild deodorization – Olive oil, typically of low quality, that has undergone a refinement process to remove unpleasant odors and flavors. By law such oil can only be sold as **refined olive oil**, but it is frequently sold, illegally, as extra virgin oil. Many cheap supermarket oils worldwide consist in large part of deodorized oil. One of the most popular deodorizing methods is the SoftColumn refining system by Alfa Laval, the leading producer of extraction equipment for olive oil and other vegetable oils; the company markets SoftColumn for seed oils, but it is reportedly used widely to deodorize olive oil as well. Because deodorization is done at far lower temperatures (40–60 degrees Celsius) than normal refining, and because a number of different deodorizing techniques exist, deodorization is often difficult to detect with chemical tests. New chemical analyses have recently been introduced (a ceiling on the amount of alkyl esters by the EU, measurement of DAGS and PPP by the Australian Olive Association) that should help to reduce the prevalence of deodorized oil—or at least force unscrupulous oil producers to develop new methods of deodorization.

Drupe – The botanical term for a fleshy fruit that usually contains a single hard stone, inside which is a seed. Drupes include olives, cherries, plums, and peaches.

Extraction – A process by which oil is removed from olives (as well as other fruits, nuts, and seeds). Two major types of extraction exist for olive oil, mechanical and solvent extraction, of which the mechanical process alone is allowed for extra virgin oil. In mechanical extraction, the olives are crushed (see **Milling**), the resulting paste is stirred to allow oil microdroplets to coalesce (see **Malaxing**), after which the oil is separated from the paste with a centrifuge or press. In modern extraction systems, centrifuges have replaced hydraulic presses as the technology of choice because they are more efficient and easier to keep clean. Nowadays very few quality oils are made with presses. (See also **Cold-pressed**.) Solvent extraction is widely used in making seed oils and in olive pomace oil.

Extra virgin – The highest quality grade of olive oil, which according to standards established by the IOC, the EU, and other governing bodies, must meet a series of chemical requirements (free fatty acidity of 0.8 percent or lower, peroxides at less than 20 milliequivalents per kilogram, etc.), and be able to pass a **panel test** which demonstrates both that it possesses some detectable level of olive fruitiness, and that it is free of taste **flaws**.

Fat – An organic compound, derived from the adipose tissues of animals and of the fruits, nuts, and seeds of plants, which is made up primarily of **triglycerides**, **free fatty acids**, and associated organic groups. The terms "fat," "oil," and "lipid" are largely interchangeable, though in common usage a fat is solid at room temperature, an oil is liquid at room temperature, and a lipid comprises both fat and oil.

Fatty acids, free fatty acids – Members of a large group of organic acids, particularly those found in animal fats and vegetable oils, which consist of a carboxyl group (COOH) and a chain of carbon and hydrogen atoms, most of which vary from four to twenty-eight carbon atoms in length. The general chemical formula of fatty acids is $CnH2n+1COOH$. When not attached to other molecules, fatty acids are called free fatty acids. Fatty acids may be saturated or unsaturated; unsaturated fatty acids, in turn, are divided into monounsaturated and polyunsaturated fatty acids. The fatty acid composition of olive oil varies depending on many factors, including the olive cultivar, climate, and fruit maturity. The primary fatty acids present in olive oil are oleic acid, which makes up between 50 and 80 percent of most olive oil, together with linoleic acid, and palmitic acid.

Filtration – The process of removing sediment—tiny bits of olive pulp, pit, and skin—suspended in the oil, as well as making an oil more brilliant by running it through a cloth or mesh filter. There is considerable disagreement even among producers about the importance of filtration: improper filtration can attenuate certain flavors and aromas, and many makers of fine oil prefer simply to **rack** their fresh-pressed oil repeatedly. Other top oil-makers swear by filtration, which can significantly increase an oil's shelf life and seems to improve its stability during storage.

First-press – An outdated term, now used for marketing purposes and devoid of meaning. A half-century ago, when oil was made with hydraulic presses, after the first pressing the nearly spent paste was sloshed with hot water and re-pressed, producing an inferior second-press oil. Nowadays, extra virgin olive oil is "first-pressed" and "cold-pressed" almost by definition.

Flavored oils – Olive oils flavored with extracts from a range of fruits, vegetables, and other agricultural products. The best are made by crushing whole fruits or peels (typically of citrus fruit) together with the olives, a process called *agrumato*. Other flavored oils are made by steeping fruit peels in olive oil or by adding extracts to the oil, the latter being the quick-and-dirty method of producing flavored oils.

Flaws, defects – Official off-flavors (and odors) in olive oil that are listed in olive oil legislation and quality protocols, and that, if present, help to determine the quality grade of the oil. They indicate the poor quality of an oil, often caused by unhealthy or overripe fruit, flawed milling techniques, faulty storage, or other errors in the oil-making chain. The sixteen official taste flaws listed by the IOC and in EU law are: fusty (or *atrojado*), mustiness/humidity, muddy sediment, winey/vinegary, metallic, rancid, heated or burnt, hay/wood, rough, greasy, vegetable water, brine, esparto, earthy, grubby, and cucumber.

Free fatty acidity (FFA), free acidity – An important chemical parameter for determining the quality of an olive oil, which is part of the olive oil grading system of the IOC, the EU, the USDA, the Australian Olive Association, and many other bodies that oversee olive oil quality. FFA measures the percentage by weight of the free oleic acid (see **Fatty acids**, **Oleic acid**) contained in a sample of olive oil. In general terms, FFA indicates the breakdown of the basic fat structure of an oil, whether because of poor-quality fruit (due to bruising, olive fly infestation, fungal attack) or, most commonly, by delays between the harvest and the crush. Although a low FFA is no guarantee of good quality, as a rule of thumb the higher the FFA, the more likely the oil is to be of poor quality. The level of 0.8 percent FFA set by the IOC and other regulatory bodies for the extra virgin grade is far too high to guarantee good oil: excellent extra virgin oil frequently has an FFA of 0.2 percent or lower, and anything over 0.5 percent is likely to be inferior.

Fruity – One of the three characteristics, together with **bitter** and **peppery (or pungent)**, which are mentioned as desirable in the definition of extra virgin olive oil endorsed by the IOC, the EU, the USDA, and many other institutions. Fruity refers to a taste or aroma reminiscent of fresh olives. An olive oil must demonstrate some level of fruitiness in order to be legally eligible for the extra virgin grade.

Fusti **(Italian** *fusto***, "tank" or "barrel")** – Stainless steel containers used to store olive oil (as well as wine and other products), typically having a large lid on top that screws off and on.

Hydrogenation, hydrogenated, partially hydrogenated – Refers to a vegetable **oil** that has undergone the industrial process of hydrogenation, during which the oil is heated to 250–400 degrees Fahrenheit, a metal catalyst is added, and hydrogen is bubbled through it. As a result, the fatty acid chains in the oil are artificially saturated with hydrogen atoms, which straightens the chains by removing the kinks that naturally occur at the sites of double bonds. Full hydrogenation yields a fat that is too hard for convenient use in food production, so the process is usually interrupted when the fat is only partially hydrogenated, resulting in a product that is firm but malleable at room temperature and melts when cooked or eaten. The resulting partially hydrogenated (or hydrogenated) fat is a **trans fat**, and has significant health risks when eaten.

Hydroxytyrosol – A polyphenol and powerful antioxidant contained in olives, olive oil, and olive leaves. Its use as a supplement or preservative is being explored by the nutraceutical, cosmeceutical, and food industries. Recent experimentation suggests that hydroxytyrosol, thanks to its potent antioxidant activity, helps prevent DNA damage and the harmful oxidation of LDL ("bad") cholesterol; medical research also suggests that it works against cardiovascular disease by inhibiting platelet aggregation and pro-inflammatory enzymes.

Invaiatura – The Italian term (in English, the French term *véraison* is often used) for the phase in the maturation of the olive, and other fruits, during which the green coloration of the young, unripe fruit gives way to the darker oranges, reds, and purples of more mature fruit. Many olive growers use the *invaiatura* as a signal to begin their harvest, because it marks a balance between the marked flavors and aromas of young, early harvest fruit and the higher oil content of later-harvest fruit.

IOC – International Olive Council, an intergovernmental agency instituted by the United Nations in 1959, aimed to supply aid and advice to growers and millers, fund research in oil quality and chemistry, and promote olive oil consumption worldwide. The IOC currently has forty-three member nations (counting the EU and EU nations), olive-growing and oil-producing countries primarily located around the Mediterranean which make 98 percent of the world's olive oil.

Lampante – Literally "lamp oil," from the Italian *lampa* ("lamp"), *lampante* is the lowest grade of olive oil in the quality grading system of the IOC. By law it is unfit for human consumption, and must be refined before it can be sold as food.

Light olive oil – A marketing term for **refined olive oil**. See also **Olive oil**, **Pure olive oil**.

Linoleic acid – One of the main **fatty acids** in olive oil. Linoleic acid is polyunsaturated, and constitutes anywhere between about 4 and 21 percent of most olive oils.

Linolenic acid – One of the main **fatty acids** in olive oil. Linolenic acid is polyunsaturated, and constitutes up to about 1.5 percent of most olive oils.

Malaxer, malaxing – The second major phase of the olive oil **extraction** process after **milling**, during which the olive paste made from ground-up olives is mixed or stirred to allow the microdroplets of oil in the paste to coalesce into larger drops that are more easily extracted. A modern malaxer is a stainless steel trough with a fan screw turning along the bottom. Malaxing lasts twenty to forty minutes, depending on the cultivar, the condition and ripeness of the olives, and other factors. Shorter malaxing times help minimize oxidation and **free acidity**, while longer times increase oil yield and may improve oil flavor but typically reduce shelf life. (The term is derived from the ancient Greek *malassein*, "to make soft.")

Milling – The first part of the oil **extraction** process, in which olives are ground or crushed using one of several different machines. Traditional mills used millstones in a number of different shapes, originally turned by animal or hydraulic power and later by motors. Motor-driven millstones are still widely used, though they are being replaced by crushing devices that grind the fruit with stainless steel hammers, disks, and other mechanisms, which cause less oxidation of the oil.

Oil – Generally speaking, an oil is a **fat** that is in a liquid state at room temperature.

Oleic acid – The primary **fatty acid** in olive oil, which is monounsaturated, and constitutes between 50 and 80 percent of most olive oils. Because of a lipid profile that is relatively resistant to oxidation, oleic acid gives olive oil a longer shelf life than most other oils. Oleic acid has been associated with some of the major health benefits of the Mediterranean diet, such as a reduced incidence of coronary heart disease and cancer, and a 2005 study done at the Northwestern University Feinberg School of Medicine showed that oleic acid can cripple a gene that causes 25 to 30 percent of breast cancers.

Oleocanthal – A **polyphenol** that naturally occurs in quality extra virgin olive oil, which is a strong **antioxidant** and a powerful anti-inflammatory with properties that resemble those of ibuprofen. The peppery throat-sting caused by oleocanthal, first discovered by a team of Unilever scientists and later studied in detail by Gary Beauchamp and colleagues at Monell Chemical Senses Center, is also very similar to that caused by ibuprofen. Research has revealed that many olive oils contain comparatively large quantities of oleocanthal, and suggests that the substance may have therapeutic effects against coronary heart disease, stroke, cancer, Alzheimer's disease, and other conditions.

Olive oil – A marketing term for **refined olive oil** that has been blended with a small amount of extra virgin olive oil to give it flavor. See also **Light olive oil, Pure olive oil.**

PAHs (polycyclic aromatic hydrocarbons) – A family of chemical compounds formed during the incomplete combustion of organic substances, which have been shown to cause cancer as well as genetic and neurological damage. While trace amounts of PAHs are present in many foods, illegally high levels of PAHs have been detected by European health officials in certain olive pomace oils.

Palmitic acid – One of the main **fatty acids** in olive oil, palmitic acid is saturated, and constitutes between 8 and 20 percent of most olive oils.

Panel test – The official sensory analysis of olive oil, performed by a **taste panel**, which, together with a battery of chemical analyses, is part of the legal method for determining the quality grade of a given sample of olive oil.

PDO ("Protected Designation of Origin," DOP in Italian) – A legal designation by the European Union, similar to the *Appellation d'origine contrôlée* designation in French wines, for foods that are produced or processed in a specific region using traditional production methods. One of these food products is extra virgin olive oil; a number of PDO oils have been designated in Italy, Spain, Greece, and elsewhere in southern Europe. The production process of PDO oils is laid down by a specific protocol and overseen by a quality control committee, which helps to ensure the quality of the oil. PDO status is legally binding within the European Union, and is gradually being extended via bilateral agreements to areas outside the EU.

Peppery (or pungent) – One of the three characteristics, together with **fruity** and **bitter**, which are mentioned as desirable in the definition of extra virgin olive oil endorsed by the IOC, the EU, the USDA, and many other institutions. Pepperiness is often associated with the presence of a number of health-promoting constituents in the oil. A recent survey of olive oil consumers in northern California performed by UC Davis sensory scientists revealed that the majority of consumers disliked oils with marked pungency or bitterness, in stark contrast to the preferences of experienced olive oil tasters.

Peroxides – An important chemical parameter for the quality of olive oil, which is part of the olive oil grading system of the IOC, the EU, the USDA, the Australian Olive Association, and many other olive oil bodies. Generally speaking, an oil's peroxide value indicates the extent to which it has been oxidized, typically through degradation by free radicals or by exposure to light. The peroxide levels for the extra virgin grade set by the IOC and many other bodies—less than 20 milliequivalents per kilogram—are far too high to guarantee good oil, which frequently has peroxides at well below 10 meq/kg.

PGI ("Protected Geographical Indication," IGP in Italian) – A legal designation by the EU which is similar to **PDO**, though less stringent. PGI status requires that at least one phase in the production of a product must occur in a given geographic region. (In the case of extra virgin olive oil, for example, the olives may be grown in the PGI region but milled elsewhere.)

Polyphenols – A generic term for a range of phytochemicals contained in olive oil and other natural substances, many of which demonstrate **antioxidant** and anti-inflammatory properties. Polyphenols are widely held by medical researchers to have a range of positive health effects against such pathologies as cardiovascular disease, cancer, and Alzheimer's disease. Because they protect against oxidation, polyphenols also protect olive oil against spoilage.

Pomace, olive pomace oil – An oil extracted from olive pomace—the solid waste left over from the **extraction** process, composed primarily of olive pits, skin, and flesh—using hexane or another industrial solvent, then highly refined. Though frequently sold in ways that lead consumers to believe it is olive oil, olive pomace oil is actually a very different substance, with far fewer health benefits and several potential health risks (food safety authorities have found certain batches of olive pomace oil to contain mineral oil and **PAHs**). The oversight of olive pomace oil production is often limited; in Italy, for example, pomace oil can be produced in facilities that are not officially designated for food production.

Pure olive oil – A marketing term for **refined olive oil** that has been blended with a small amount of extra virgin olive oil to give it flavor. See also **Light olive oil**, **Olive oil**.

Racking – After olive oil is extracted from the olives (see **Extraction**), it is commonly left in a tank for a period of weeks to allow the tiny pieces of olive pulp, skin, and pit that are suspended in the oil to settle out. During the racking process, the oil-maker decants the oil several times and removes the sediment at the bottom of the tank, which could otherwise give the oil off-flavors.

Rancid, rancidity – Unpleasant odor or taste from an olive oil (or other oil or fat) that has undergone extensive oxidation. See also **Flaws**.

Refined olive oil – Olive oil that has undergone a chemical and physical refinement process, rendering it tasteless, odorless, and colorless. In sales jargon, "refined olive oil" is a blend of refined olive oil and a small portion of extra virgin olive oil, which gives the resulting mixture flavor, aroma, and color. See also **Light olive oil**, **Olive oil**, **Pure olive oil**, and **Refining**.

Refining – Vegetable oil refining is the series of chemical and physical steps by which odors, tastes, colors, and other characteristics, typically unpleasant, are removed from olive oil or any other oil made from seeds, fruits, or nuts. These steps typically include alkali refining, water refining (or "degumming"), bleaching, winterizing (or "destearinating"), and deodorizing (see also **Deodorized oil**). During alkali refining, the oil is heated and mixed with an alkaline substance such as sodium carbonate or sodium hydroxide, which causes free fatty acids (see **Free fatty acidity**) and other undesirable elements to settle out of the oil in the form of soap. Water refining or degumming involves treating the oil with hot water, steam, or water mixed with acid, followed by centrifugation, which removes gummy phospholipids contained in the oil. During the bleaching process, an oil's pigments are elimated with filtering agents like fuller's earth or activated carbon. In winterizing or destearinating, an oil is rapidly chilled and filtered, thereby lowering the temperature at which it will begin to solidify. Deodorization involves heating an oil (typically to temperatures between 175 and 250 degrees Celcius), placing it under high vacuum, and blowing steam through it to distill out unpleasant tastes and aromas. Olive oil is one of the very few vegetable oils that does not require refining; since the refining process removes tastes, aromas, and many health-promoting attributes of olive oil, no refined olive oil can legally be sold as extra virgin oil.

Smoke point – The heat at which olive oil, or any other cooking fat or oil, begins to produce an acrid, bluish smoke. This event signals the degradation of the flavor and nutritional characteristics of the oil; when cooking with a given oil, care should be taken to keep the temperature below the smoke point of that oil. Generally speaking, the higher the quality of an extra virgin olive oil—and in particular the lower its **free fatty acidity**—the higher its smoke point. Fine oils have a smoke point of about 210 degrees Celsius, while lower-grade quasi–extra virgins begin to smoke at about 185 degrees Celsius.

Strippaggio – The slurp made by an oil-taster after taking an oil sample into his mouth, which allows a more complete sensory impression of the oil than would be possible by simply tasting it. During *strippaggio*, air drawn in rapidly at the corners of the mouth creates an emulsion of air, oil, and saliva, and distributes it evenly over the tongue's papillae. *Strippaggio* also draws the aromatic molecules of the oil up into the nasal passages, where, through a process known as retro-nasal olfaction, a far wider range of aromas can be perceived than in the mouth itself—and with far greater precision (at a parts-per-trillion level with certain aromas). (The term *strippaggio* derives from the English word "stripping," which in the context of chemistry is a separation process by which a liquid substance is transferred into its vapor phase by physical means.)

Super-high-density (SHD) – A system of olive cultivation in which 700 to 900 trees are planted to the acre, set in hedgerows like row crops, and the olives are picked by large, over-the-row harvesters. (Traditional olive groves, which are picked by hand or with simpler shaking or combing devices, contain about 100 trees to the acre, while medium-density groves hold between 200 and 400 trees per acre.) At present only a few olive cultivars are compatible with the SHD model, so the range of oils that can be made in this manner is limited; some critics also suggest that the extensive irrigation and fertilizers used in SHD and the violence of the mechanical harvesting system itself may impair oil quality. However, after the high initial costs required to set up an SHD orchard, harvests are quick compared to those in traditional groves, which reduces costs and minimizes the time between picking and crushing.

Taste panel – The team of eight tasters and one panel leader who perform the **panel test** on olive oil. The tasters and panel leader have all been trained to recognize the official characteristics of olive oil, both positive and negative, and to assess the relative intensities of these characteristics.

Tocopherols – A group of organic compounds which, together with related compounds called tocotrienols, are collectively referred to as "vitamin E." Tocopherols have pronounced antioxidant properties, and have been used in the cosmetics industry to shield the skin from sun damage.

Trans fat – A **fat** containing one or more unsaturated **fatty acids** which have a transisomer, produced (with a few minor, naturally occurring exceptions) through the industrial process of **hydrogenation**. Trans fats are widely employed in processed foods because of their superior workability and shelf life as compared to naturally occurring fats and oils. Health authorities worldwide recognize that consumption of trans fats increases the risk of coronary heart disease, because trans fats raise the level of LDL ("bad") cholesterol in the blood and lower HDL ("good") cholesterol. According to the National Academy of Sciences of America, there is no safe level of trans fat consumption.

Triglycerides (or triacylglycerols) – The main constituent of vegetable and animal fats, and a vital energy storage source for plants and animals. Triglycerides consist of three fatty acids bonded to a glycerol molecule.

Unfiltered oil – Olive oil that has not undergone **filtration**. The choice between unfiltered and filtered oil is mainly a matter of taste.

While filtration does extend shelf life and appears to improve stability during storage, it may slightly reduce the intensity of tastes and aromas in certain oils. Among premium extra virgin olive oils, the consumer's main choice is between the clarity and brilliance of filtered oils and the cloudy density of unfiltered oils.

Virgin – The intermediate quality grade of olive oil between superior **extra virgin** and inferior *lampante*, all three of which are technically known as **virgin olive oils**. Once common in stores, virgin olive oil has largely disappeared in recent years, as the de facto quality (and price) of extra virgin oil has dropped, and many virgin oils are now being labeled as extra virgin.

Virgin olive oils – Oils made from olive fruit with mechanical methods alone, such as washing and crushing the olives, malaxing and centrifuging their pulp, and filtering the resulting oil. No chemical, thermal, or other nonphysical methods, such as reesterification, are allowed in the production of virgin oils. Within the category of virgin oils, **extra virgin** oil is the highest grade, **virgin** is the next highest, and *lampante* is the lowest.

Appendix

. . . .

CHOOSING GOOD OIL

- See www.extravirginity.com for extensive information and up-to-date resources for buying and enjoying good oil.

- Find a store where you can taste olive oils before you buy them, and where the staff can answer a few basic questions about how, where, and by whom they were made. Specialty olive oil stores and oil bars are becoming more common, and a growing number of delicatessens, markets, and supermarkets have an oil bar. Four model institutions are the Olive Press in Sonoma, California, Amphora Nueva in Berkeley, California, Eataly in Manhattan, and Zingerman's Delicatessen in Ann Arbor, Michigan. Nationwide franchise chains like Oil & Vinegar (www.oilandvinegarusa.com) and We Olive (www.weolive .com) need to continue to concentrate on maintaining high quality in their oils, but they do offer a wide selection and knowledgeable salespeople.

- When you have to buy oil without being able to taste it first, choose a store that performs stringent quality control in its production and selection of oils, such as the Olive Press (www.theolivepress.com), Zingerman's (www.zingermans.com), Beyond the Olive (www.beyond theolive.com), or Corti Brothers (www.cortibros.biz).

- Unlike many wines, which improve with age, extra virgin olive oil is perishable: like all natural fruit juices, its flavor and aroma begin to deteriorate within a few months of milling, a decline that can accelerate when the oil is bottled. To get the freshest oil, and cut out middle-men who often muddy olive oil transparency and quality, buy as close to the mill as possible. If you can't actually buy at an olive mill, find a seller who purchases excellent oil in bulk rather than in bottles or tins, and stores it in clean, temperature-controlled stainless steel containers topped with an inert gas like nitrogen to keep oxygen at bay. Failing this, look for olive oil purveyors that store their bottled oil in a cool, dark warehouse and have high turnover, which helps to ensure that the oil is fresh.

- When choosing bottled oil, prefer dark glass bottles or other containers that protect against light, and buy a quantity that you'll use up quickly. Even an excellent oil can rapidly go rancid when left sitting under a half-bottle of air.

- Don't pay much attention to the color of an oil. Good oils come in all shades, from vivid green to gold to pale straw, and official tasters actually use colored glasses to avoid prejudicing themselves in favor of greener oils. Both in flavor and aroma, genuine extra virgin oils have a marked fruitiness reminiscent of fresh olives, and typically some level of bitterness and pepperiness. In great oils these characteristics are harmoniously balanced, together with complex aromas, flavors, and aftertastes that bloom gradually on the senses.

- Don't be put off by bitterness or pungency—remember that these are usually indicators of the presence of healthful antioxidants—unless one of these characteristics is overwhelming and disproportionate to the others.

- Above all, seek out freshness, choosing oils that smell and taste vibrant and lively, and avoid tastes and odors such as moldy, rancid, cooked, greasy, meaty, metallic, and cardboard. Also pay attention to mouthfeel: prefer crisp and clean to flabby, coarse, or greasy.

- Labels: If you aren't able to taste an oil or get help from a knowledge-able salesperson, you'll have to rely on the label for information about the oil. To begin with, ensure that your oil is labeled "extra virgin," since other categories—"pure" or "light" oil, "olive oil," not to mention "olive pomace oil"—have undergone chemical refinement which strips away olive flavors and many of the oil's health benefits.

- To ensure freshness, look for bottles with a "best by" date, or better still a date of harvest. Try to buy oils only from this year's harvest. "Best by" date are usually two years after an oil was bottled, so if you see a date that is two years away, the oil is more likely to be fresh. That said, many olive oils, particularly in the EU, are stored for years before being bottled, yet their "best by" dates are (wrongly) determined by the date of bottling, not of harvest. In fact, most supermarket extra virgins are blends of fresher oil from more recent harvests with flatter oil from earlier harvests. So far, no system has been found to calibrate the "best by" date to the chemical freshness of the oil when it is packed.

- Phrases like "packed in Italy" or "bottled in Italy" do not mean that an oil was made in Italy, much less that it was made from Italian olives. Italy is one of the world's major importers of olive oil, much of which originates in Spain, Greece, Tunisia, and elsewhere, so don't be taken in by Italian flags and scenes of the Tuscan countryside on the packaging. Some of the oil imported into Italy is consumed by Italians, but much of it is blended, packed, and re-exported. Generally speaking, avoid oils whose precise point of production—a specific mill—is not specified on the label.

- Chemical parameters like free fatty acidity (FFA) and peroxides are sometimes mentioned on olive oil bottles. In general terms, FFA indicates the breakdown of the basic fat structure of an oil, whether due to poor-quality fruit (bruising, olive fly infestation, fungal attack) or, most commonly, by delays between harvest and extraction of the oil; a low FFA doesn't guarantee high quality, but high FFA almost always means poor oil. An oil's peroxide value indicates the extent to which a young oil has been oxidized, typically through breakdown by free radicals or by exposure to light. The levels set by the IOC and the EU (and followed recently by the USDA) for the extra virgin grade— 0.8 percent FFA and a peroxide value of less than 20 milliequivalents per kilo—are by no means stringent enough to guarantee a good oil, which frequently has 0.2 percent or lower FFA and peroxides at well below 10 meq/kg.

- An oil's polyphenol content contributes significantly to its anti-oxidant properties, and is therefore an important indicator of a range of health-giving characteristics, taste qualities, and shelf life (polyphenols work to preserve the oil as well as the bodies of those who consume it). The IOC recently approved a method of measuring an oil's polyphenol content, so this indicator may become increasingly common on olive oil labels. At least in health terms, the higher the rating the better, with numbers below 300 being low, and above 500 high—though the latter can be too bitter, peppery, or both for many consumers. (Some oils rate as high as 800 in polyphenols.)

- Though not always a guarantee of quality, several certifications mentioned on olive oil labels should provide a level of confidence that an oil has been properly made.
  - PDO and PGI status (see Glossary)
  - Organically grown
  - Olive oils certified by national and state olive oil associations, such as the Australian Olive Association, the California Olive Oil Council, and the Association 3E. The North American Olive Oil Association and the International Olive Council also run certification programs.

- Oils that scored well in recent, reputable olive oil contests are often a good choice, especially when the oil you are buying is from the same harvest as the oil that won the award (and not from a decade or more later). Leading olive oil contests include:
  - Sol d'Oro (Verona, Italy): www.sol-verona.com
  - Mario Solinas: www.internationaloliveoil.org/estaticos/view/227-mario-solinas-quality-award-of-the-international-olive-council
  - Ercole Olivario: www.ercoleolivario.org

- Los Angeles International Extra Virgin Olive Oil Competition: www.fairplex.com/wos/olive_oil_competition
- Yolo County Fair Olive Oil Competition: www.yolocountyfair .net/html/olive_oil_competition.html
- The National Extra Virgin Olive Oil Show run by the Australian Olive Association: www.australianolives.com.au/web/ index.php?option=com_content&task=blogcategory&id=61&I temid=321

For information on some of the more prominent olive oil competitions around the world, see www.oliveoiltimes.com/reviews-opin ions/extravirgin-olive-oil-competitionsandwww.oliveoilsource.com/ competitions.

- Start noticing the cultivars of olives that are used to make the oils you like best, as you do the grape varietals of your favorite wines. (See Glossary under **Cultivar**.)
- Certain terms commonly used on olive oil labels are anachronistic, and sometimes indicate that the producer is paying more attention to the image of an oil than to what's actually inside the bottle. Take the terms "first pressed" and "cold pressed," for example. Since most extra virgin oil nowadays is made with centrifuges, it isn't "pressed" at all, and all true extra virgin oil comes exclusively from the first processing of the olive paste. EU regulations state that "cold pressed" can be used only when the olive paste is kept at or below 27 degrees Celsius during the malaxing process, a level respected by nearly all serious producers—and when the oil is actually extracted with a press, not a centrifuge.
- Unfiltered oil and filtration: Some consumers view unfiltered olive oil, with tiny bits of olive pulp and skin floating in it, as more authentic and flavorful. Improper or excessive filtration can attenuate certain flavors and aromas, and most makers of fine oil prefer simply to rack their fresh-pressed oil repeatedly, removing sediment, rather than to filter it. However, other top oil-makers swear by filtration, which can significantly increase an oil's shelf life. In either case, be on

the lookout for a layer of sediment at the bottom of the bottle, which often spoils faster than the oil itself, and can produce the taste flaw of muddy sediment.

- As you would with a wine, choose a style of oil that fits the role it will play in your meals. Pick a powerful oil—variously described as "robust," "early harvest," or "full-bodied"—to accompany foods with strong or distinctive flavors, such as pepper steak; *bruschetta* or *fett'unta* (toasted bread with oil and salt, often rubbed with garlic); fresh, flavorful vegetables like arugula; or to drizzle over vanilla ice cream (try it before you scoff!). Choose a milder oil—often called "mild," "delicate fruit," or "late harvest"—for foods like fish, chicken, or potatoes.

- Olive oils may be flavored with a range of fruit, vegetable, and other extracts; some of the most popular are made with lemons, blood oranges, and other citrus fruits. While many olive oil cognoscenti (and most Europeans) turn up their noses at these oils, they have a wide following in North America and Down Under. The best are made by crushing whole fruit or peels together with the olives, a process called *agrumato*. Make sure that the base oil flavor isn't rancid, and that the flavoring itself is fresh and not artificial tasting.

- Avoid bargain prices, because producing genuine extra virgin oil is expensive. Though high prices don't guarantee great oil, low prices—under about $10 for a liter—strongly suggest that the oil you're buying is inferior. Having stated these general guidelines, it's worth considering two potential exceptions. First, new, mechanized methods of olive growing and harvesting (such as super-high-density cultivation—see Glossary) are reducing production costs, allowing excellent oils to be made at lower prices than with traditional methods. Second, government subsidies to olive growers and oil-makers in the European Union and elsewhere allow subsidized producers to charge far lower retail prices for their oils than producers in the US and Australia, where no subsidies exist.

- Once you've bought your oil, store it in a place where it's protected from light, heat, and oxygen, the three enemies of good oil, which speed spoilage. And don't hoard it! Even great oils deteriorate with each passing day, and all too soon will become ordinary, even rancid, if not used quickly.

- There is a great deal of disagreement, and a fair bit of misinformation, concerning whether to use extra virgin olive oil, rather than refined ("pure," "light") olive oil, for frying. Quality extra virgin olive oil is a fine choice for sautéing and shallow frying, so long as its flavor doesn't overpower the food; an aggressive early harvest oil would be a poor choice to sauté fish, for example. Using extra virgin olive oil for deep-fat frying at higher temperatures is uneconomical and can even be counterproductive, because the cooking process sometimes accentuates the harsh flavors in the oil, and many of the flavors and aromas of fine oils will volatilize and disappear. Refined olive oil is probably a better choice for deep-fat frying, though there are undoubtedly many milder extra virgin olive oils that hold up well to frying—the lower an oil's free fatty acidity, the higher its smoke point (the temperature at which it begins to smoke and produce unpleasant, unhealthy by-products), and the more times it can be reused. (Each time the oil is heated its acidity rises, meaning that its smoke point and quality both decline.)

- Depending on their composition, most olive oils harden when chilled to around 3 degrees Celsius. As they cool, a waxy sediment settles out of them. Freezing does not harm an oil—in fact, it's a good way of preserving oil—but may reduce its shelf life if substantial sediment is produced. The idea that the freezing point of an oil indicates whether an oil is adulterated is a myth. For more details see the excellent précis at www.oliveoilsource.com/page/freezing-olive-oil.

- See www.extravirginity.com for a wide range of web resources about oil. Websites for further information on extra virgin olive oil include the following:

  - Olive Oil Times (www.oliveoiltimes.com): The best source for daily news from the olive oil world.

- Olive Oil Source (www.oliveoilsource.com): An excellent and diverse array of resources covering many aspects of olive oil chemistry, tasting, and production.

- Teatro Naturale (www.teatronaturale.it in Italian and www .teatronaturale.com in English; the Italian site is better and more comprehensive): Olive oil news from many European perspectives, sometimes taking the side of larger producers and bottlers.

- UC Davis Olive Center (http://olivecenter.ucdavis.edu/): The new olive oil research center at one of America's most important agricultural universities, which has an IOC-recognized taste panel and performs important research into sensory analysis. The UC Davis Olive Center has the potential to become one of the world's leading voices regarding extra virgin olive oil.

- Slick Extra Virgin (www.aromadictionary.com/EVOO_blog/): A highly entertaining and informative blog by Richard Gawel, Australian chemist, oil taster, and consultant who is as meticulous about facts as he is caustic about slippery behavior in oil. Gawel also sells an ingenious plasticized wheel laying out the terms used in oil tasting, which is a convenient reference tool.

- ONAOO (www.oliveoil.org): A good site, in Italian and English, by one of the premier olive oil associations in the world, the National Organization of Olive Oil Tasters, located in Imperia, Italy.

- Association 3E (www.super-premium-olive-oil.com): A perceptive look at both the philosophical and the pragmatic aspects of quality in olive oil, and an introduction to "super-premium olive oil," which 3E proposes as a new designation for top-quality oil, to replace the by now meaningless adjective "extra virgin."

- Modern Olives (www.modernolives.com.au): The premier laboratory for the chemical analysis of olive oil in Australia, and in the world.

- California Olive Oil Council (www.cooc.com): The leading

association of olive growers and oil producers in America, which compiles a list of certified oil producers (www.cooc.com/pro ducers_certified.html) and offers a range of other useful information. The COOC has its own taste panel.

- North American Olive Oil Association (http://naooa.org/): The trade association of the olive oil importers in the United States, which runs quality tests and a certification program, and recently encouraged the USDA to upgrade its trade standard for olive oil to meet international norms.

- The Olive Press (www.theolivepress.com): The slick website of the equally slick Sonoma oil mill and shop.

- Australian Olive Association (www.australianolives.com.au/web/) The trade association of the Australian olive oil industry, whose stress on olive growing and oil-making skills as well as innovative chemical testing has pushed the envelope of olive oil quality throughout the world.

- *Merum* (www.merum.info): The superb, opinionated, highly informed website of Andreas März, which considers a wide range of Italian oils and wines (in German).

- Zingerman's (www.zingermans.com): One of the best selections of olive oils—and a great many other exotic foods—available by mail-order in America.

- Harold McGee (http://news.curiouscook.com/): Journeys through the science of food, including olive oil, led by a world authority in the chemistry of food and cooking.

- International Olive Council (www.internationaloliveoil.org): The historic intergovernmental olive oil body representing growers in countries around the Mediterranean, whose tasting protocol helped create the modern definition of extra virgin.

- Corporazione Mastri Oleari (www.mastrioleari.it): An authoritative group of top extra virgin olive oil producers (in Italian).

- Veronica Foods (www.evoliveoil.com): A high-quality source of olive oil for a growing number of specialty stores across America, as well as its own outlet Amphora Nueva in Berkeley, California (http://amphoranueva.com).

- Marco Oreggia (www.marco-oreggia.com/default/htm): An independent olive oil taster who writes one of the more important yearly guides to top olive oils worldwide (in Italian and English).

- UCCE Sonoma (http://cesonoma.ucdavis.edu): High-class technical resources for olive growers and millers.

- Slow Food (www.slowfood.com): The global food NGO offers important information on top oils and oil producers, and compiles a yearly guidebook (in Italian) that is required reading for oil aficionados.

- Gambero Rosso (www.gamberorosso.it): A leading Italian wine and food association whose new guide to Italian extra virgins, updated each year, is a useful reference.

ACKNOWLEDGMENTS

Though olive oil has been made for millennia, little has been written about producing good oil, and surprisingly few generally accepted truths exist, even among generally accepted experts, about oil quality, production, nutrition, chemistry, regulation, labeling, crime, and punishment. Therefore, the vast majority of the data on which this book is based came not from written sources, but from conversations on the front lines of oil, with growers, oil-makers, salesmen, and scholars. Because of the absence of canonical wisdom about olive oil, these authorities themselves often disagree, even violently, about the basic truths of oil. I've frequently had to navigate among their widely disparate views, while endeavouring to avoid the treacherous shoals of opinion, rumor, and half-truth. The satisfactions of making great oil (and even bad oil) normally go far beyond money, since earning a living in high-quality oil has become extremely difficult in many countries. Olive oil soaks into people's family histories, their cultural roots, their mythic and poetic imaginations. Oil is a substance of strange intimacy, and making it is a very personal occupation.

For all these reasons, *Extra Virginity* is as much about the people who produce olive oil, good and bad, as it is about the oil itself. While writing this book, I've had the good fortune to meet many hundreds of oil people, some larger-than-life, others soft-spoken and shy, but most with a deep pride and conviction in what they do. I've walked with them through olive groves and oil mills on four continents, watched them perform chemical analyses, heard them explain marketing strategies and tease out legal arcana. Above all I've tasted their oil, sometimes humble, other times magnificent, as they've looked on expectantly; then we've discussed their views on this mysterious foodstuff. Even where I disagree strongly with their beliefs about oil, or object to their activities, they have taught me much. I wish to thank some of these people here, publically and gratefully. Many more I can't identify, because they spoke to me on condition of anonymity, but my heartfelt thanks go to them nonetheless—you know who you are!

I am grateful to numerous officials of the Carabinieri, the Guardia Forestale, the Fraud Repression and Quality Control office of the Italian Agriculture Ministry, and other Italian police forces and investigative corps, who took time off from more pressing activities and investigations to speak with me. Particular thanks go to the Guardia di Finanza, without whose superb investigative work and frequent, generous help, from corporals and major generals alike, I wouldn't have been able to write large sections of this book. Likewise Domenico Seccia, Pasquale Drago, Michele Ruggiero, and a number of other investigative magistrates in Italy provided invaluable information and interpretations, and functionaries in various district courts and appeals courts throughout Italy, including the Supreme Court in Rome, helped in locating and parsing court documents. Officials of OLAF, the anti-fraud office of the European Union, likewise supported my work, notably the impressive Alessandro Butticé and the former director of the agriculture unit, Elisabeth Sperber. Regarding the generous assistance I received from EU officials, I wish in particular to acknowledge Paulo Casaca, Vincenzo Lavarra, Michael Mann, Antonio Bellucci, and Umberto Guidoni. Thanks to Rudy Filko and Mike Drewniak at the New Jersey district attorney's office for details on oil adulteration cases in America, and members of the Food and Drug Administration, past and present, including Martin Stutsman, David Firestone, and Michael Herndon, for vital data on US government oversight of olive oil and, more broadly, on the American food supply. I received essential legal advice from Ed Davis of Davis

Wright Tremaine; Alberto Russo of Studio Legale Associato Russo; Giorgio Fontana of Studio Legale Associato Avvocato Fontana Giorgio; Tim Macht of Macht, Shapiro, Arato & Isserles; Marvin L. Frank of Murray, Frank & Sailer; Bruno Cova of Paul Hastings; and Mark Greenberg at UCLA.

Regarding the history of olive oil from classical times to the present, a number of scholars gave me the benefit of their vast erudition, including David Mattingly at the University of Leicester, Nigel Kennell at the American School of Classical Studies at Athens, Tom Scanlon at the University of California, Riverside, Angelo Bartoli at the Centro di Archeologia Sperimentale "Antiquitates" di Blera, Giordano Sivini at the University of Calabria, Massimo Montanari of the University of Bologna and Andrea Brugnoli at the Centro di Documentazione per la Storia della Valpolicella. Henry Blackburn at the University of Minnesota told me amusing and illuminating anecdotes about the work of Ancel Keys in the Mediterranean. While I was in Cyprus, Maria Rosaria Belgiorno of the Italian Consiglio Nazionale delle Ricerche was an inexhaustible source of information and splendid images (not to mention *meze*), particularly regarding the excavations she directs at the Bronze Age site of Pyrgos. Jean-Pierre Brun of the Centre Jean Bérard of the University of Naples and the French Centre National de la Récherche Scientifique, in addition to the treasure trove of his four-volume history of olive oil and wine, generously provided images for my book, as did José Remesal at the University of Barcelona, a leading authority on the amphorae of Monte Testaccio. More help with amphorae came from David Williams at the University of Southampton, and the impressive Amphora Project web resource which he helps to run. Tina Mirra, Paolo Imperatori, Denise Gavio, Simonetta Serra, and the rest of the team at the American Academy in Rome, my old stomping ground, furthered my research in this project, as they have in many others, and dosed me with espresso and fine oil when my energies flagged.

A number of distinguished olive oil organizations aided and guided me. Among these I wish to thank the Corporazione Mastri Oleari in

Milan and its indomitable director, Flavio Zaramella, sine qua non. Dan Flynn and his staff at the University of California, Davis, Olive Center helped me understand the vagaries of the US oil market and of California olive-growing. Bob Bauer at North American Olive Oil Association shared important information on the US market and its various players. Thanks also to the International Olive Council in Madrid, especially Francesco Serafini and former director Fausto Luchetti, and to Fabrizio Vignolini and the staff of ONAOO in Imperia.

Thanks to Marco Mugelli and Lamberto Baccioni, two independent oil-making consultants (Mugelli also makes superb oil), for insights on cutting-edge oil processing technology; Andrea Giomo for a range of erudition about olive oil processing, tasting, sex, statistics, and marketing; and Roberto D'Auria at the Istituto di Servizi per il Mercato Agricolo Alimentare (ISTAT) for a valuable overview of olive oil economics. Freelance olive oil consultant and educator Alexandra Kicenik Devarenne has instructed me in oil-making in California and beyond, and assisted me in countless other ways. Journalists and writers who furthered my work include Bernardo Iovene at RAI 3, Toni Mira of *Avvenire*, Roberto De Petro of TeleNorba, Giuseppe De Tomaso of *La Gazzetta del Mezzogiorno*, wine and culinary critic Isao Miyajima, and Luigi Caricato at *Teatro Naturale*, who shared acute observations and valuable contacts drawn from a lifetime of thinking about olive oil, both good and bad. Claudio Peri, founder and president of Association 3E, challenged me to think more clearly about the technology of food quality, and the philosophy of excellence in olive oil. Don Celso Bidin, monk and olive-miller at the Monte Oliveto Maggiore abbey in Tuscany, and Don Luigi Ciotti, founder and president of Libera, Associazioni, Nomi e Numeri Contro le Mafie ("Associations, Names and Numbers Against the Mafias"), taught me about the spiritual and liturgical roles of olive oil, past and present, while Alessandro Leo, head of the Terre di Puglia agricultural cooperative, demonstrated for me the courage needed to make oil on lands formerly owned by, and still under the shadow of, organized crime. While on the subject of bravery, I salute Antonio

Barile, president in Puglia of the Italian farm union CIA, an expert, ingenious, and tireless force in defense of farmers and consumers alike.

A number of lipid chemists and food quality specialists patiently taught me olive oil from the inside out and the molecules up. Most notable among these are Lanfranco Conte at the University of Udine and Alissa Mattei, formerly of Carapelli and now of Casa Montecucco, two people whose hospitality and wit are as finely tuned as their science. Thanks also to Giovanni Lercker at the University of Bologna; Ed Frankel at the University of California, Davis; Gary Beauchamp at Monell Chemical Senses Center; and Giorgio Cardone at Chemiservice. Agronomists Paul Vossen at the University of California Cooperative Extension, Zeev Wiesman at the Ben-Gurion University of the Negev, Gianluigi Cesari at the Istituto Agronomico Mediterraneo di Bari, and David Lee at the National Institute of Agricultural Botany in the UK helped firm up my grasp of the botanical and genetic enigmas of the olive tree itself, just as sensory scientist Erminio Monteleone of the University of Florence inducted me into the arcana of astringency, umami, and mouthfeel. For recent research into the nutritional and health properties of olive oil, I've consulted Francesco Visioli at the Madrid Institute for Advanced Studies, Antonino De Lorenzo at the Università degli Studi di Roma "Tor Vergata," and Atul Gawande of the Brigham and Women's Hospital and *The New Yorker*. Greg Drescher and Bill Briwa at the Culinary Institute of America helped me think more clearly about olive oil's role in cooking and eating, and together with the charismatic chef/restaurateur Paul Bartolotta, showed me how great chefs can be opinion leaders (and cheerleaders) for fine oil. Members of Slow Food provided valuable information and contacts throughout Italy—thanks especially to Diego Soracco, Pasquale Porcelli, Elisa Virgillito, and Paola Nano. Mark Wickens kindly gave me access to his magnificent private collection of historic olive oil labels, and spent many thankless hours at the scanner on my behalf (mawickens@yahoo.com, http://pages.infinit .net/wickens/).

To name all the olive growers and oil-makers who, over the years, have set aside their important work to field my ignorant questions would require a dozen densely printed pages, and a far better memory than I possess. What follows is a very incomplete list, organized by country, of those who have improved my knowledge of how olives are grown and how oil is coaxed from them.

In Italy, where I live and first encountered fine oil, I want to thank the De Carlo family, Andreas März, Angelo Guarini, Paolo Pasquali, Gemma Pasquali, Marzia Massari, Gregorio Minervini, Marco and Lorenza Pallanti, Giuseppe Mazzacolin, Tony Sasa, and Gino Celletti, for stimulating conversations and many magnificent meals. Thanks to Leonardo Colavita and Marco De Ceglie for insightful commentary on the oil business at the industrial as well as the family level, and to Sabino Angeloro, Francesco Caricato, Leonardo Marseglia, Laura Marvaldi, Domenico Ribatti, Nicola Ruggiero, and Silvestro at Ottava Piccola, for their often contradictory but always engaging views of the oil business.

In Spain, Rosa and Francisco Vañó of Castillo de Canena were the ideal ambassadors to premium olive oil, in Andalucía and beyond. Thanks also to Brigida Jiménez Herrera of IFAPA, Carlos Falcó of Pagos de Familia Marqués de Griñón, and Luis Rallo Romero of the University of Córdoba.

In Greece, the aid of Rhea Spyridou and Vassilis Zampounis of Axion Agro was essential to my work. Thanks also to Nikos Zachariádes and the people of the village of Kritsa, as well as to Aris Kefalogiannis of Gaea, all of whom welcomed me into their homes and taught me several life lessons. Nikos Psilakis provided information on olives and oil in Minoan and classical Crete, and generously allowed me to use his photographs; Zoe Nowak of Cretan Quality Agreement contributed great logistical help.

In Israel and the West Bank, heartfelt thanks to Ehud and Dove Netzer for their hospitality in Jerusalem and their companionship and advice elsewhere in the Middle East; Ehud's tragic death in October 2010 prevented him from reading this book. Thanks to the resolute Father Firas Aridah, parish priest of Aboud, and the quieter but no less impressive Father Ra'ed Abu Sahlieh, parish priest of Taybeh, for sharing their stories of olive-growing and oil-making in two West Bank villages. Thanks also to Elia Sides at Lily Film for his wisdom, companionship, and common sense, and to Yaakov Kalman and his son, M-16s in hand, for security.

In Australia, I'm grateful to Paul Miller of the Australian Olive Association for sharing his immense experience of the olive oil market Down Under, and freelance oil expert Richard Gawel for his unique blend of hard data, sharp analysis, and knee-slapping humor. Carmel Ross and Gordon Smyth at the Benedictine monastery of New Norcia provided an admirable introduction to 150 years of life and oil-making in a monastic community in the far west of Australia.

In South Africa, thanks in particular to Guido and Carlo Costa of F. Costa and Son, "The Olive People," in Paarl, for their authoritative view of the South African oil market, as well as information on oil chemistry, the dangers of olive pomace oil, and the wiles of South African fraudsters. Andries Rabie at Willow Creek shared his experiences of growing olives at the extreme southern tip of the African continent, and of the spiritual resonance of making olive oil, which Rabie, a fervent Christian, first imagined making in a dream.

In the United States, the energy and the Rolodex of Ed Stolman at the Olive Press made much of my research in California possible, and Deborah Rogers took time out from the crush to answer countless questions, about olive oil and Polish grandmothers alike. During a memorable evening in Lodi, Dino Cortopassi and Brady Whitlow of Corto Olive showed me how agricultural horse sense, top Napa wines, and Texas hold 'em intuition can combine to make excellent oil in California's Central Valley. Gregg Kelley gave me a look behind the scenes of the secretive and super-efficient California Olive Ranch. During scores of meetings and conversations, Mike Bradley of Veronica Foods has shared his knowledge of world oil—among the most encyclopedic I've encountered anywhere—and expressed his conviction, which I now share, that the shortest route to oil quality runs through consumer education, still more than through fighting fraud (though a few arrests would help). I'm grateful to Mike Madison for a stimulating talk (and a much-needed breath of serenity) on Putah Creek, to Mustafa Altuner for the inside story on Los Angeles oil, and to John J. Profaci for insights into the early years—and the future—of extra virgin olive oil in America.

Many specialists in words have contributed to the actual writing of this book. Emily Eakin at *The New Yorker* guided my early writing about olive oil and Marina Harss checked every last fact with rigor and intelligence. My agent Sarah Chalfant at the Wylie Agency got the project off the ground as a book. Alane Salierno Mason, my editor at W. W. Norton, has earned my heartfelt gratitude for her deft and patient work at every stage of the book, from hewing the first draft out of a formless mass of material to adding progressively finer finishes and polishes in successive manuscripts. Thanks also to Denise Scarfi for her hard work throughout, and to Allegra Huston for a sharp-eyed copyedit.

Thank you to my neighbors, the Olivieri—Gino and Rosetta, Danilo and Silvia, Egidio and Daniela, Iose and Raffaella, Marilena and Piercarlo—who have welcomed me into their family. Thanks to Lyn Mueller and Chad Mueller for unstinting patience, advice, and stiff shots of *Monty Python, The Simpsons,* and Stephen Colbert. Last, but far from least, I thank on bended knee my wife, Francesca, and children, Nicholas, Jeremy, and Rebecca, who have suffered with my oil obsession for many years now, and have in turn been infected with it . . . hopefully to their lasting good.

INDEX